IMAGES of America

CLEARFIELD COUNTY

In memory of George A. Scott and Ed Morgan.

IMAGES
of America

CLEARFIELD COUNTY

Julie Rae Rickard

ARCADIA
PUBLISHING

ISBN 978-0-7385-3453-4

Published by Arcadia Publishing
Charleston, South Carolina

Printed in the United States of America

Library of Congress Catalog Card Number: 2003110800

For all general information contact Arcadia Publishing at:
Telephone 843-853-2070
Fax 843-853-0044
E-mail sales@arcadiapublishing.com
For customer service and orders:
Toll-Free 1-888-313-2665

Visit us on the Internet at www.arcadiapublishing.com

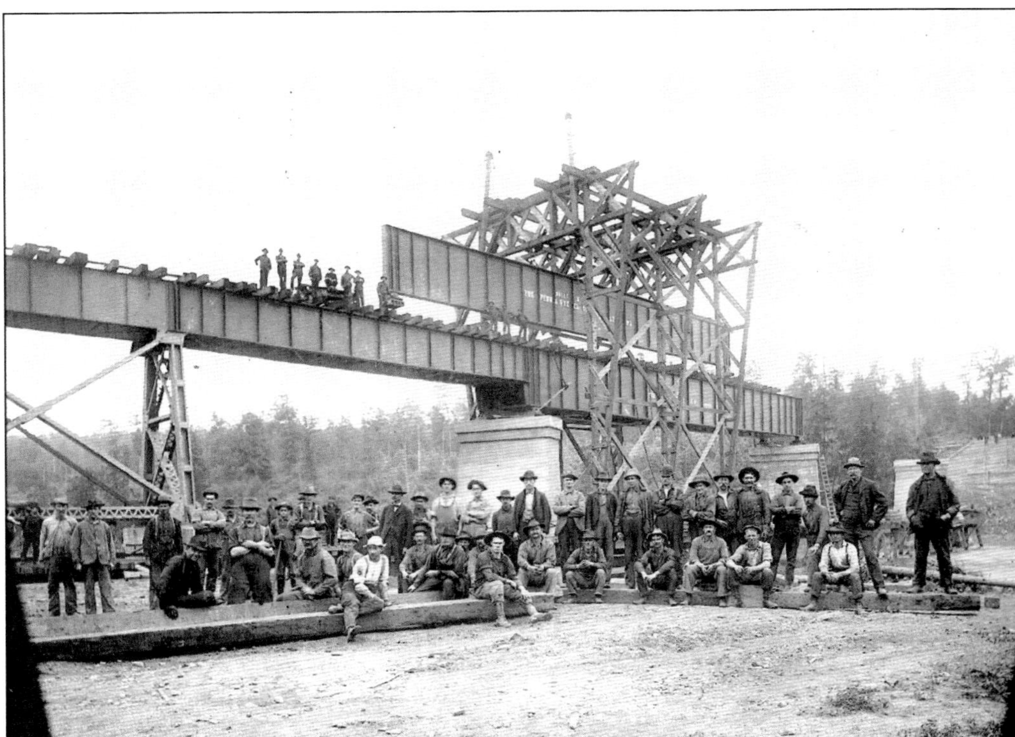

Men take a break from working on the Arnoldtown Railroad Bridge near Curwensville to pose for this 1917 photograph. The railroads were very important to the early development of Clearfield County. Towns that had railroad stations prospered. (Courtesy Clearfield County Historical Society.)

CONTENTS

ACKNOWLEDGMENTS

Several people are responsible for helping me compile this historic record of Clearfield County. They are Pat Murphy; Warren Fox; Robert M. Kurtz Jr.; the Clearfield County Historical Society; J. Duane Test; Jim and Lois Leitzinger; Evo G. Facchine, Judith Leech, and Audrey A. Lott of the DuBois Area Historical Society; Richard Snyder of the Coalport Area Coal Museum; Dan of the Osceola Mills Public Library; Doe Augustine and the Curwensville Public Library; Bill Williams and the Curwensville-Pike Township Historical Society; Scoot Grice; Brian Witherow; Autumn Watson; Tina Shadduck; Tim Harley; Paul Rishell; Glee Norman; Duane Rowles; Scott P. Crago; Eugene Williams; Emma Guarino; Marietta Ross; Cortland Peacock; Shawn K. Inlow; and Erin Loftus at Arcadia. Thanks to all of you who trusted me with your photographs, helped me find the correct information, or just loaned me computer discs. I must also thank Luan C. Smith Jr. of El Paso, Texas, who donated his father's photographs to the Clearfield County Historical Society. Many of those great images are used here.

Research materials include *History of Clearfield County*, by Lewis Cass Aldrich; *Clearfield County, Pennsylvania: Past and Present*, by Thomas Lincoln Wall; *DuBois Where and When*, *DuBois Now and Then*, by Janice Flood Nichols; *Curwensville in Celebration of 200 Years*, edited by Ed Morgan, *150th Anniversary Curwensville; A View From*, Vols. 1 and 2, from *The Progress*; *Railroads of the Area*, by George A. Scott; the Harry Truman Presidential Library (Web site); and various articles and information found at the Clearfield County Historical Society.

INTRODUCTION

Happy birthday, Clearfield County! For 200 years, the people of Clearfield County have lived, loved, and grown. Businesses may have come and gone, but what we have left here is a resilient people whose ancestors have survived some turbulent times. Included in this book is a record of some of those times.

We start with the pioneers, the people whose sense of adventure and courage is hard to imagine today. They came from all over Europe to a land that had unfamiliar weather, plants, and wildlife. It is a wonder they survived at all. They not only survived, they thrived. Many found fortune in lumber and coal. Others started successful retail businesses. But most of the early settlers were generous in sharing their good fortune with their communities. Without the men featured in the first chapter, it is hard to imagine what our early schools, churches, parks, or fire companies would be like. Because these men contributed to so many ventures, it was impossible to list them all. But trust that they played a large part in the creation of all facets of their communities.

Clearfield County's first century was an interesting one, with many towns springing up overnight. Lumber brought profit and prosperity in the early years as the West Branch of the Susquehanna River filled with logs. Curwensville had the largest mill in the state. Life was hard and most men worked long hours. The railroad slowly moved into the area, connecting residents in the local areas and statewide and providing a faster mode of transportation. Schoolchildren were able to attend high school because of the trains that took them from rural areas to the bigger towns.

Education was important, for even the smallest community had a school. The residents themselves built some of these schools.

In the 20th century, in addition to being known for fine timber and coal, a few businesses made their mark nationally. The Clearfield Cheese Company, Clearfield Furs, the DuBois Brewery, Kurtz Brothers, and the Grice Gun Shop are good examples of this.

A few Clearfield County residents were able to find fame. These range from movie stars (Tom Mix) to war correspondents (Nora Waln) to composers (Philip Bliss and George Rosenkrans) to Secret Service agents (Floyd Boring) to commanders of the president's yacht (Rear Adm. Donald MacDonald).

Putting together a book that covers 1,147 square miles and 200 years of history was extremely difficult. I was unable to find photographs of all the important people, dairies, quarries, and other businesses that were important to the county's development.

I tried to include as many towns as I could, but it was impossible to include them all. Each town and village has between 100 and 200 years of stories and photographs. It would take a much larger book to tell it all.

This book is dedicated to George A. Scott and Ed Morgan because I realize now how difficult it is to put together a historical publication. Both of these men were great writers and historians. I thank them for leaving us such a great legacy of information. Scott, an editor at *The Progress*, had access to vast amounts of information that he generously donated to the Clearfield County Historical Society. As I worked, I felt his spirit with me since his name is on so much of the information I have gathered for this book. I like to think this book is something he and Ed Morgan would have enjoyed and that it will inspire the next generation of historians.

One

THE FOUNDERS

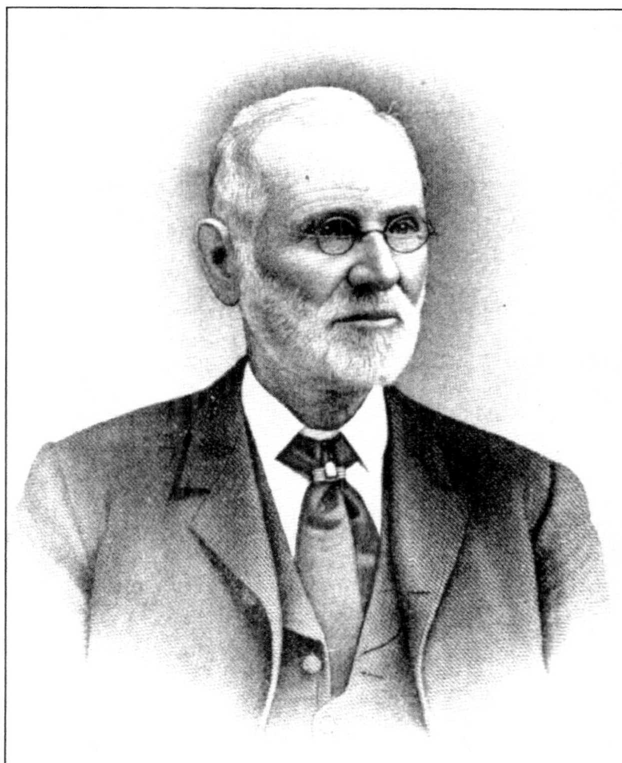

Lumber baron John DuBois (1809–1886) came to Clearfield County from Williamsport in 1871. This portrait is one of the best-known images of him. The town he settled in, then known as Rumbarger, became DuBois in 1876. When he died, he left his lumber interests and fortune to his nephew, John E. DuBois. (Courtesy DuBois Area Historical Society.)

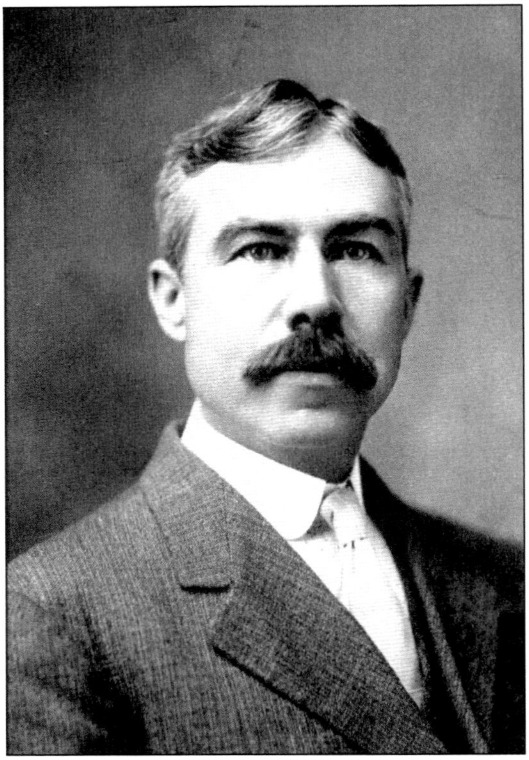

John E. DuBois (1861–1934) was known as a generous, caring man. If his lumber business was slow, he found other work for his men. Those who worked for him or his uncle were never hungry. He made many contributions to the community, including lumber and stone for the Presbyterian church, land for the Maple Avenue hospital, pipeline for the reservoir, and many parks and playgrounds. This portrait of him was taken in 1907. (Courtesy DuBois Area Historical Society.)

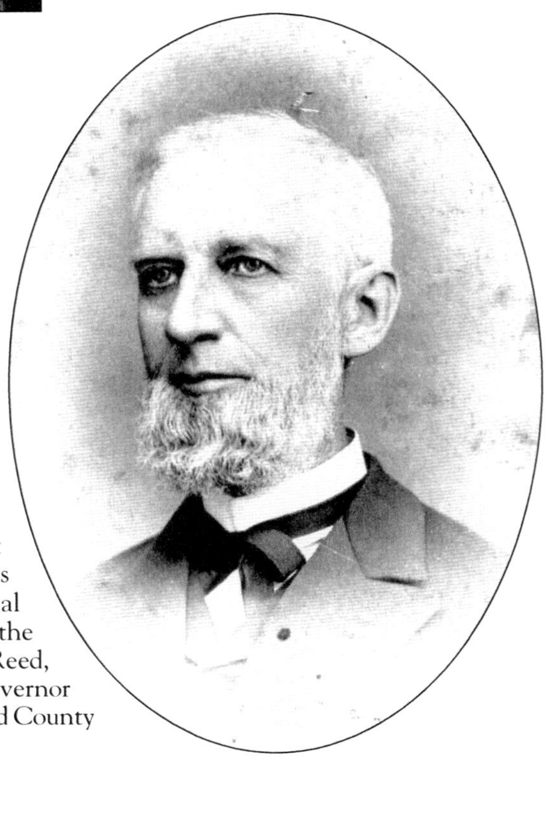

George Latimer Reed (1825–1905) was the son of Alexander B. Reed, an agent for Abraham Witmer who helped lay out Clearfield in the early 1800s. George was an influential man who served in many local offices and on the board of directors of the County National Bank. His sister, Maria J. Reed, married William Bigler, who was elected governor of Pennsylvania in 1851. (Courtesy Clearfield County Historical Society.)

Gen. John Patton (1823–1897) was an important factor in the growth of Curwensville. After a humble start as an errand boy for William Irvin, he became known as one of the most successful businessmen in the area. In addition to his other ventures, he organized the First National Bank of Curwensville. Very generous to the community, he gave money for the building of a railroad, the Patton School, and many other community projects. (Courtesy Clearfield County Historical Society.)

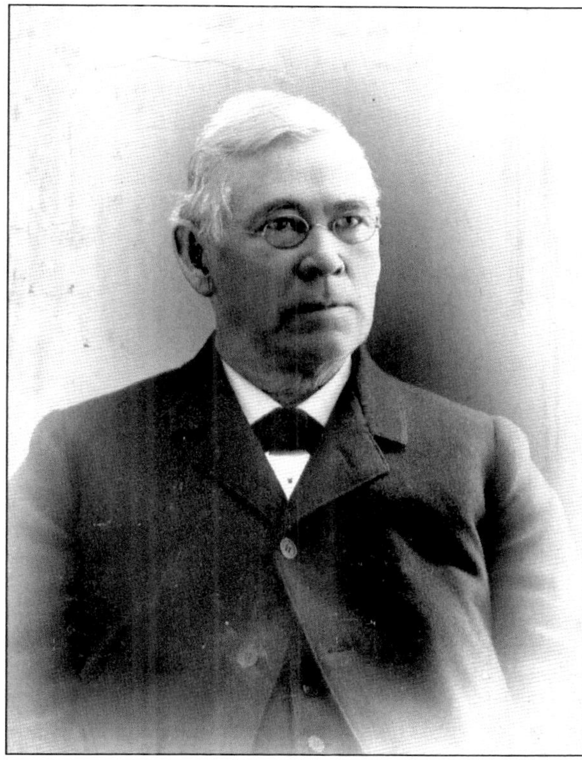

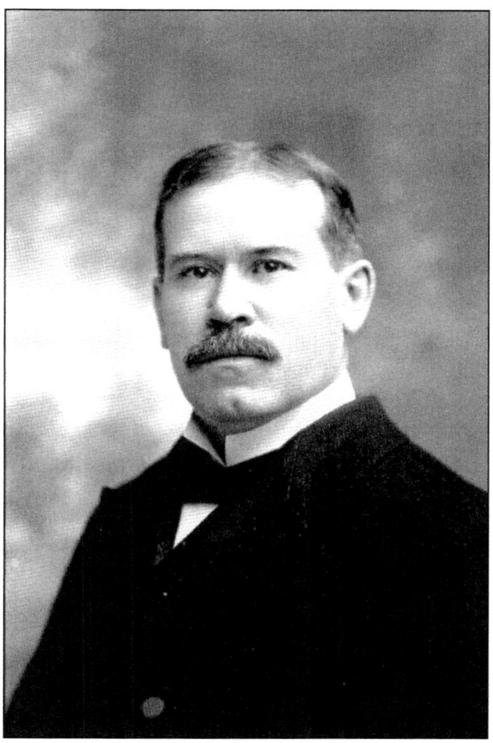

Alexander Ennis (A.E.) Patton (1852–1904) was the son of John Patton. Following the tradition his father began, he was responsible for many of Curwensville's improvements, including a good water system. He was a state senator and once entertained Pres. Benjamin Harrison at his home. It is said that "as a citizen he displayed a public spirit worthy of all praise." (Courtesy Clearfield County Historical Society.)

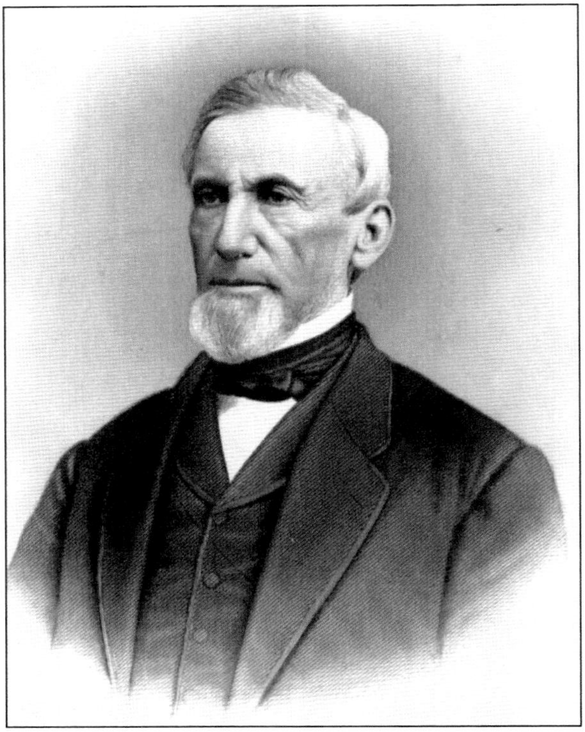

William Irvin Jr. (1801–1869) was a key player in the building of the Tyrone and Curwensville railroad. He was also a vital contributor to Curwensville, giving money for a brick schoolhouse, a church, and many other causes. His wife, Jane Patton, was also very giving, and during the Civil War, she spent time tending to the sick on the Union lines. (Courtesy Clearfield County Historical Society.)

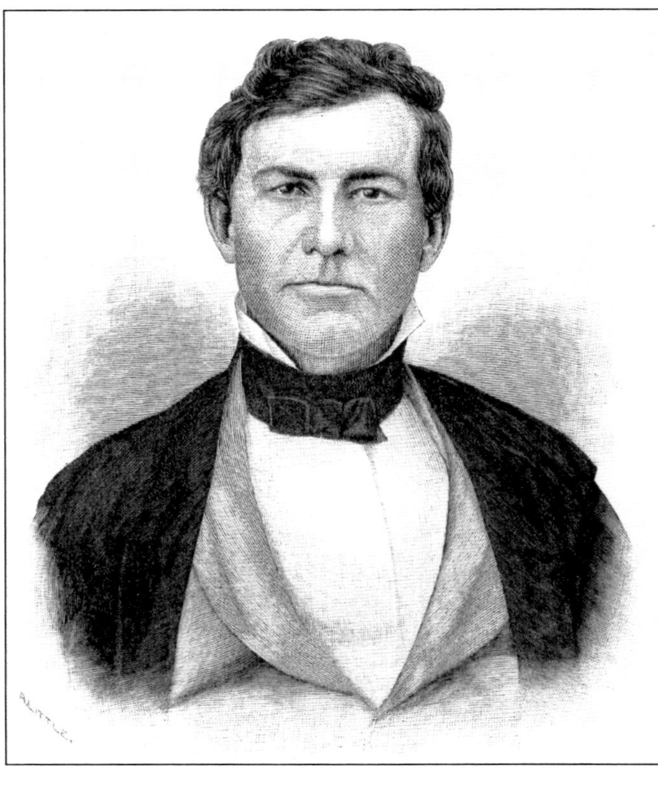

Alexander Irvin (1800–1874) worked in his brother William's store for a few years before moving to Clearfield in 1825. After marrying Elizabeth Bloom, he became involved in politics. He was elected to Congress in 1846, and he was, therefore, the first representative from Clearfield County. He also served as a state senator, county prothonotary, and U.S. marshal for the western district of Pennsylvania. (Courtesy Clearfield County Historical Society.)

Col. Edward Anderson (E.A.) Irvin (1838–1908), son of William Jr., was a successful businessman when the Civil War began. Answering the president's call for volunteers, Edward and many other men marched to Tyrone to begin their military service. The company was eventually known as Company K of the Pennsylvania Bucktails. Edward was wounded twice before he retired. The flag that his mother, Jane Patton Irvin, made was carried in many of the bloodiest battles of the war. (Courtesy Clearfield County Historical Society.)

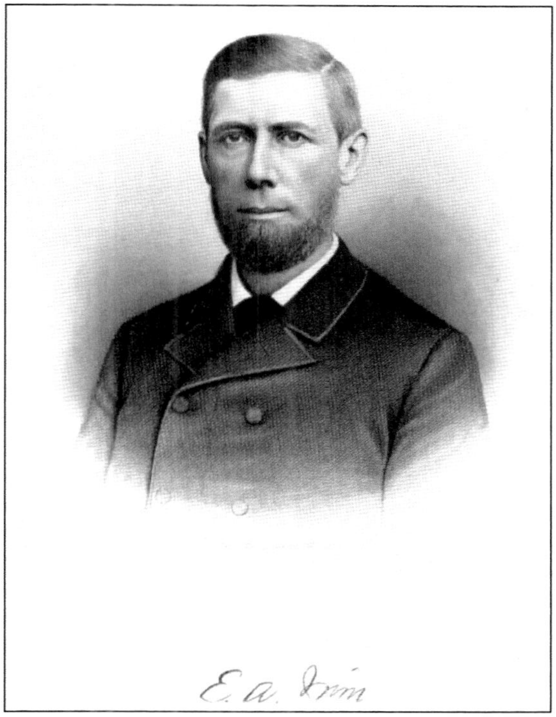

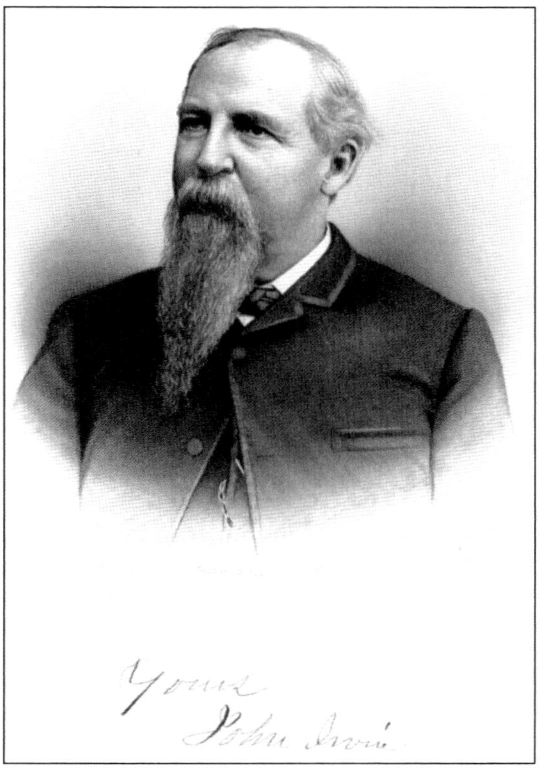

Col. John Irvin (1836–1897), cousin of Edward, also served in the Civil War. He was wounded in the Battle of Gettysburg but later returned to his regiment, Company B, 149th Pennsylvania, another Bucktail group. After the war, he and his brothers ran several businesses, including mercantile, lumbering, and milling concerns, under the name John Irvin and Brothers. (Courtesy Clearfield County Historical Society.)

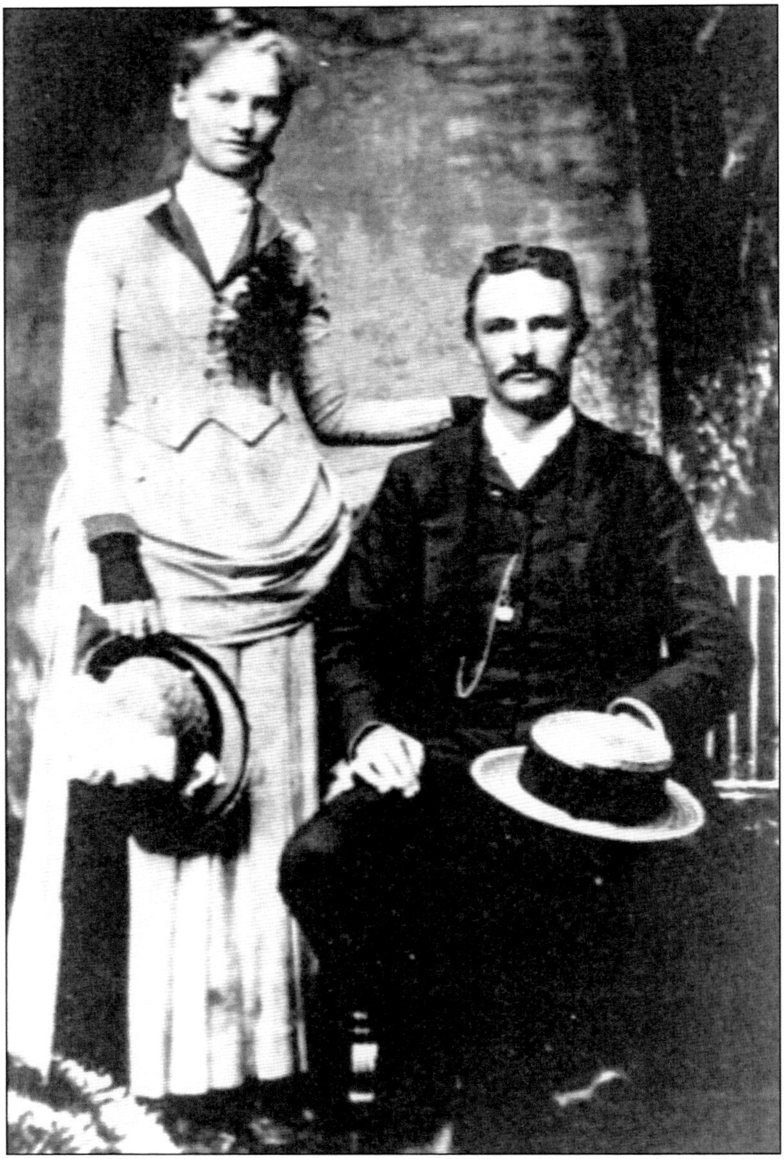

Samuel and Josephine Bell Hegarty built the house at Hegarty's Crossroads in the 1870s. He was an important businessman in the Coalport area and was involved in both lumber and coal. He also started a bank, the Hegarty Bank (later the Coalport Bank), and ran the Hegarty Company Store. His grandfather, also named Samuel, was one of the first settlers in this area. He arrived in 1811, bringing his family, including a son, John (this Samuel's father), who was only 11 at the time. The eldest Samuel built one of the first Presbyterian churches in the area in 1832. It is said that those attending the church brought their guns because of the abundant wildlife surrounding the building. Josephine's grandfather was Arthur Bell, one of the first settlers in the county. Her father, Grier, is said to have been the first white child born in Clearfield County. The couple had three sons: Allison, Wade, and Clair. The mansion at Hegarty's Crossroads, rumored to be haunted, is being remodeled as a bed and breakfast. (Courtesy Coalport Area Coal Museum.)

Two

The First Century

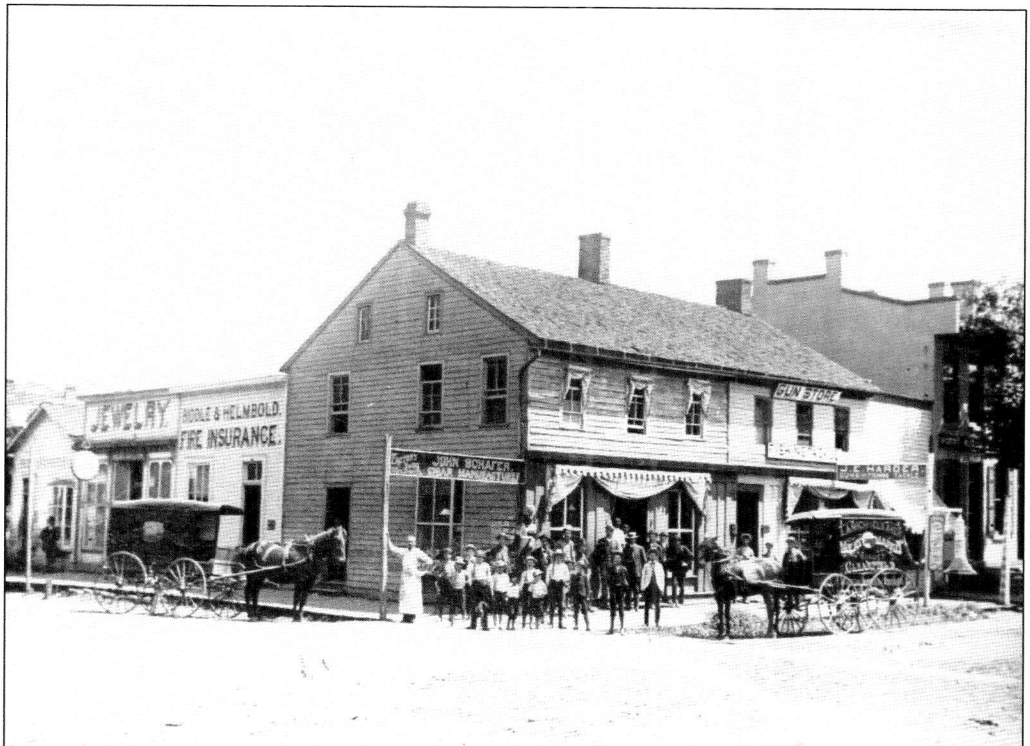

Clearfield's corner of South Second and East Market Streets looked a bit different in 1884. Seen here are, from left to right, the dental practice of Jim Stewart, the jewelry store of S.I. Snyder, Biddle and Hembold Fire Insurance, John Schafer Cigar Manufacturer, the delivery wagon of Lanich and Cleaver Meat Market, J.E. Harder Guns and Fishing Tackle, and the First National Bank. (Courtesy Clearfield County Historical Society.)

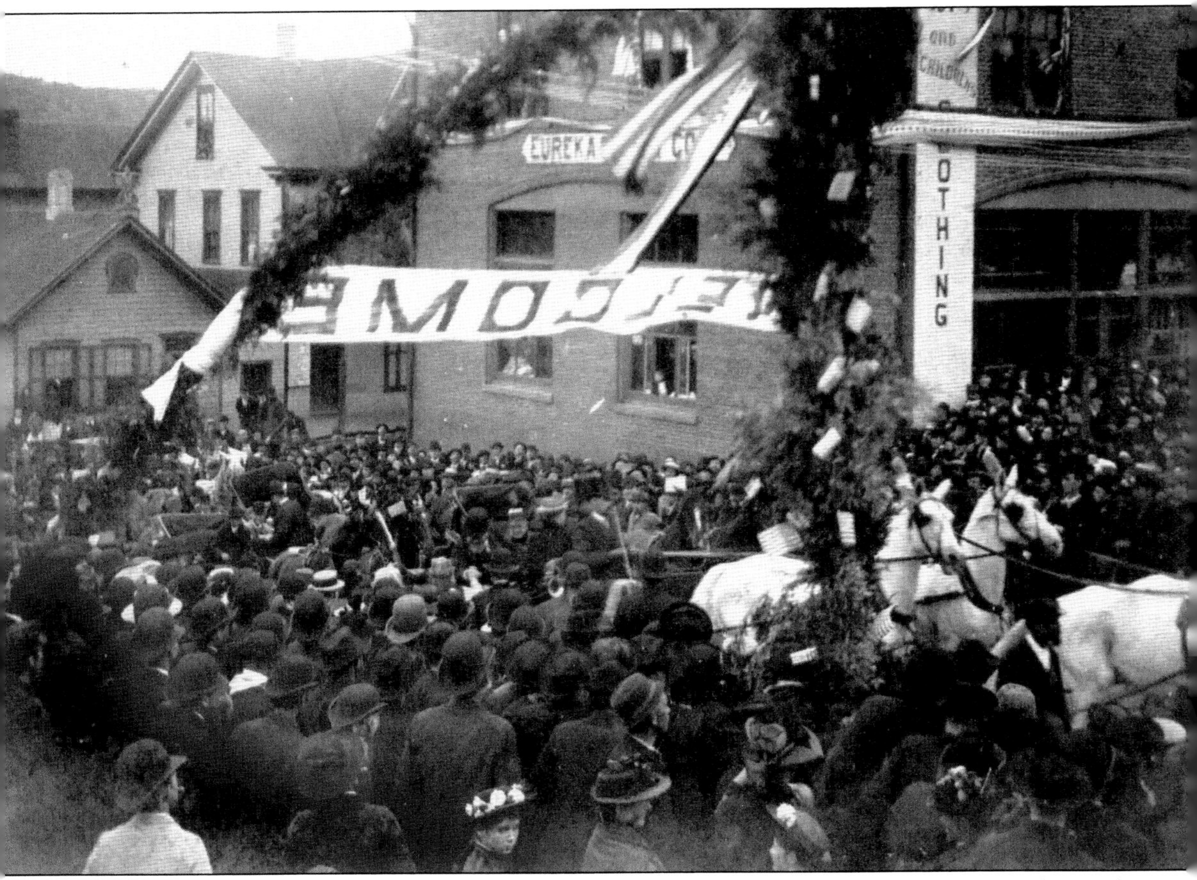

Pres. Benjamin Harrison visited Clearfield County in September 1890. While here, he made stops in Osceola Mills, Houtzdale, Philipsburg, Clearfield, and Curwensville. This photograph shows Harrison as he rides down Brisbin Street in Houtzdale and a crowd of 10,000 overwhelms the procession. The president, who is wearing a bowler hat and has his head down, can be seen in the center as he leans from the first carriage to shake hands with his supporters. Seated next to him is his wife, Carrie Harrison. The Eureka store and the town lockup are in background. Later, he addressed the crowd from a platform in front of R.R. Fleming's hardware store: "As I have passed along the streets, and as I now look into your eyes, I have read welcome in every face." In honor of the president's visit, all business was suspended from 11:00 a.m. to 2:00 p.m. (Courtesy Clearfield County Historical Society.)

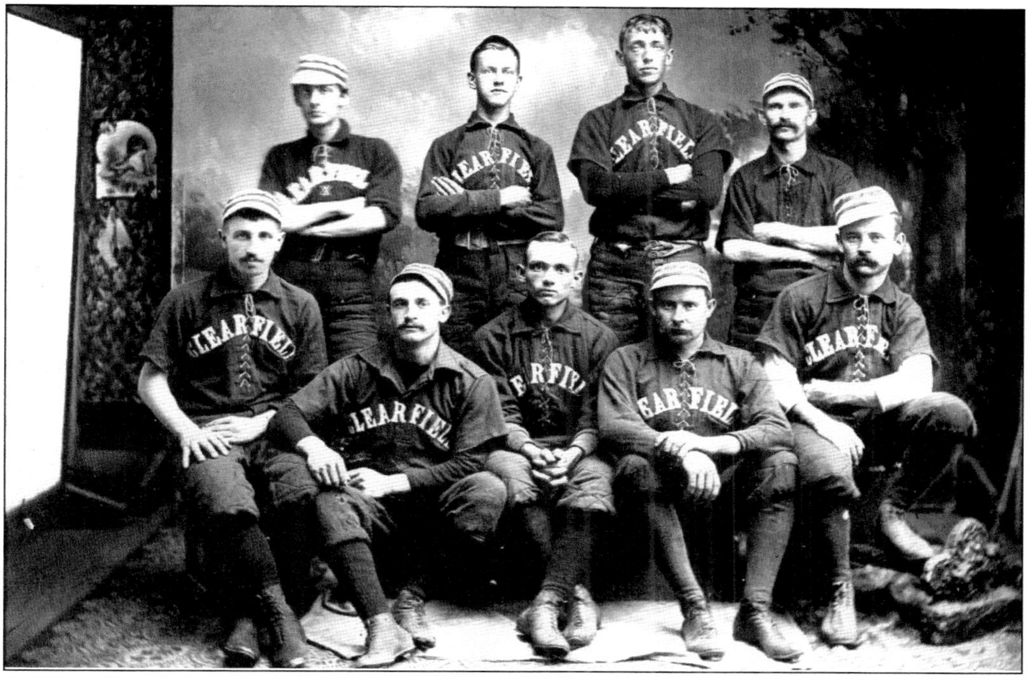

In 1892, Clearfield and many other communities had their own professional baseball teams. The members of this group are identified by last name only. They are, from left to right, as follows: (front row) Kramer, Summers, Moore, Bradley, and Connelly; (back row) Dill, Gearhart, Bigler, and Watts. (Courtesy Clearfield County Historical Society.)

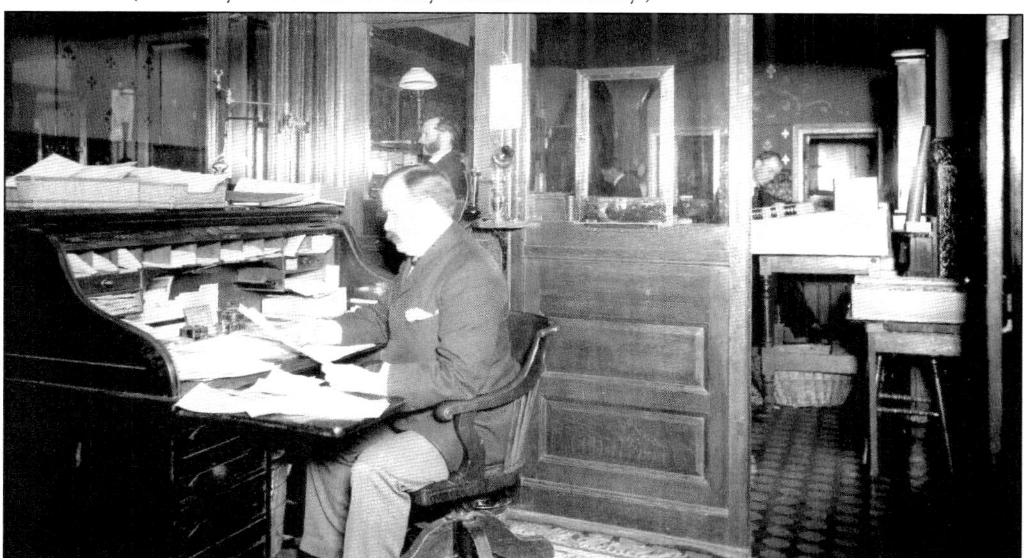

Hard at work in this 1895 Curwensville Bank photograph are, from left to right, Alexander E. Patton, C.S. Rishell, Joel McKeehen (barely visible in the background), and Anthony Hile. The Curwensville Bank became the Curwensville National Bank in 1904, and in 1945, it merged with Curwensville State Bank, which is known today as CSB. (Courtesy Clearfield County Historical Society.)

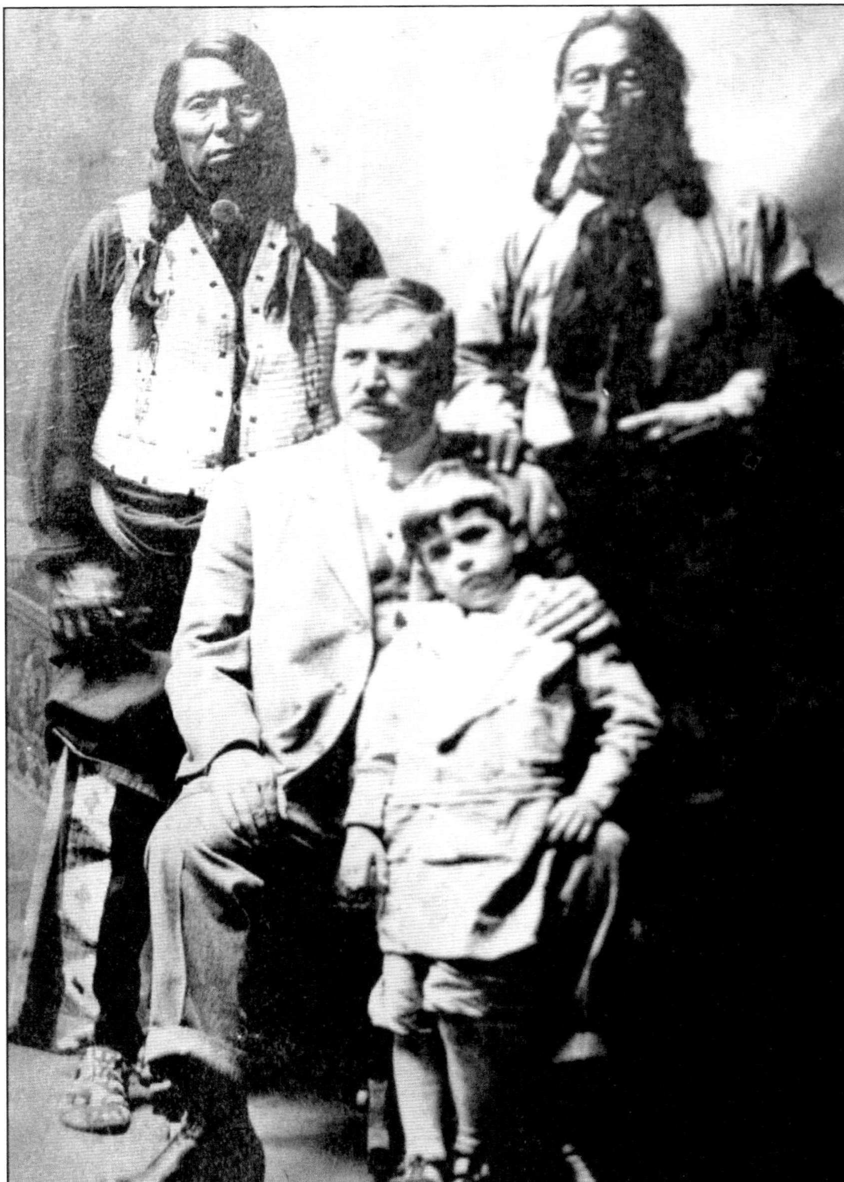

Major Israel (M.I.) McCreight, seen here with his son and a few friends, was known for his great relationship with Native Americans. In the mid-1880s, he spent time in the West, where he made many lifelong connections. His collection of memorabilia included Crazy Horse's gun that killed Gen. George Custer and an autographed photograph of Buffalo Bill Cody. His Sandy Township home was nicknamed the Wigwam. Many of his Native American friends visited there over the years. Joe Bluehorse, a world champion rider, lived for three years in a tepee on the Wigwam estate. After returning from the West, Major McCreight became a banker and wrote about his many adventures. "Major" was only a nickname and did not represent any military title. His other famous friends included Thomas Edison, Luther Burbank, and Henry Ford. (Courtesy DuBois Area Historical Society.)

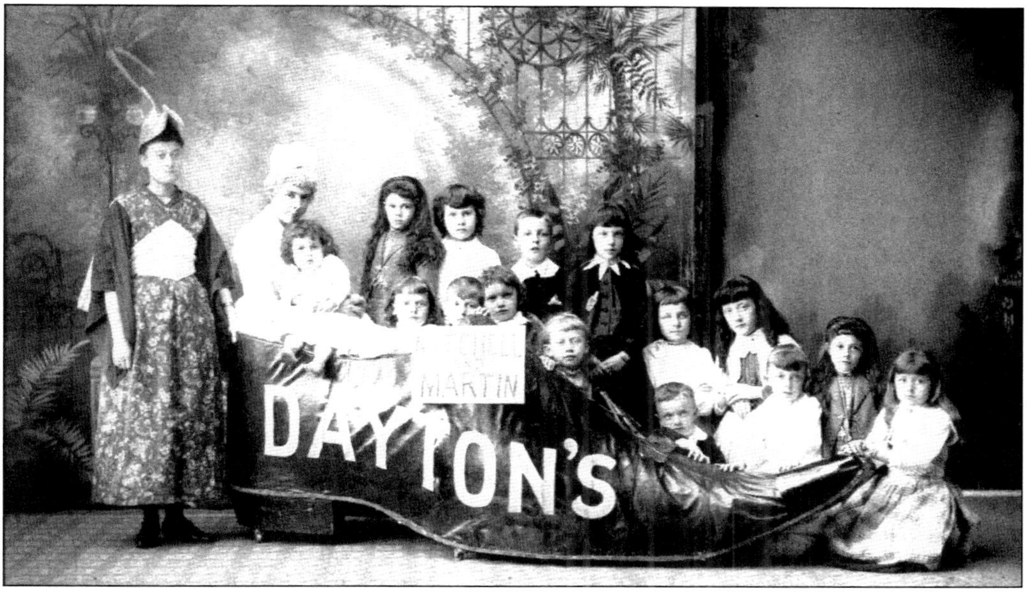

This scene is from the Businessmen's Jubilee, presented by the Women's Christian Temperance Union in May 1890. Seen here are, from left to right, the following: (front row) Lizzie Youngman, May Burchfield, Bess Hughes, May Cardon, Gordon Weaver, and Mabel Townsend; (back row) Cora Cardon (Mrs. Charles Null), Nell McCullough, (Mrs. Arthur Row), Nan Hughes, Sarah Leavy, Kate Gearhart, Clark Snyder, Blanch Cardon (Mrs. John R. Gearhart), Iva Mitchell (Mrs. Frank Ellis), Madie Snyder, Anna Leavy (Mrs. Don Gingery), and Floy Row. (Courtesy Clearfield County Historical Society.)

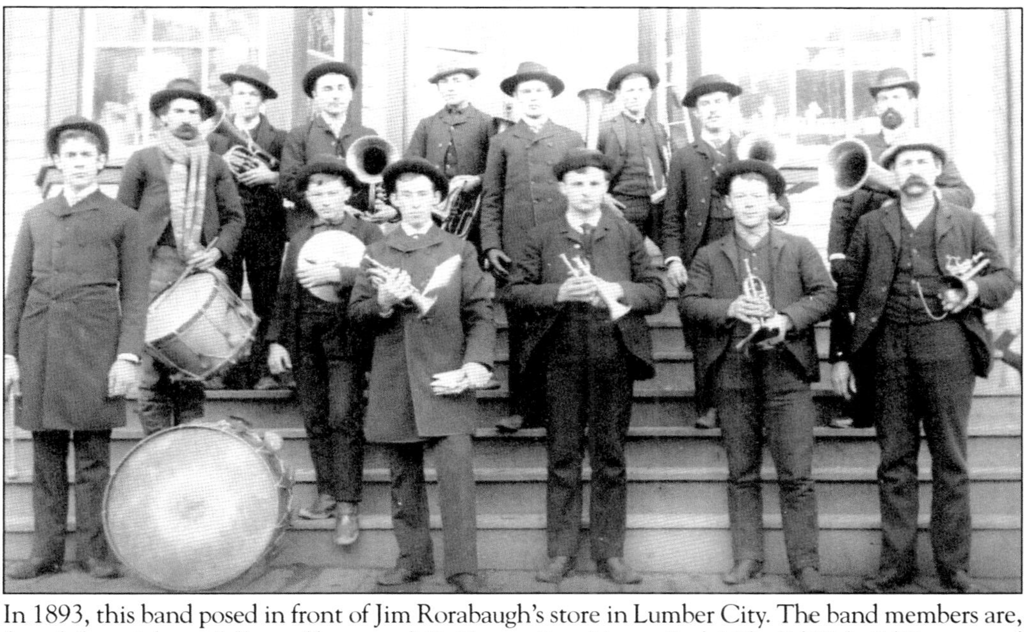

In 1893, this band posed in front of Jim Rorabaugh's store in Lumber City. The band members are, from left to right, as follows: (front row) D. Guppy, Bart Limen, Jack Hile, Ed Kirk, Ed Young, and Alfred Russell; (back row) Al Hile, Jack Limen, Dorse Hile, William Hipps, Ed Mertz, Jim Hile, Gurney Hile, and W.B. Hile. (Courtesy Clearfield County Historical Society.)

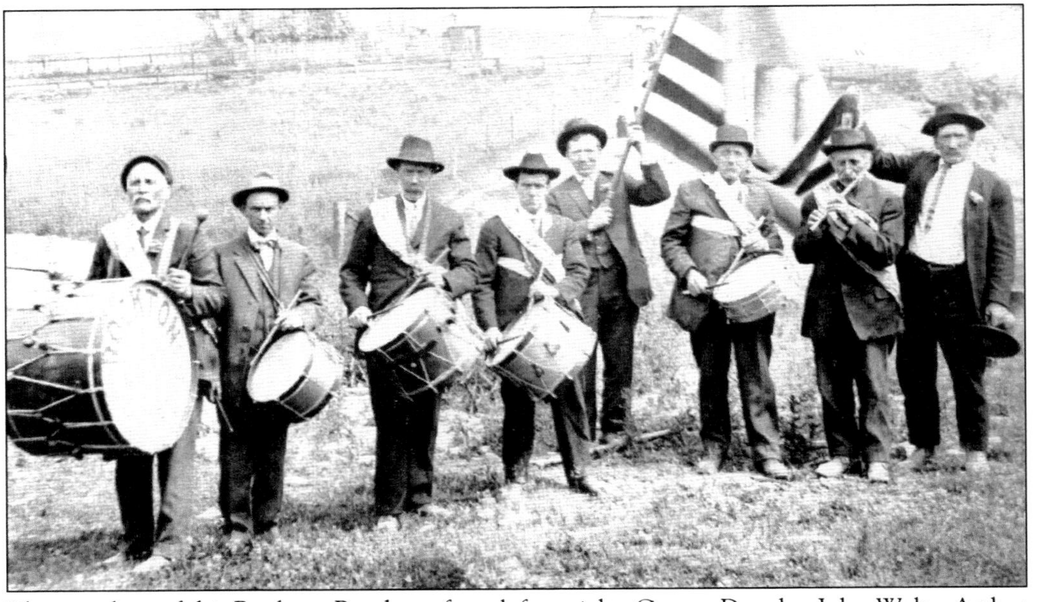

The members of this Rockton Band are, from left to right, George Dressler, John Welty, Arthur Schofield, Everett Welty, Joe Kirk, Simon Welty, Harrison Fridley, and Grant Kirk. Travelers to Rockton via stagecoach often speculated on the weight of a giant rock they saw on the way into this small town. Some said the rock weighed a ton, and thus the town became Rockton. (Courtesy Clearfield County Historical Society.)

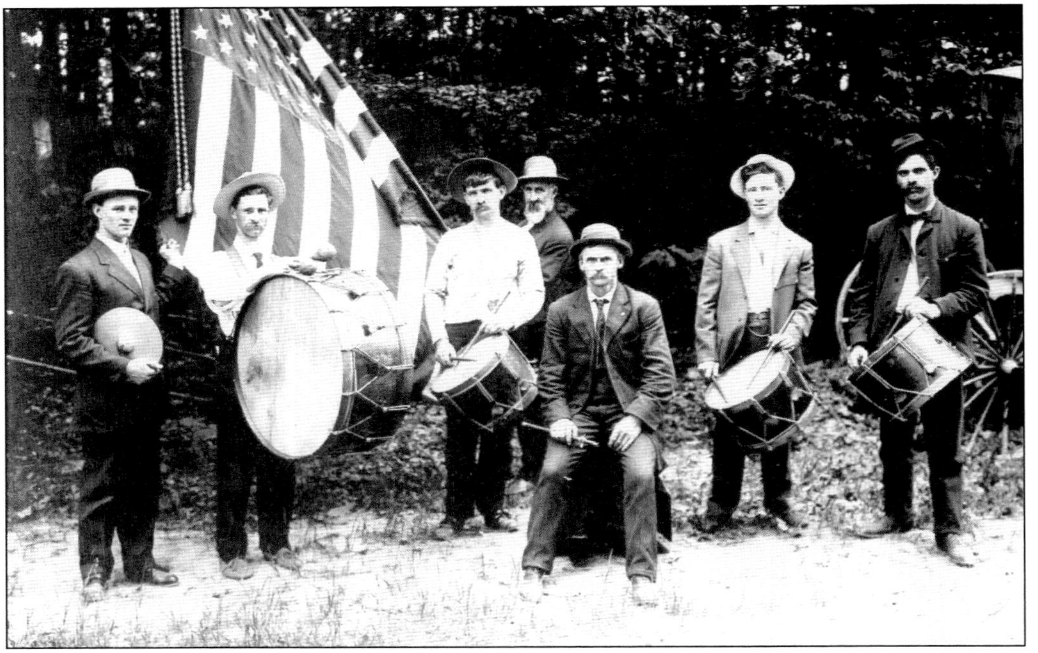

This group was known as the Ogden Drum Corps. In this photograph, taken at Eden, the members are, from left to right, Lloyd Ogden, Ralph Ogden, Clyde Ogden, Pemberton Luzier, Issac Shirey, Oswald Maines, and John Ogden. These men are most likely descendants of Daniel Ogden, who settled near Clearfield in 1797. (Courtesy Clearfield County Historical Society.)

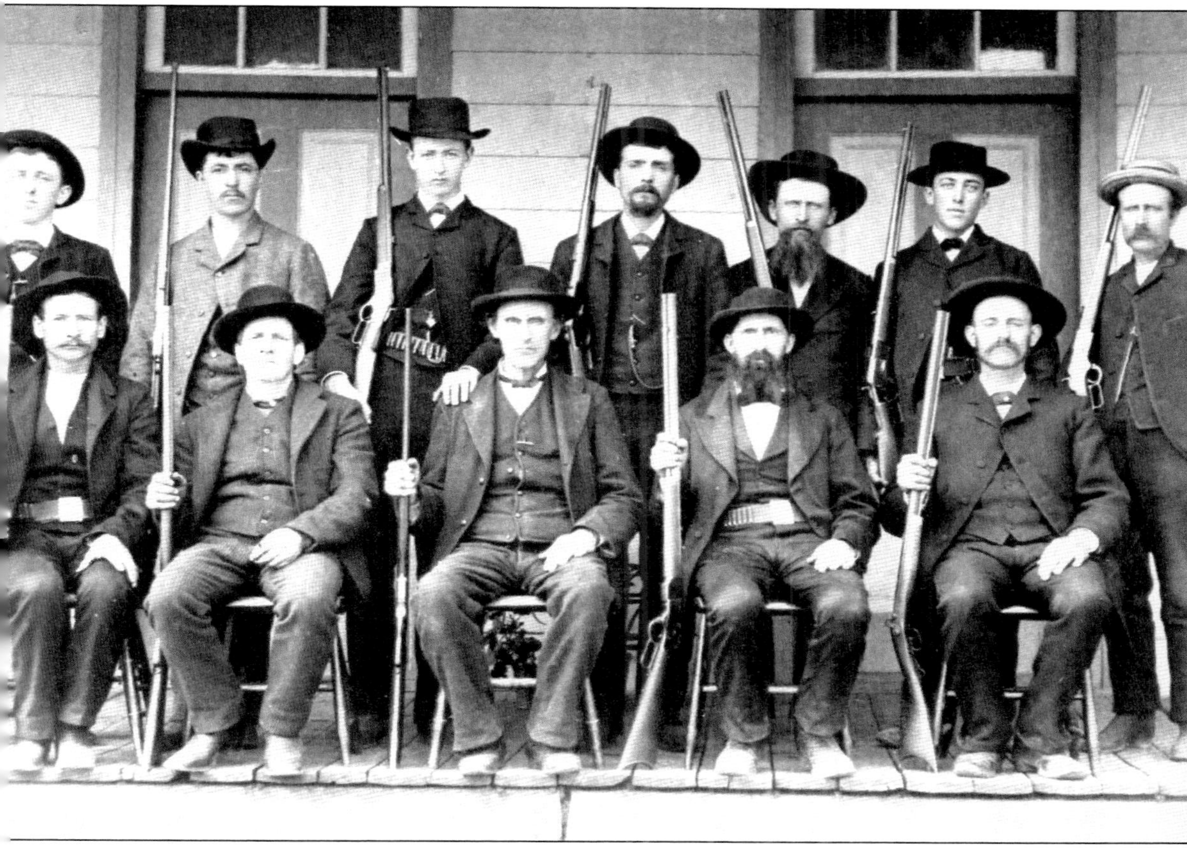

Members of the Luthersburg Rod and Gun Club pose outside the Old Eagle Hotel, originally the Cream Hill Hotel, in Luthersburg. This photograph was taken on July 31, 1885, as Luthersburg was celebrating the 100th anniversary of its first settler, James Woodside, coming into Brady Township. Seen here are, from left to right, the following: (seated) John Parrish, Elias Woodward "Woody" Kelly (the first game warden in Pennsylvania), Joseph Shugarts, Henry Michael Seyler, and George Shugarts; (standing) James Boyd Kirk Jr., Christian Laborde, William Fisher Kirk, Milton Ezra Miles, Herbert Tracy Luther (grandson of Lebbeus Luther, founder of Luthersburg), Johnson Thomas Kirk, and George Spencer. In 1820, Lebbeus Luther paid only $5 an acre for the land the hotel and town were built on. (Courtesy Clearfield County Historical Society.)

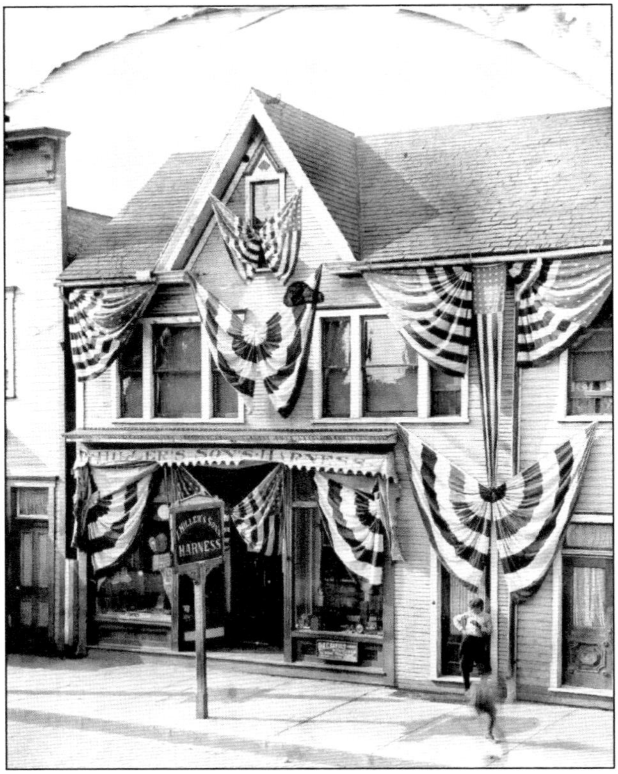

I. Hiller's Son's Harness Shop in Houtzdale was established in 1884. Here, we see it decorated for the Fourth of July. Early photographs took a long time to expose. On the bottom right, note the shadow and legs of an unidentified child who did not stand still long enough to be shown completely. (Courtesy Clearfield County Historical Society.)

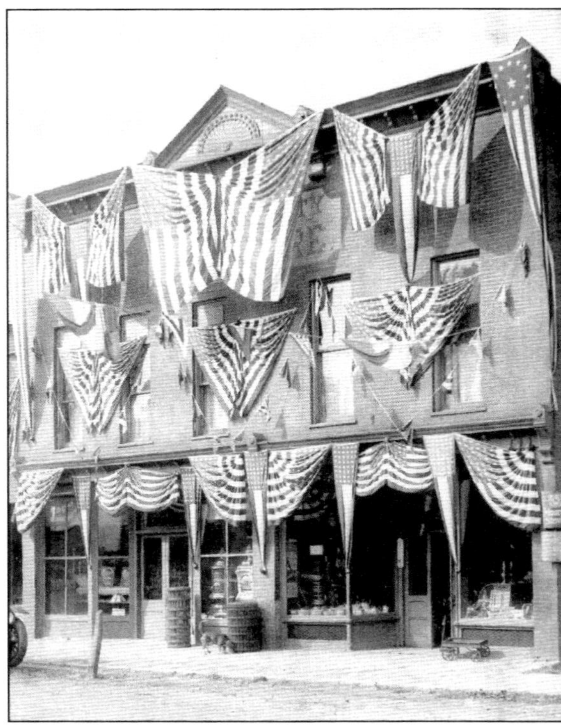

There is an amazing similarity between the previous photograph and this one of a hardware store in Coalport, which is also decorated to celebrate the Fourth of July. Perhaps all of the buildings on the street were dressed up this way. Hugh McNulty bought this hardware store *c.* 1900 from John Holden. Today, the fourth generation of the family, Jim McNulty, is doing business there. (Courtesy Coalport Area Coal Museum.)

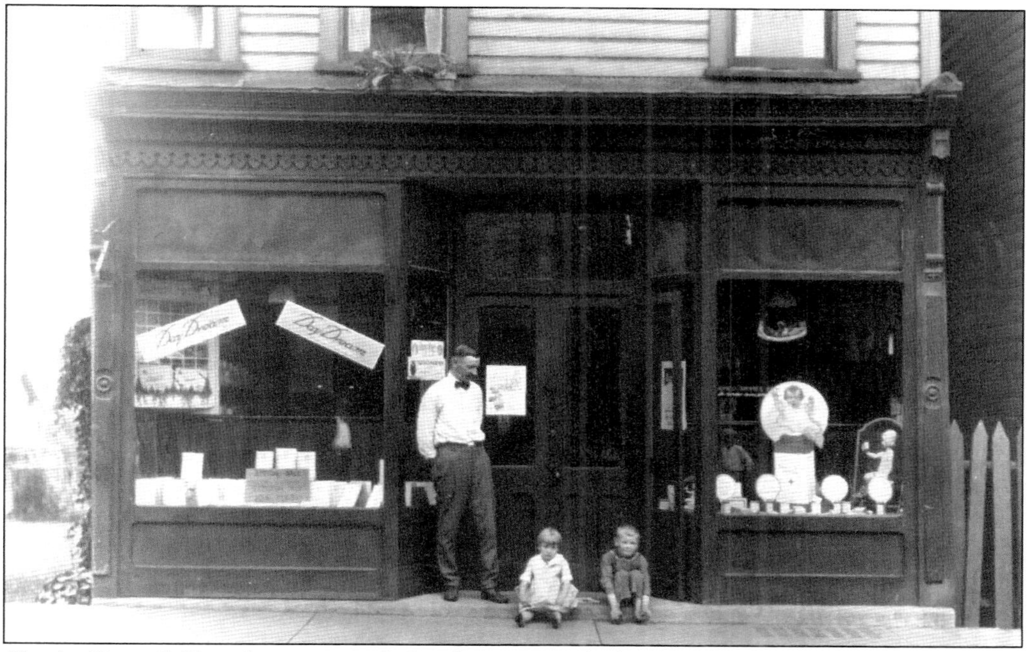

Charles Ryan Eckbert lingers outside his drugstore with daughter Sarah (Sally) Louise and son Bobby. The store was originally established in 1884 as McCartney's Drug Store. Charles bought the business in 1924 and ran it until 1947. It was then sold to Thomas E. Bell Sr. and was known as Bell's Drugstore until it closed in September 2001. (Courtesy Coalport Area Coal Museum.)

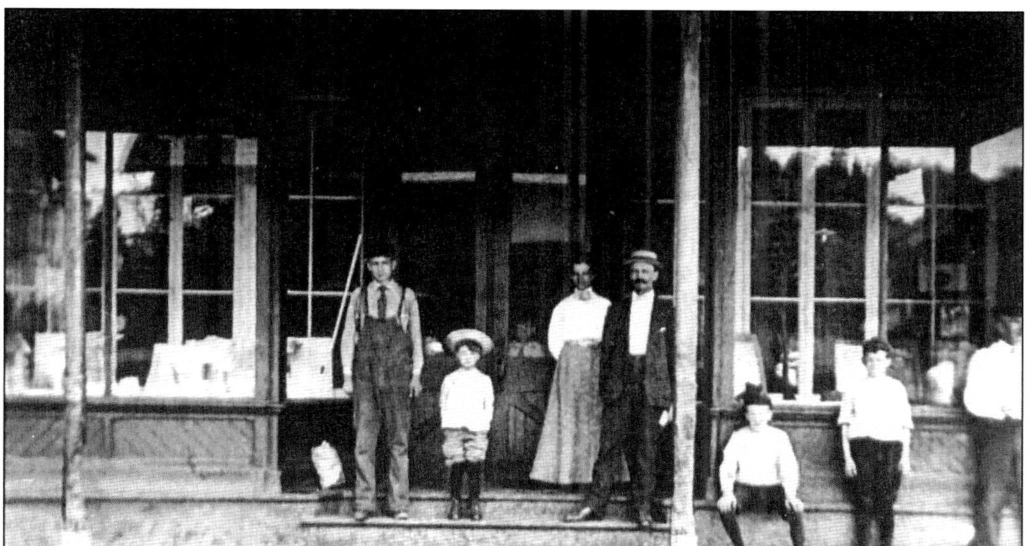

The (Samuel) Hegarty Company Store in Coalport opened in 1884 was later known as S. Hegarty's Sons. Pictured are, from left to right, Cloyd Westover (a clerk), L. Covert Hagerty, Mae Bell (a clerk who later married Allison Hegarty), and Wade Hagerty. The people on the right are customers. Note the wooden sidewalk outside of the store. (Courtesy Coalport Area Coal Museum.)

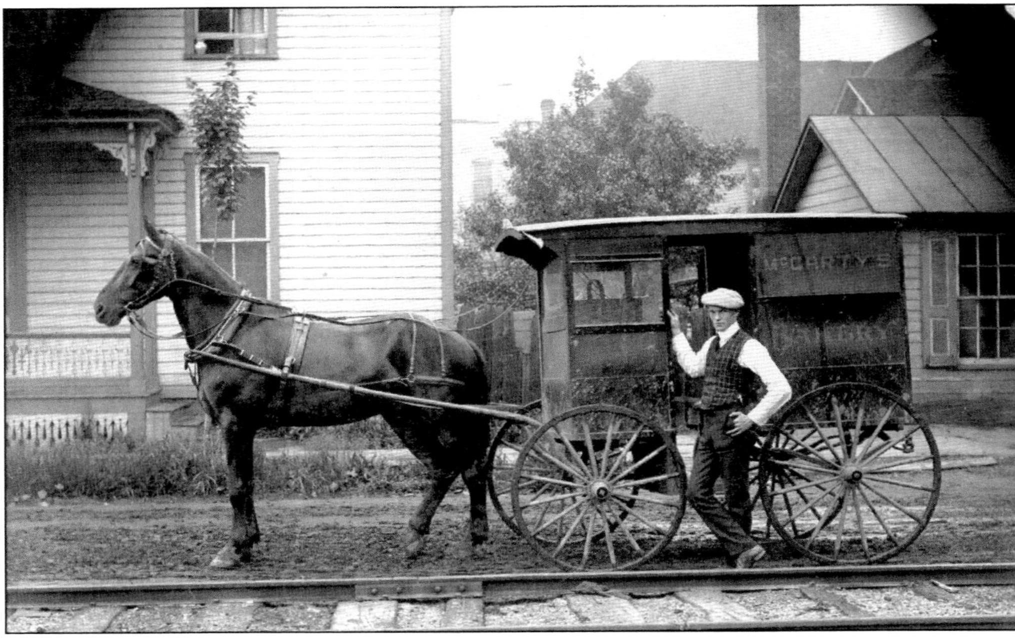

Driver Von Charlton stands by his delivery vehicle for McCarty's Bakery, which was once located on Nichols and West Front Streets in Clearfield. Owned by D.B. McCarty, the bakery operated at various locations on West Side in the early part of the 20th century. (Courtesy Clearfield County Historical Society.)

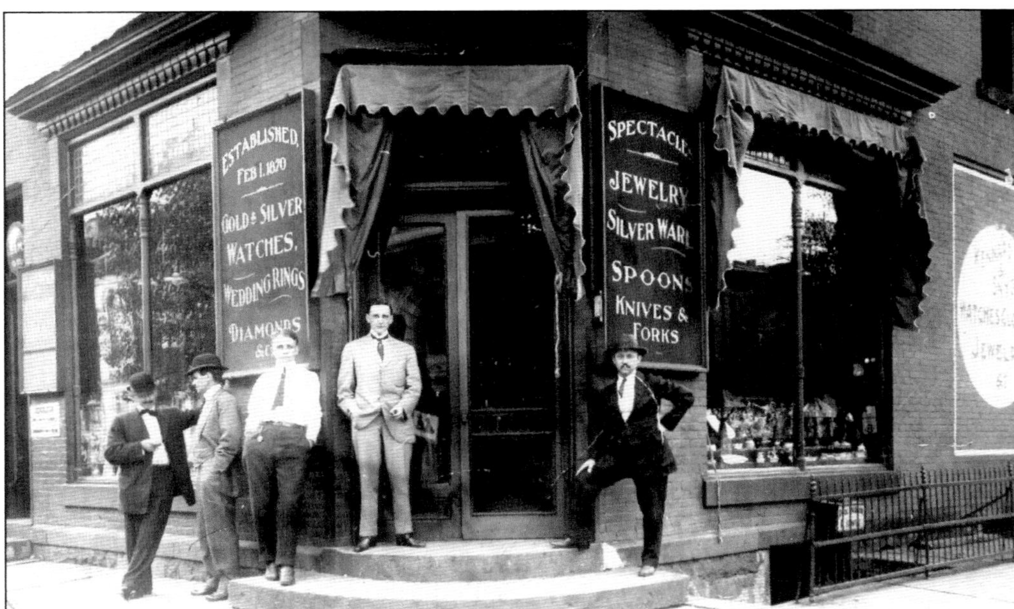

The Kennard and Snyder Jewelry Store, on the corner of Second and Market Streets in Clearfield, was started in 1870 by S.I. "Jersey" Snyder. Later, it was run by his son, J. Clark Snyder, and Richard Kennard for 40 years. In 1920, it returned to its original name of Snyder Jewelry Store. (Courtesy Clearfield County Historical Society.)

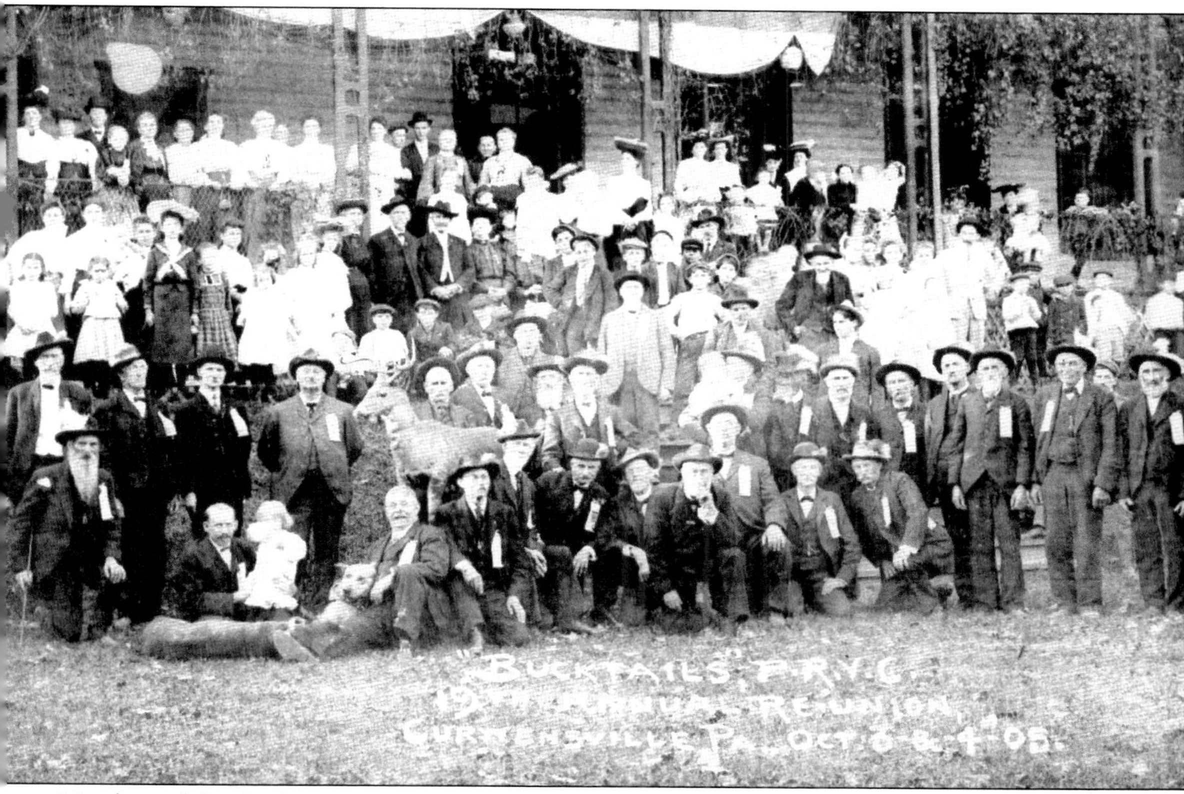

Members of the Civil War's Pennsylvania Bucktail regiment and their families gathered at the 19th annual reunion, which was held on October 3 and 4, 1905, in Curwensville. Known for their fine marksmanship and courage, the Bucktails were involved in many of the key battles of the Civil War, including Antietam, Gettysburg, and Fredericksburg. At Fredericksburg, they made it further into enemy lines than any other Union group. Col. E.A. Irvin of Curwensville hosted this reunion event. When it ended, Colonel Irvin and a committee traveled to Gettysburg for the dedication of a special monument. This monument marked the place where Col. Charles F. Taylor, a Bucktail, was killed. Colonel Irvin also donated a plot of land in Curwensville for a Bucktail monument. This plot was used for *The Doughboy*. Colonel Irvin's wishes were finally fulfilled in October 2003, when a Bucktail monument was added to the plot. (Courtesy Curwensville-Pike Township Historical Society.)

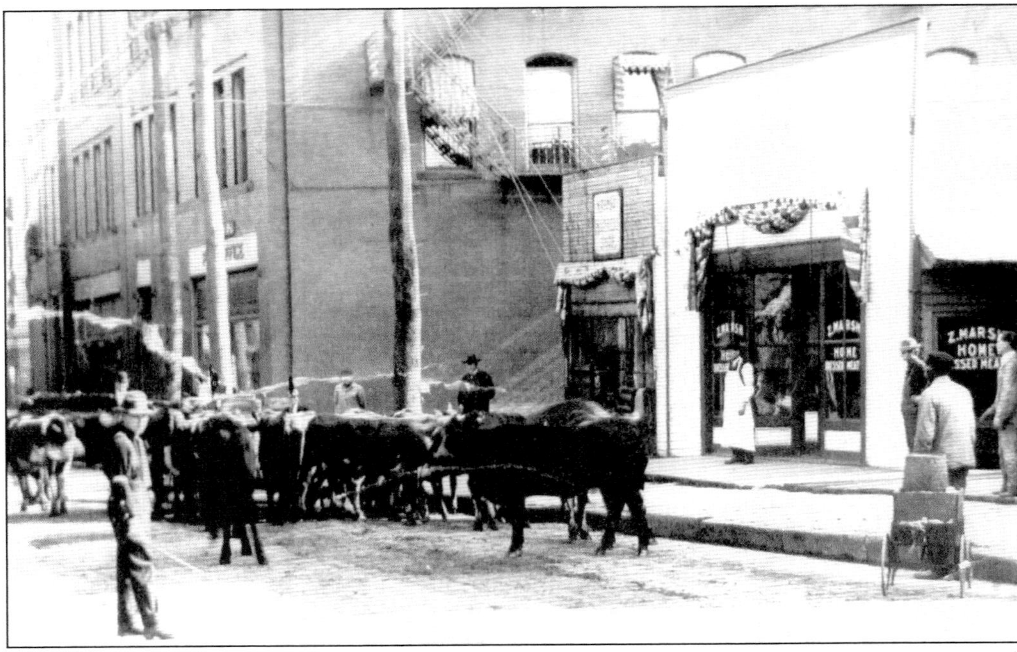

These cattle are really going to town in this c. 1900 photograph from DuBois. On South Brady Street at that time were, on the right, Young's Harness Shop and Zachariah Marsh's Market. There is no record as to when the cows went home. (Courtesy Clearfield County Historical Society.)

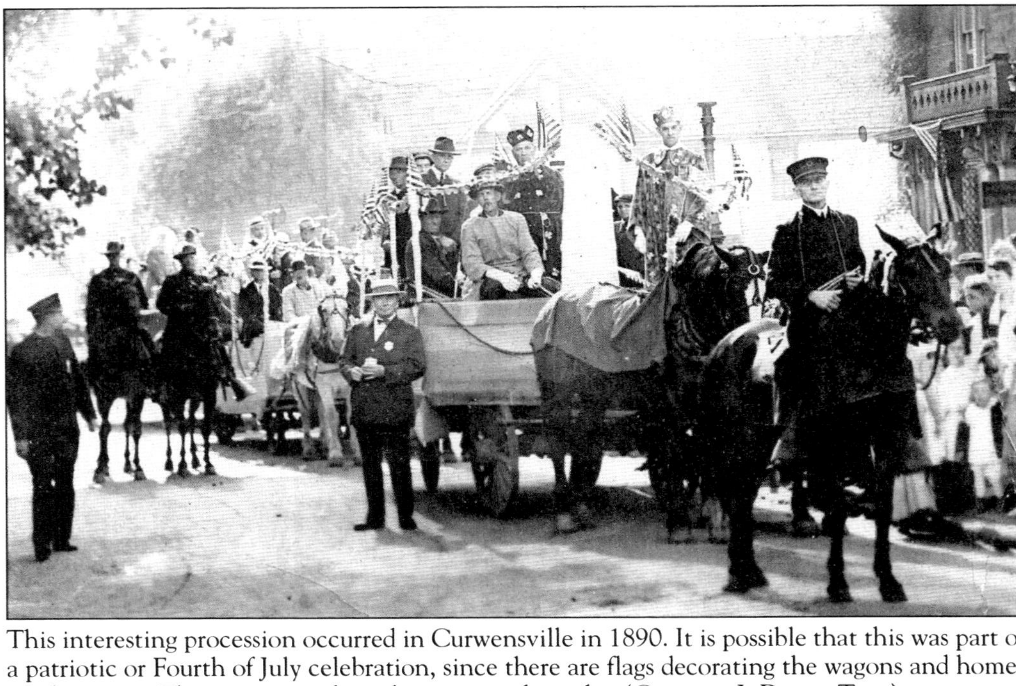

This interesting procession occurred in Curwensville in 1890. It is possible that this was part of a patriotic or Fourth of July celebration, since there are flags decorating the wagons and homes on the street. The eager crowd can be seen on the right. (Courtesy J. Duane Test.)

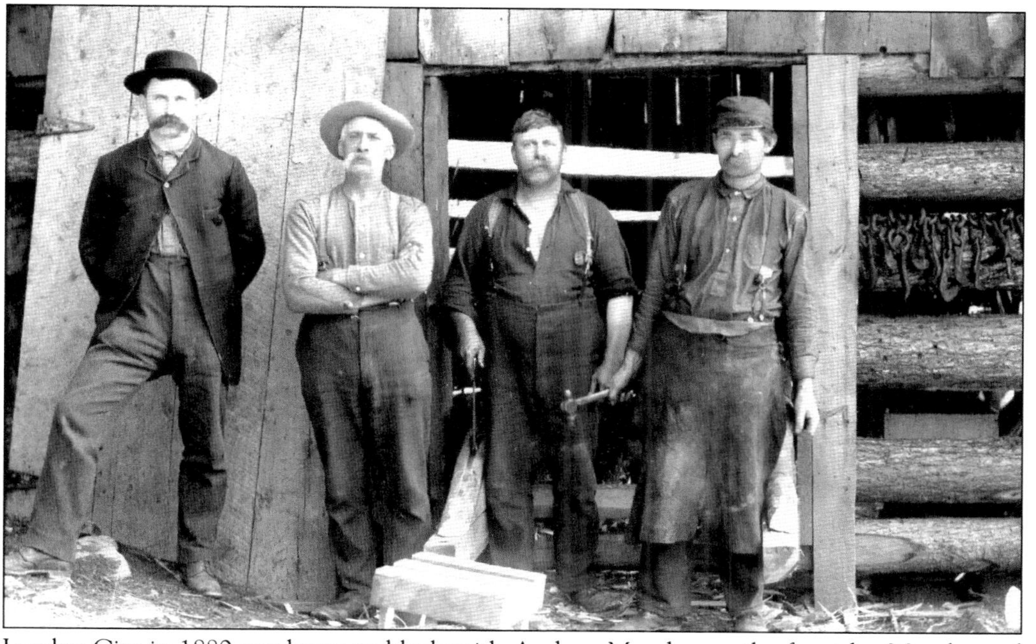

Lumber City in 1880 was home to blacksmith Andrew Murphy, on the far right. Murphy and his brother, John, came from Red Bank, Canada, looking for work. Andrew found employment as a blacksmith for the Bard and Cassaday lumber camps. In the off-season, he worked for a farmer. He also found a wife, Elizabeth Bostic, who worked at the boardinghouse where he lived. (Courtesy Clearfield County Historical Society.)

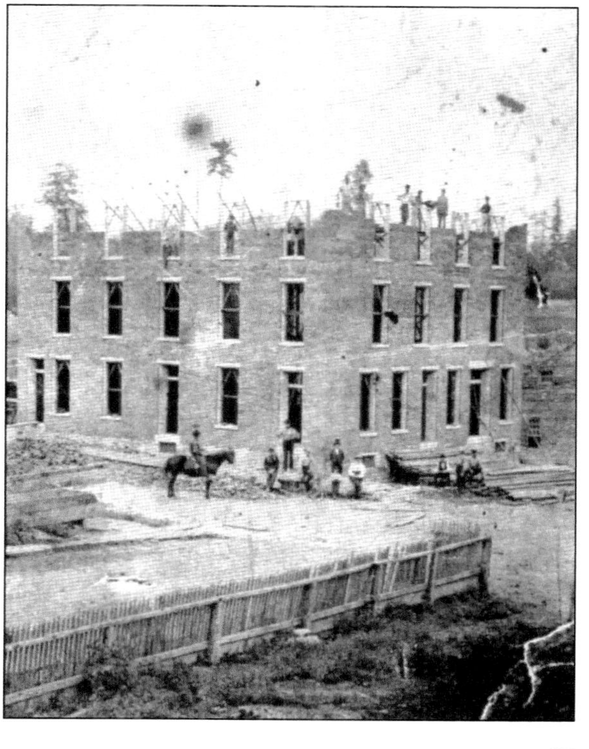

This photograph shows the building of a hotel at Glen Hope c. 1850. It is said the view from the hotel encompassed three counties. It was listed as a bomb shelter by civil defense during World War II because it was 90 percent bomb-proof due to the basement being five bricks thick. In the early 1980s, it was turned into an apartment house. (Courtesy Clearfield County Historical Society.)

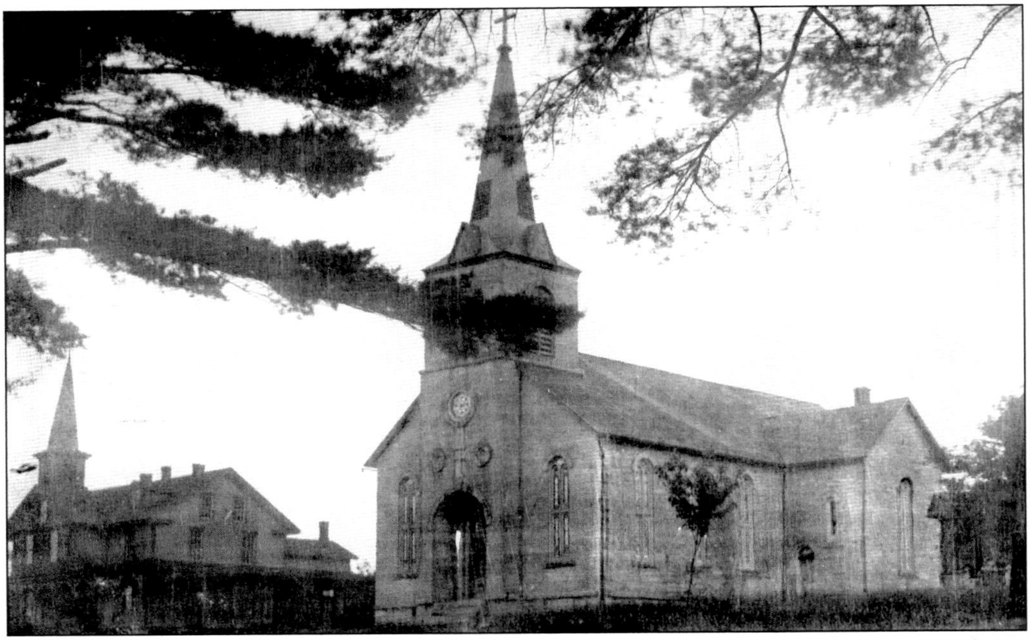

Frenchville was without a church until 1846, when Fr. John Baptiste Berbigier arrived. He coordinated the building of a church, rectory, and convent. When the church was struck by lightning in 1863, a new one was built. Its completion in 1870 was celebrated with a community picnic. Today, that tradition continues with the annual Frenchville picnic, which is held in July. This photograph shows the St. Mary's Church with the old convent. (Courtesy Tim Harley.)

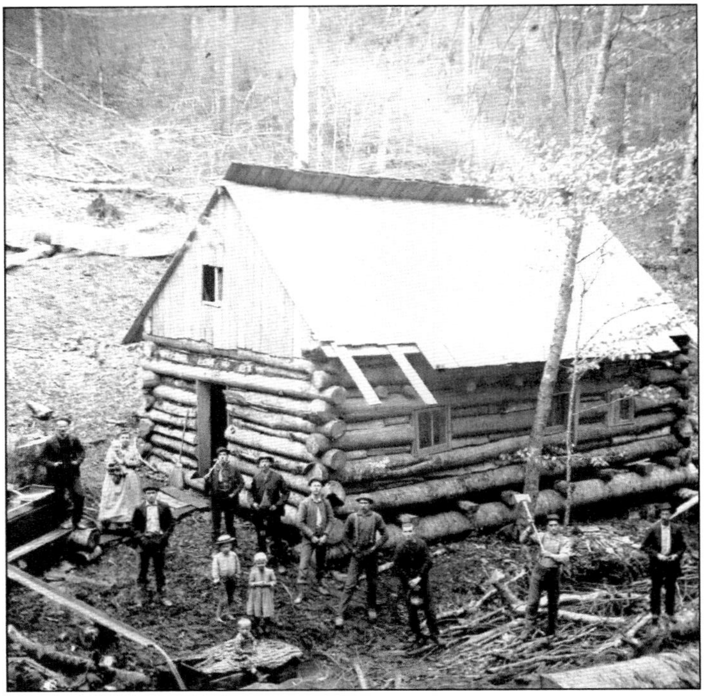

This early log home was located in LeContes Mills. This area, near Frenchville, was where Augustus Leconte chose to build his mill, thus the name. The mill, built in the 1840s, was both a saw and gristmill. It ground feed for cattle as well as cornmeal. (Courtesy Clearfield County Historical Society.)

Three

Lumber and Other Early Industries

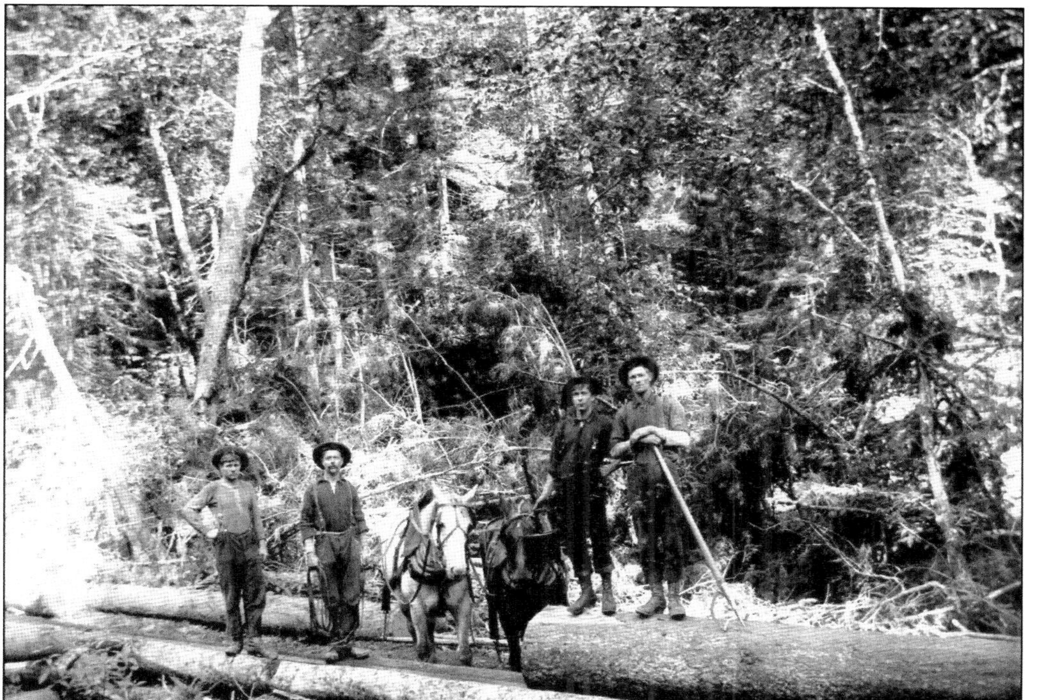

The lumber business was the predominant business in Clearfield County from 1840 to 1890. It was estimated that over 12 billion board feet of lumber was cut during that time. In addition, many tall and straight pine trees were cut for use as spars or ship masts. (Courtesy Clearfield County Historical Society.)

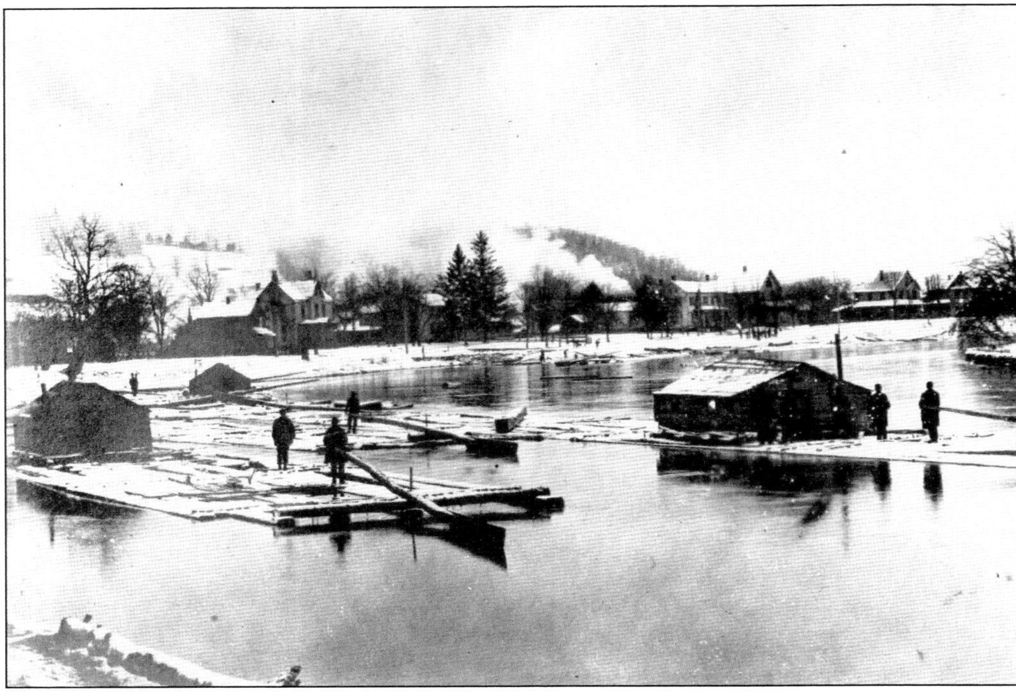

Raftsmen journey on the West Branch of Susquehanna at Clearfield c. 1889. Rafting was a common means of transporting logs from the forests to market. In the spring, log drives moved large amounts of lumber downriver. This view looks southwest on Old Town Road from the Point. (Courtesy Clearfield County Historical Society.)

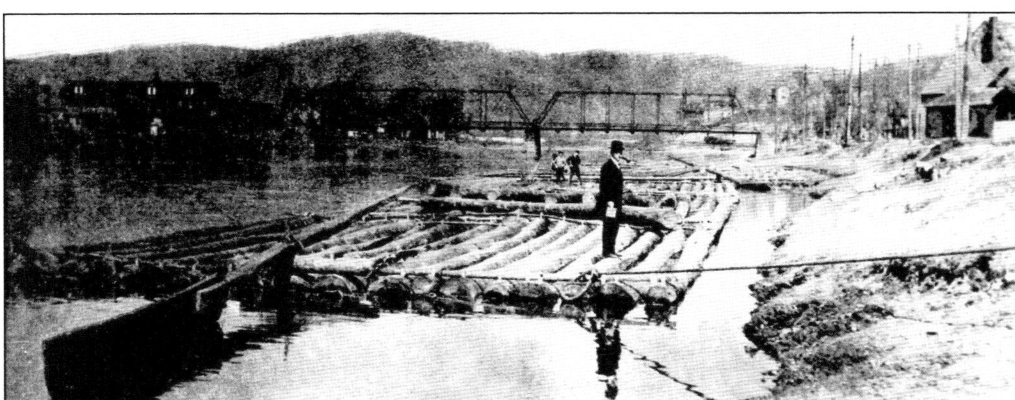

This raft is traveling past Pine Street as it heads toward the Nichols Street Bridge. Rafts were made by fastening the logs together with bows of white oak pinned over lash poles into holes bored in the timber sticks. The rafts were guided by oars located on each end. (Courtesy Clearfield County Historical Society.)

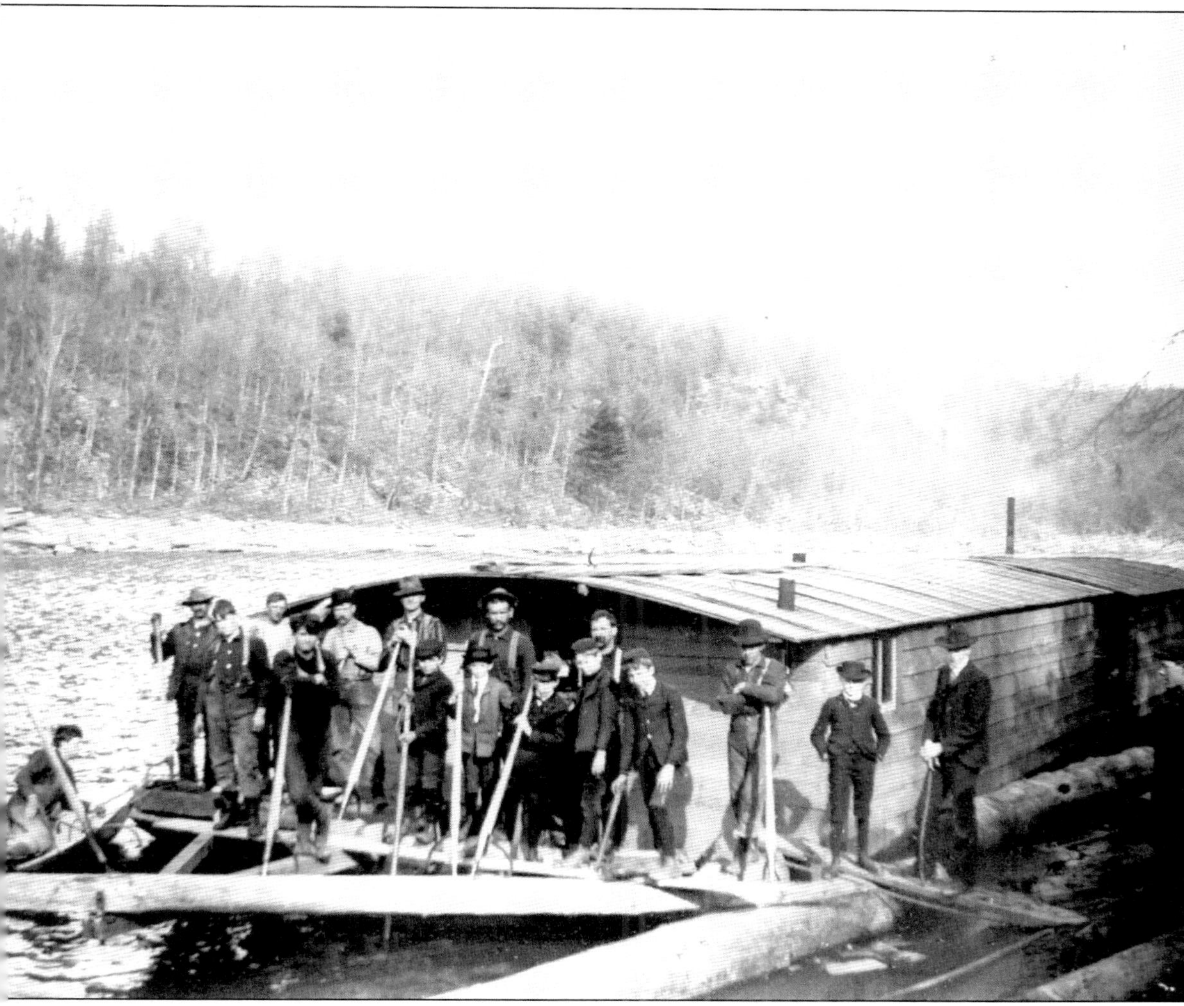

This *c.* 1890 photograph shows raftsmen posing on a trip down the Susquehanna. Raftsmen were paid $1 for a trip from Lumber City to Curwensville while the pilots received $2. For a trip from Lumber City to Lock Haven, a pilot got $20 while a hand got $12 to $15. The prices for the wood varied. Pine went for 30¢ per cubic foot while the best oak could bring 35¢. Rafting was a seasonal occupation, with most trips happening in the spring. The men had other jobs during the remainder of the year. Many of them worked in the woods, cutting timber, and they also farmed. (Courtesy Clearfield County Historical Society.)

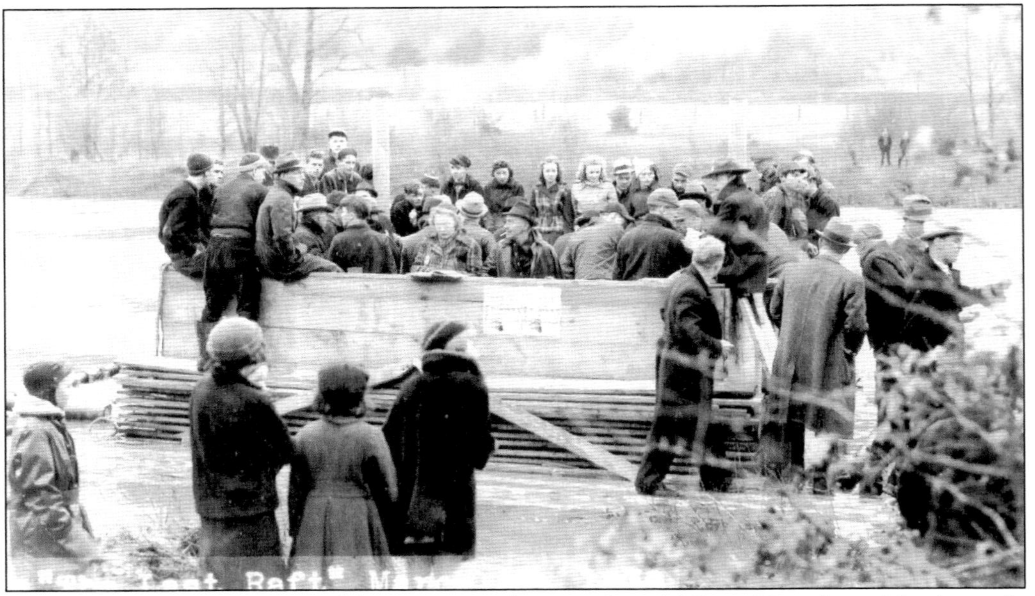

In 1938, a raft was constructed for a journey from McGees Mills to Harrisburg. The last raft, as it was known, was sponsored by R. Dudley and Ord Tonkin. Curwensville teacher Hilda Passarelli had her students present two American flags to the crew for the trip. The flags were visible on the front and back of the raft as spectators followed it through the county. The price for riding it from Curwensville was reportedly $8. Above, the raft leaves McGees Mills, and below, it passes near Clearfield. The Tonkins also sponsored the 1912 excursion raft from Cherry Tree to Williamsport. (Courtesy Clearfield County Historical Society.)

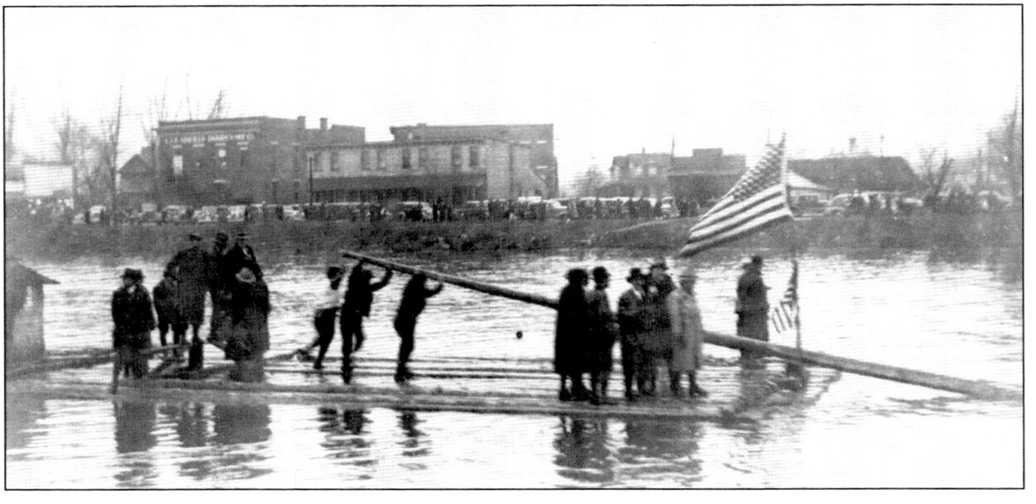

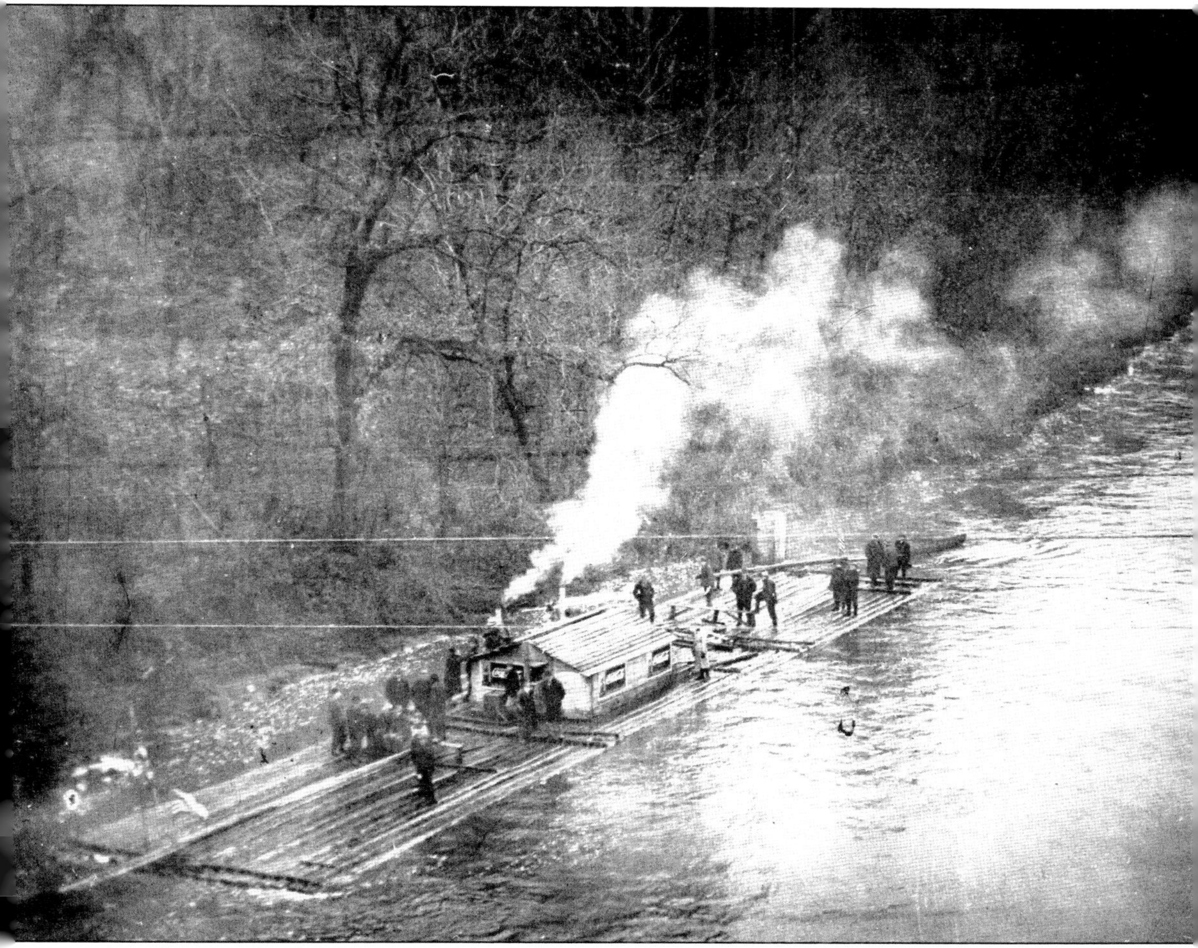

In this photograph, the last raft is about to pass under the railroad bridge near the Fulton Tunnel. The raft was 112 feet long and 28 feet wide and was made of white pine timbers. Many people, in addition to several reporters and photographers, followed the progress of the raft. However, this celebration of the Tonkin family's 100 years of rafting was ill fated. On March 20, shortly after noon, the raft crashed into a railroad bridge at Muncy and 7 of the 45 people aboard were killed, including the pilot, Harry "Spot" Conner, and newsreel cameraman Thomas Proffitt. Otis M. Fulton took this photograph on March 16, 1938. (Courtesy Clearfield County Historical Society.)

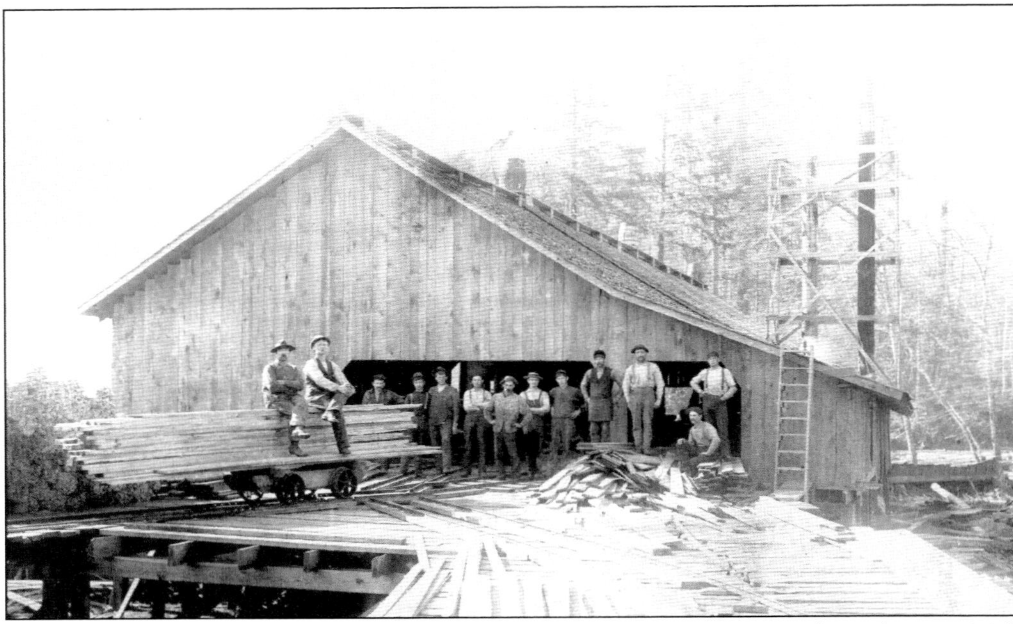

In 1892, the Watson and Clark Mill in Glen Campbell was one of many mills in the area. Mills were usually built near small streams and rivers, as they were run by waterpower. They were busy in the spring and fall during the wet seasons but shut down during the farming season. (Courtesy Clearfield County Historical Society.)

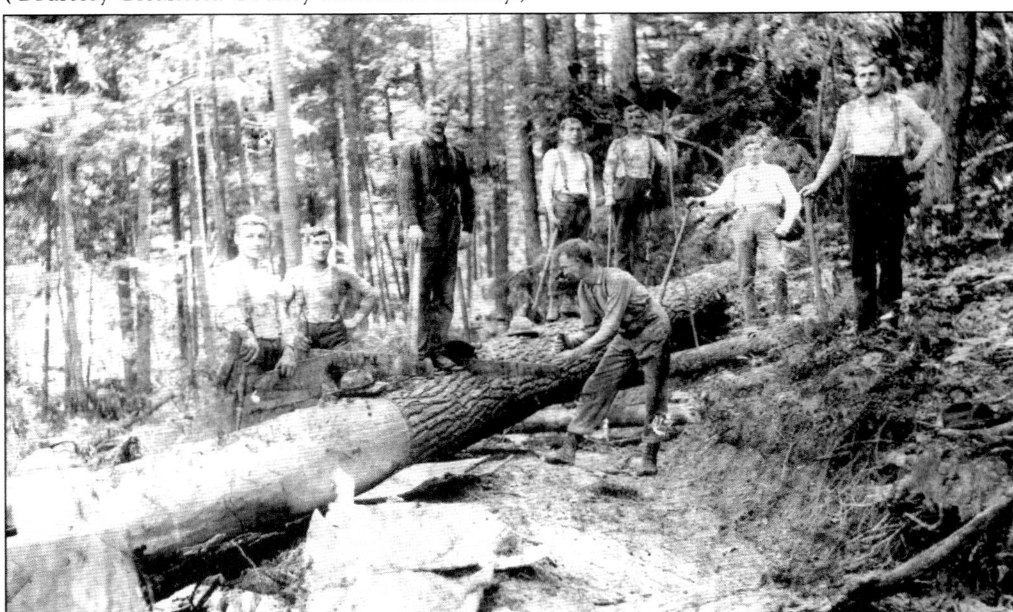

Trees had a variety of uses. These men, working near the DuBois-Rockton Road, are removing Hemlock bark to use in tanning leather. A new way to tan leather was developed c. 1940, and the bark was no longer needed. Seen here are, from left to right, Charles Peoples, Bill Kirk, Arthur Schofield, Jesse Dressler, Charles Sphicher, Austin Hendricks, Floyd Shaffer, and Woody Kelly. (Courtesy Clearfield County Historical Society.)

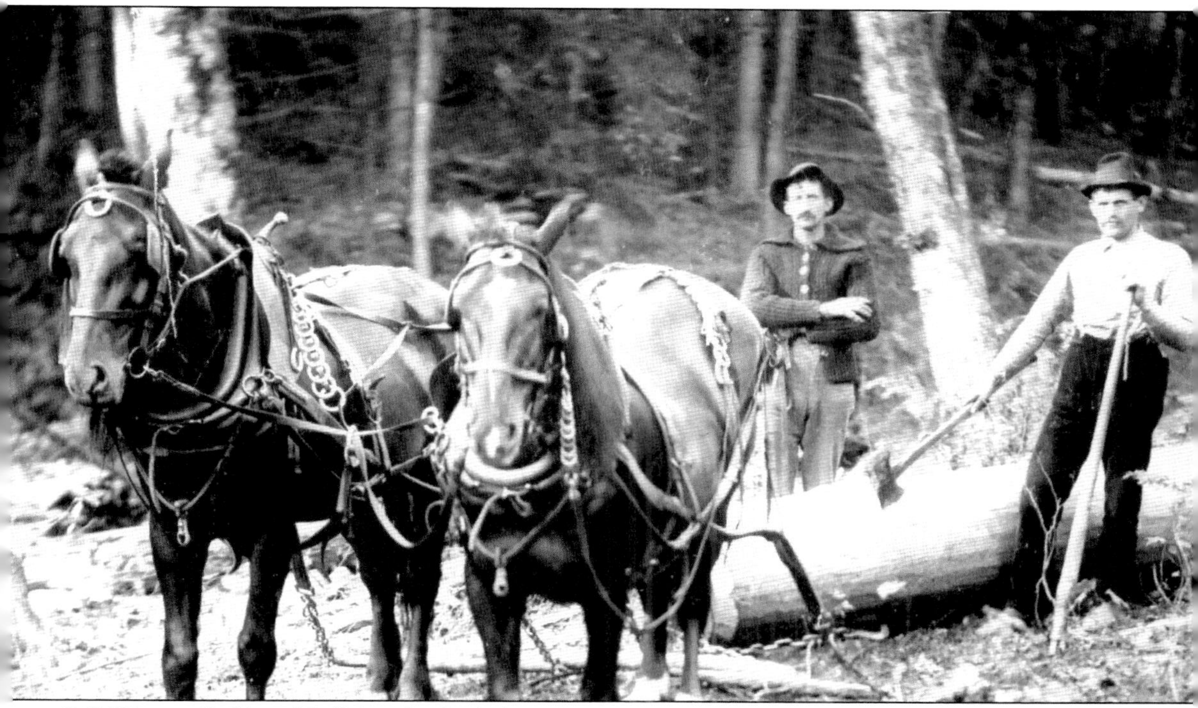

Bill Weaver (left) and Bill Brooke (right) work together on Adam Marshall's crew at Bell Run c. 1900. Weaver is the driver, or swamper, who dragged logs from the spot where the tree fell to the logging area. Brooke was a swamp dog, or the one who located logs, cut the brush and roots so the logs could be hauled out, and leveled the end of the log so it would not catch on roots or dig into soft soil. The swamp dog also drove the grabs, or hooks used for hauling, into the logs. Here, the grab has already been driven into the log and is almost under it. (Courtesy Clearfield County Historical Society.)

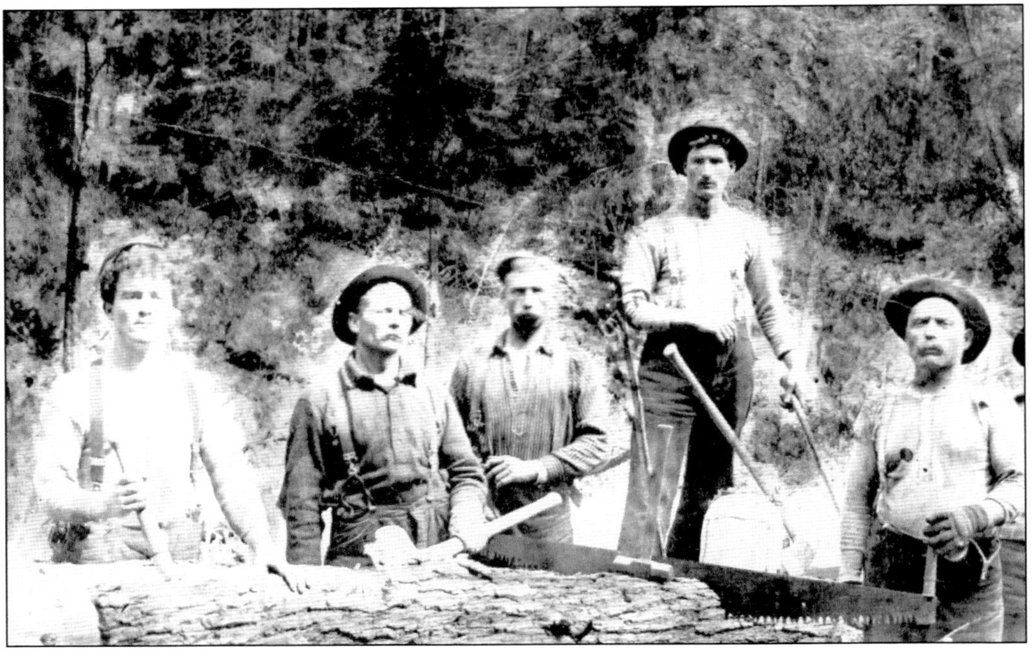

Each man on a cutting crew had a specific job, as illustrated in this photograph of a Bell Run crew. The men sawing are sawyers. The man standing highest is a bumper, or someone who cuts the limbs and knots away. The length of the log is measured by the man with the ax, who also loosens the bark for the spudder. The spudder then removes the bark. (Courtesy Clearfield County Historical Society.)

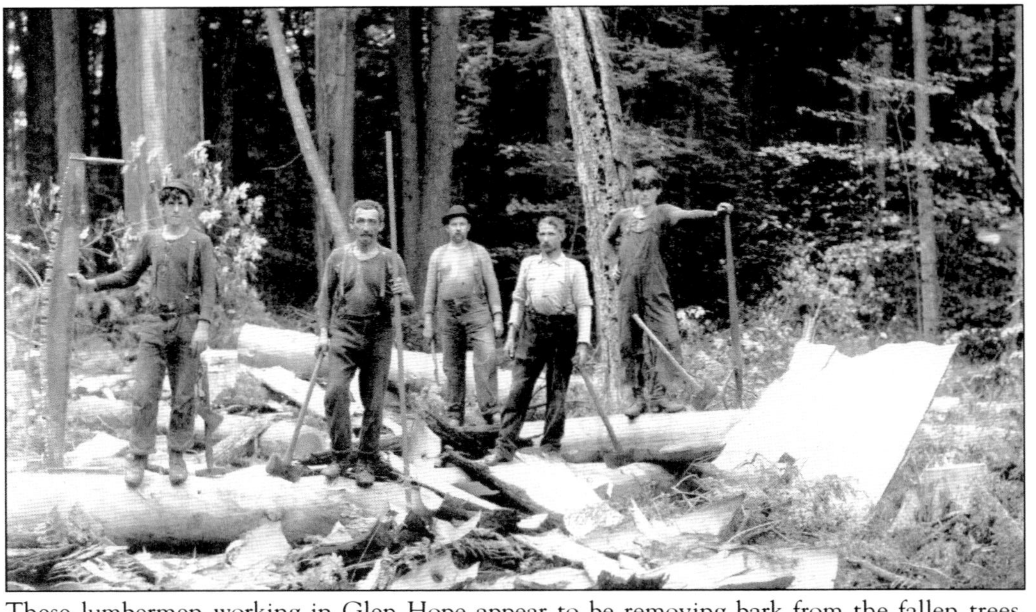

These lumbermen working in Glen Hope appear to be removing bark from the fallen trees. Note the large saw held by the man on the far left. On Route 53 near Glen Hope is a monument marking where one of the first men in the county, Capt. Edward Ricketts, settled in 1784. (Courtesy Coalport Area Coal Museum.)

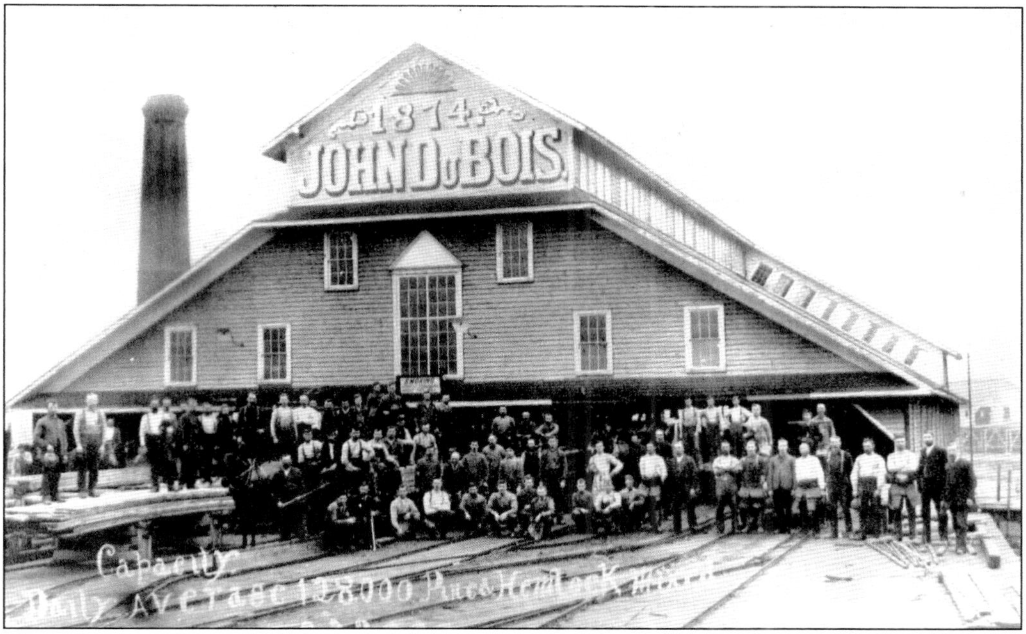

This lumbermill, owned by John DuBois (above), was 250 feet long and 80 feet wide, with a 250-horsepower engine and a production capacity of 120,000 board feet, 60,000 shingles, 40,000 lath, and 10,000 pickets per day. It was built in 1874. Prior to this, most of the timber was floated to his Williamsport mills. DuBois is said to have treated his employees well, paying them higher than normal wages. In slower economic times, when it was suggested he lower these wages, he decided not to, saying he and his managers could probably take a pay cut easier than his men could. When DuBois died, he left his holdings to his nephew, John E. DuBois. Below is a postcard showing his lumber camp. (Courtesy Clearfield County Historical Society.)

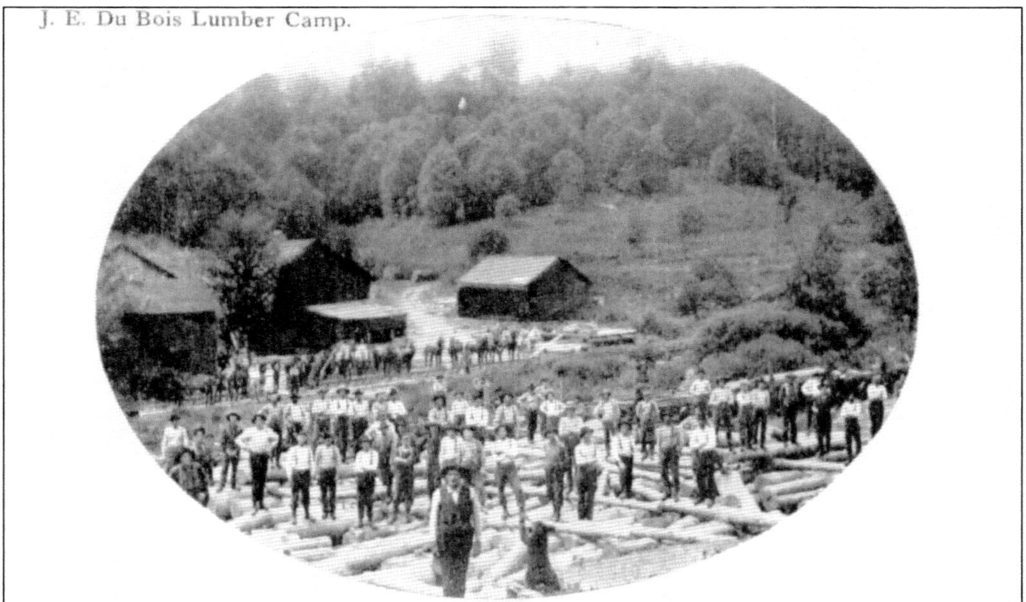

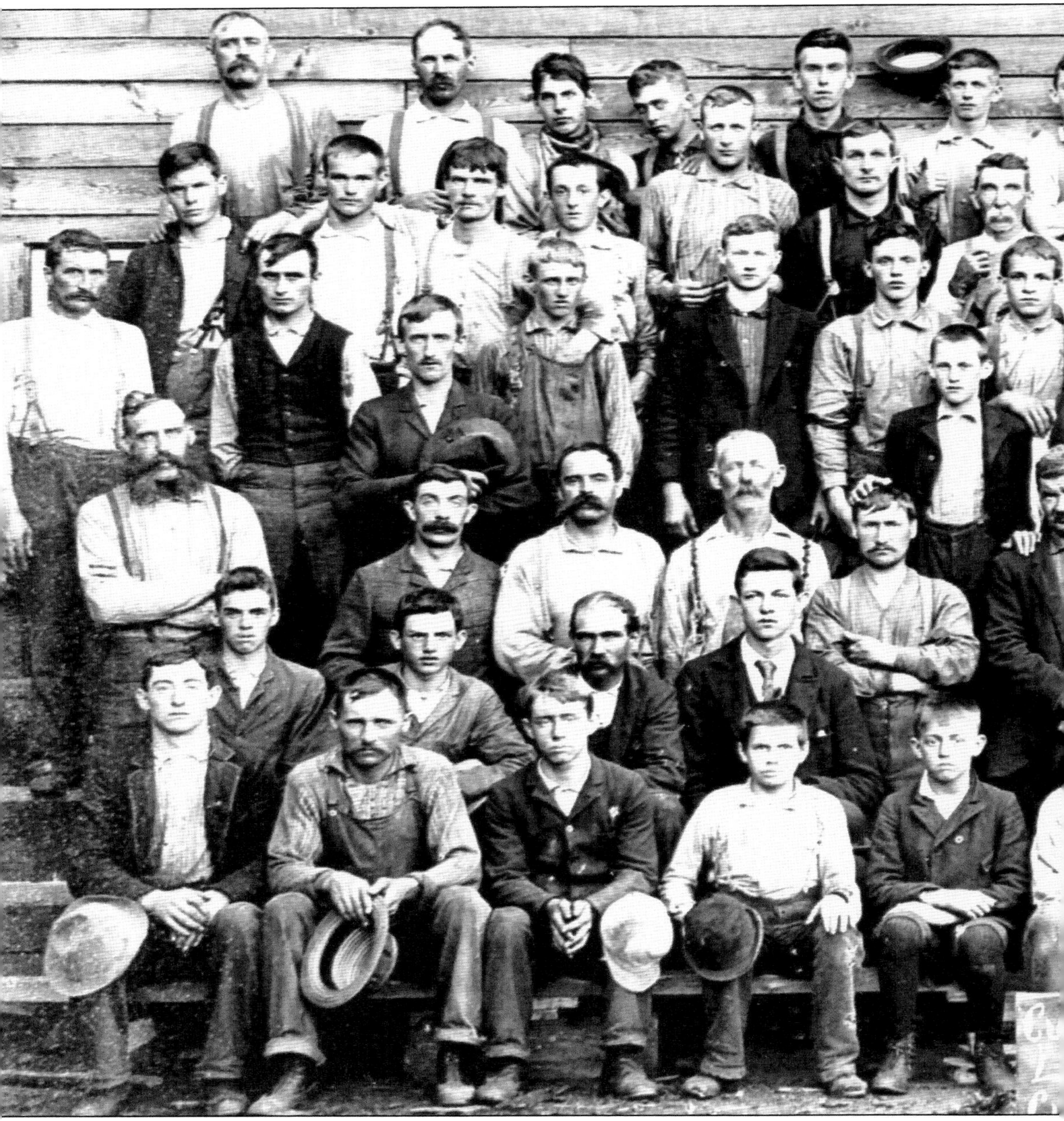

The employees of the Big Mill in Curwensville (*c.* 1891) pose for a photographer. They are, from left to right, as follows: (first row) Robert Durnell, John Spinney, Edward Peters, William R. Daugherty, Ned Bloom, Oscar B. Ardary, Clarence Young, Clarence King, Frank Miller, Scott King, Zelotus A. Strickland, Charles Stockbridge, Frank Hooven, and Nat Maurey; (second row) George Lewis, George King, Joseph Chilcote, Fred Stockbridge, J.C. Dunkle, Harry Caldwell, Thomas E. Evans, Edward Tate, Herbert Shearer, and William Tate; (third row) John H. Cole, Thomas Barnes, George Williams, Alonzo E. Benson, Perry Picketts, Thomas Long, unidentified, David Maurey, Edward Williams, Sepherious E. Deering, Archie Cole, and George E. Daugherty; (fourth row) "Roddy" Fullerton, Charles Cole, Frank Brown, T. Millard

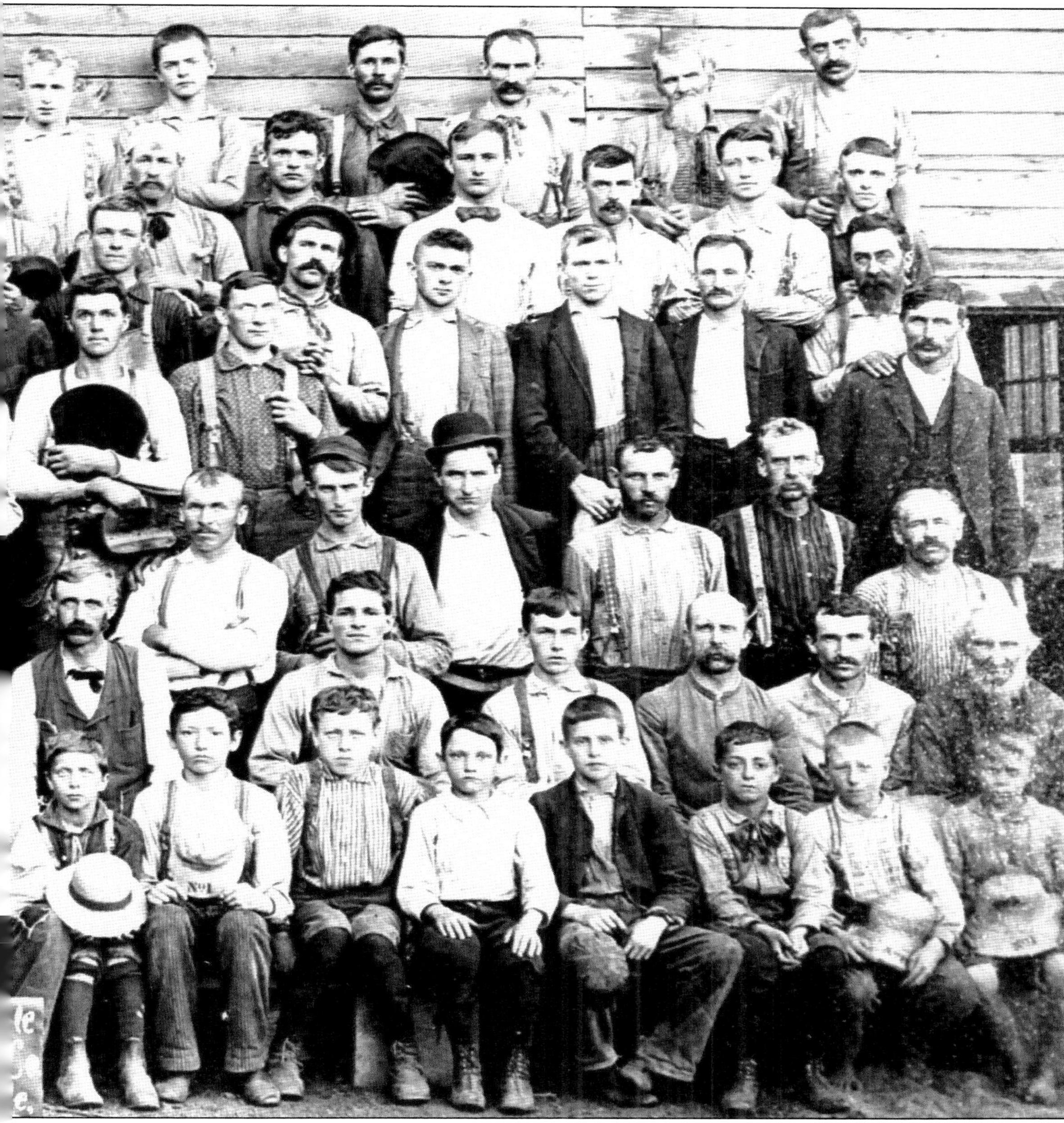

Bloom, Thomas B. Scott, and Michael Cassidy; (fifth row) George Strickland, William Rider, Harvey Maurey, Bruce Bennett, Charles King, Port Wise, Samuel Keyser, Albert Mellott, Harry S. Brown, Percy E. Smith, George Philips, Samuel Freeze, and Samuel S. Moore; (sixth row) Mart Robison, Orvis Bloom, Frank Frantz, Fred H. McKendrick, Warren Price, Harry Shirk, David C. Scott, Perry Shirk, Samuel Starr, James Rider, Frank Rider, William Ammerman, D. Newton Shirey, and David Young; (seventh row) William Durnell Sr., George Warren, David Wilson, Oliver F. Smith, Charles Wells, William Young, William Durnell Jr., Jacob Maurey, Edward Lender, Robert Wilson, John Lender, William Dorbit, and John Cronmiller. (Courtesy Clearfield County Historical Society.)

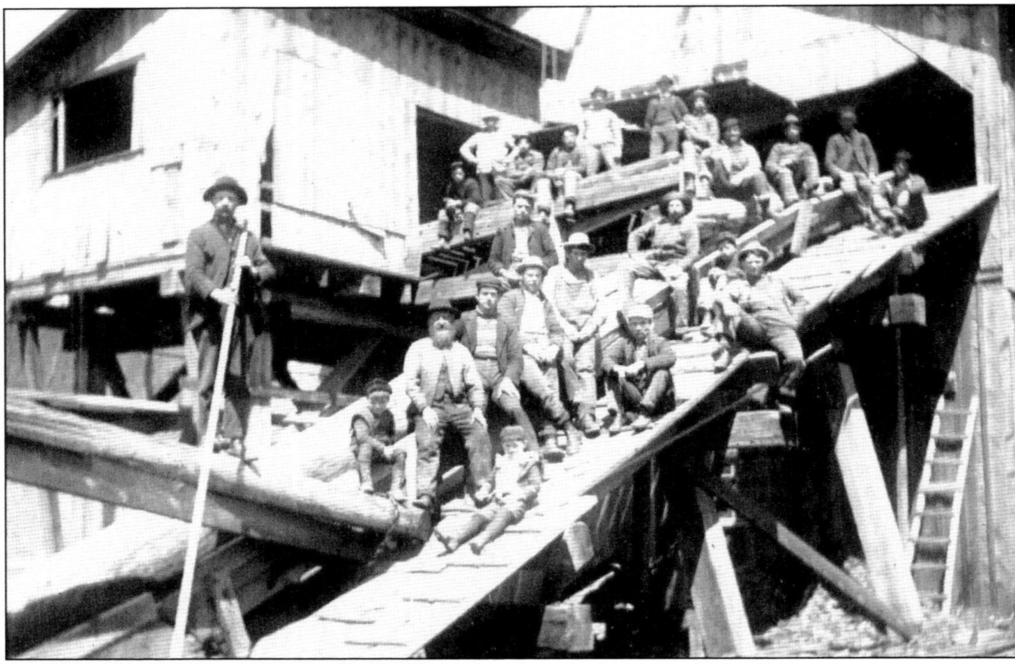

Men pose outside of the Hall and Weiss sawmill in Curry Run in July 1905. A railroad hauled logs to the mill, and the timber was then cut and floated down Curry Run to the Susquehanna River. The mill is reported to have been able to cut 100,00 feet of lumber per day. It closed in 1908. (Courtesy Clearfield County Historical Society.)

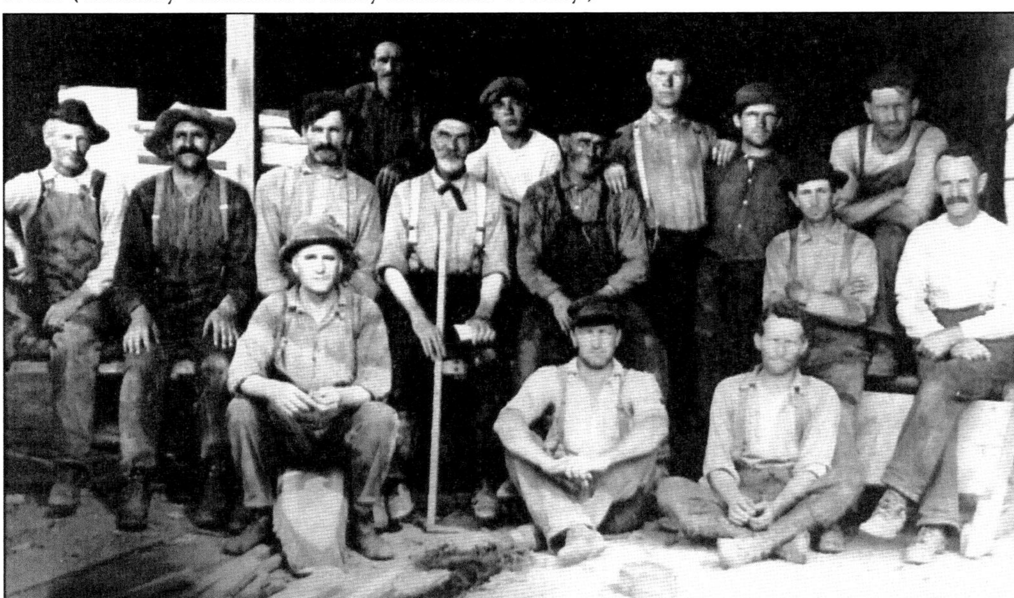

The crew poses at Hegarty's sawmill. Allison Hegarty is the one on the right in a white shirt. The Hegartys had mills in Coalport and Madera as well as several coal mines and a company store. Allison and his wife, Mae Bell, lived in the old mansion at Hegarty's Crossroads. (Courtesy Coalport Area Coal Museum.)

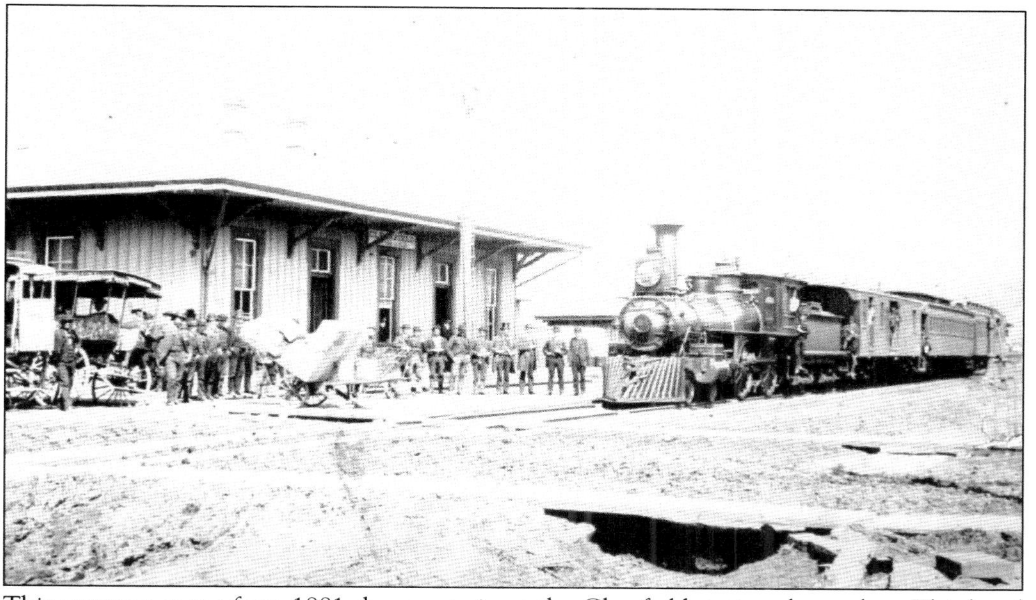

This common scene from 1881 shows a train at the Clearfield station, located on Third and Reed Streets. A legend that claims the railroad company snuck into town in the middle of the night to lay the Third Street tracks is untrue. The tracks were actually laid starting on September 13, 1873. (Courtesy Clearfield County Historical Society.)

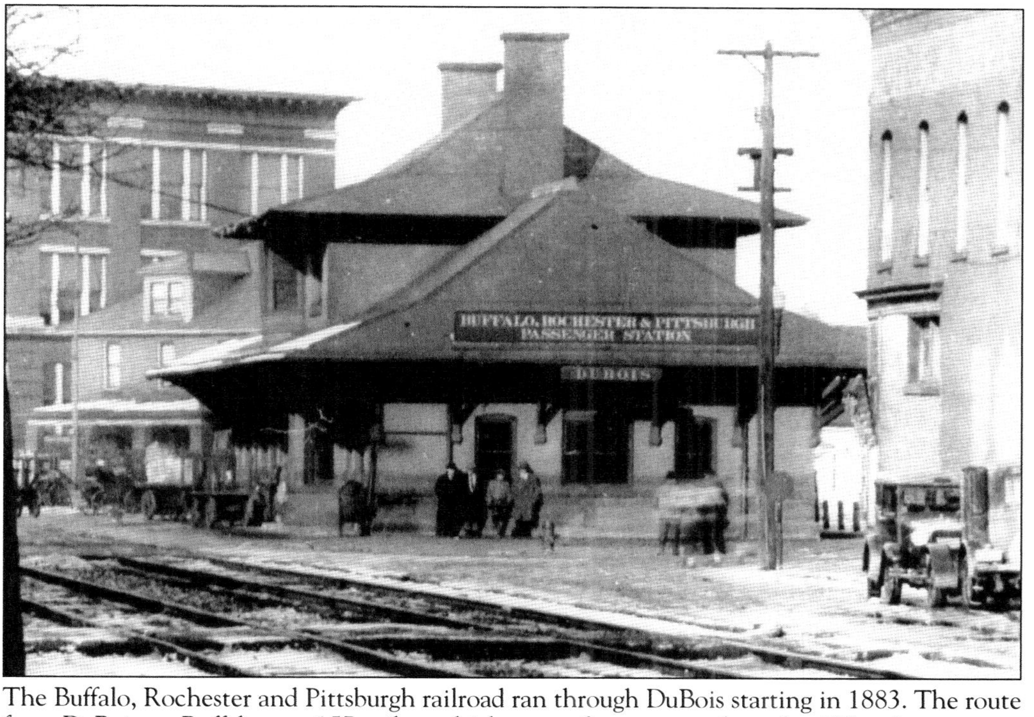

The Buffalo, Rochester and Pittsburgh railroad ran through DuBois starting in 1883. The route from DuBois to Buffalo was 157 miles, which was a faster route than the 185-mile route via Driftwood and Emporium. This station was built in 1894 and is now home to the Cherry law offices. (Courtesy Clearfield County Historical Society.)

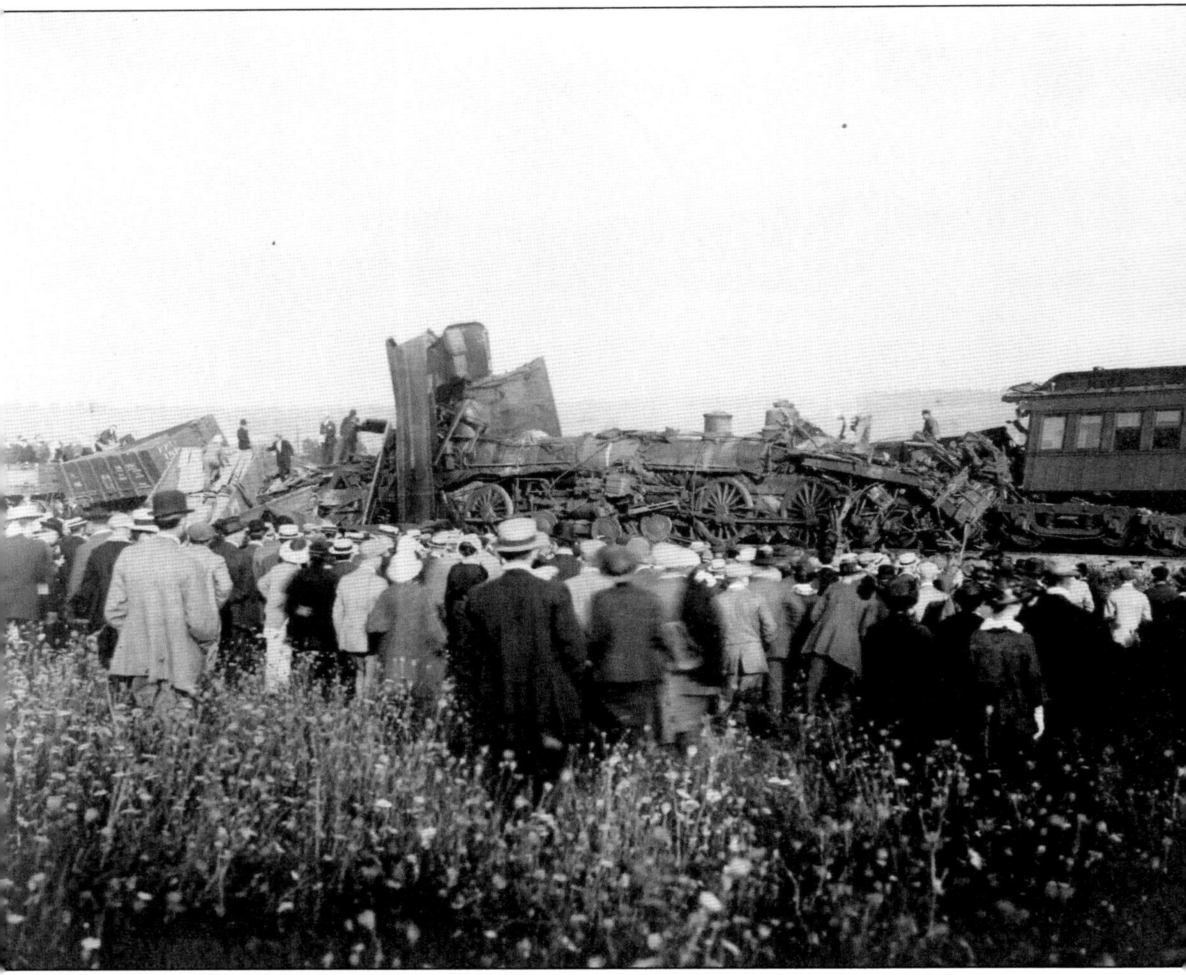

The Altoona and Philipsburg Connecting Railroad was nicknamed the Alley Popper. This name stuck with the 15-mile line even after several mergers and name changes. At the end of the line's existence, in 1936, it was the Pittsburgh and Susquehanna Railroad.

In 1914, the Alley Popper staged a train wreck for a movie called *The Valley of Lost Hope*. The two trains started about a mile apart. Once the engines got going, the engineers leaped to safety. It is reported that the two trains crashed with a tremendous roar. Thousands of people gathered to watch the event. (Courtesy Clearfield County Historical Society.)

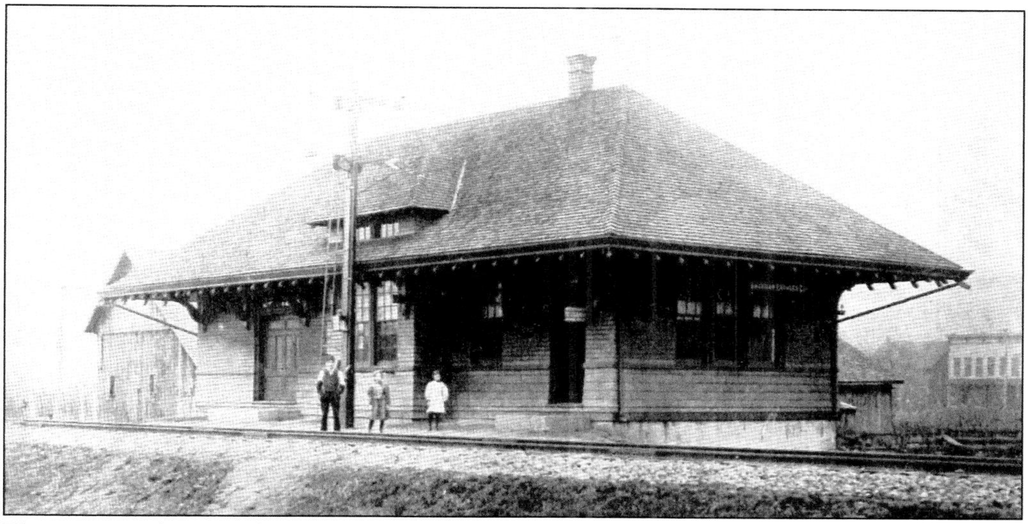

The New York Central Railroad came to Irvona in 1904, building the above station. The Pennsylvania Railroad was there first, in the 1880s, and had a separate station in town. The Pennsylvania Railroad line ran from Cresson to Punxsutawney. The town Irvona was named for Col. E.A. Irvin of Curwensville. He was a Civil War veteran who was a member of the famed Pennsylvania Bucktails. (Courtesy Coalport Area Coal Museum.)

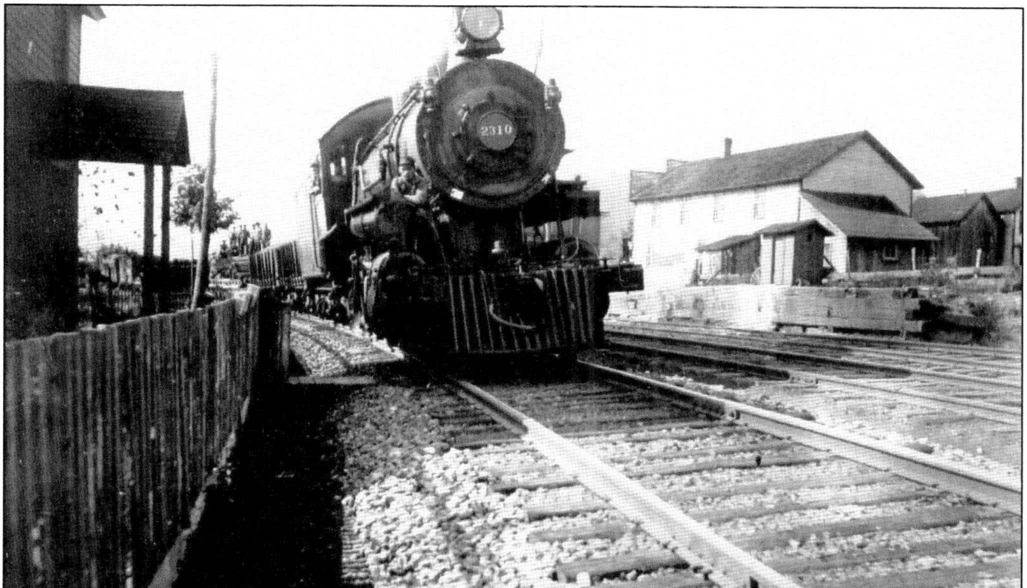

Many little towns sprang up because of the railroad. In 1884, it was Olanta that benefited from the traffic of the Beech Creek, Clearfield and Southwestern Railroad. In this 1902 photograph, a locomotive passes through the town. When the railroad left in 1938, so did many of the businesses. (Courtesy Clearfield County Historical Society.)

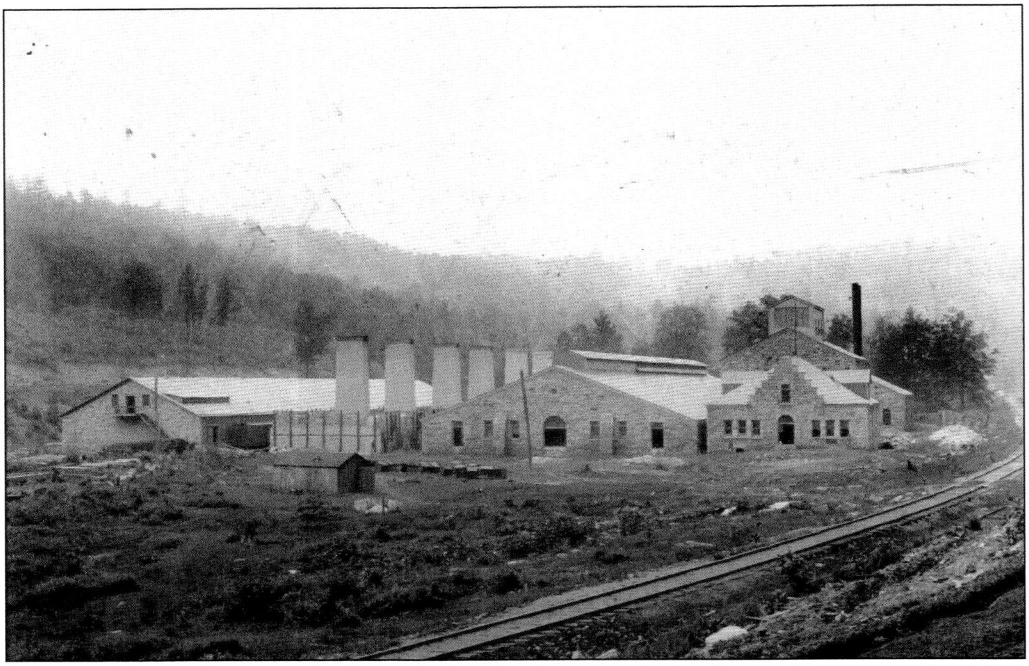

The brickyard at Curwensville was completed in 1900 and started manufacturing in the fall of that same year. At first, it was the Curwensville Fire Brick Company and then the Hamond Burkey Company, the Bickford Fire Brick Company, and the Crescent Refractories Company. In 1929, that company merged with the North American Refractories Company, which eventually became known as NARCO. (Courtesy J. Duane Test.)

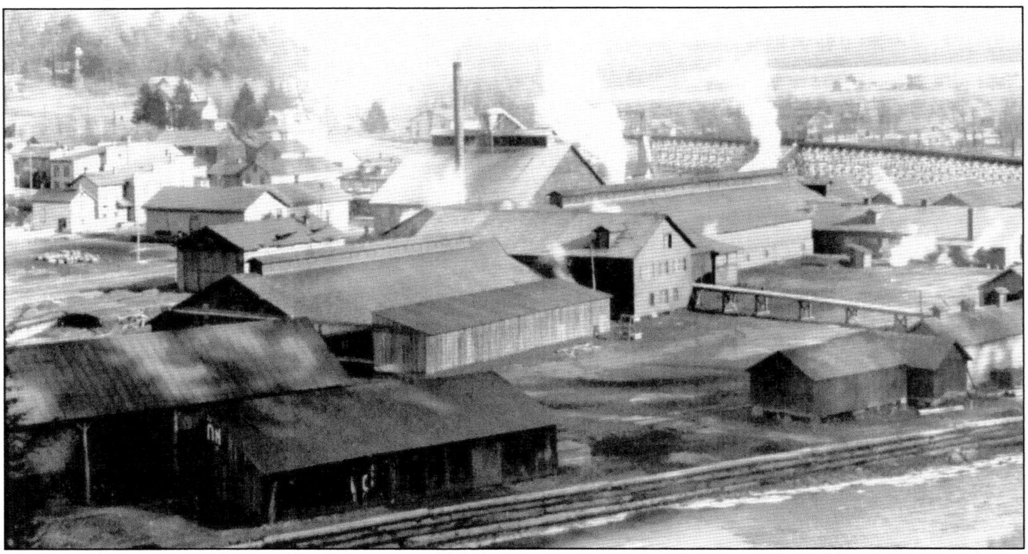

Since 1819, Curwensville has always had a tannery. This is Curwensville's first steam tannery, which started in 1877 as William S. White and Sons. It had several owners and was the Elk Tanning Company when a big fire damaged it in 1897. By the time this photograph was taken, it had been rebuilt. A few years later, another fire destroyed the business completely. (Courtesy Curwensville-Pike Township Historical Society.)

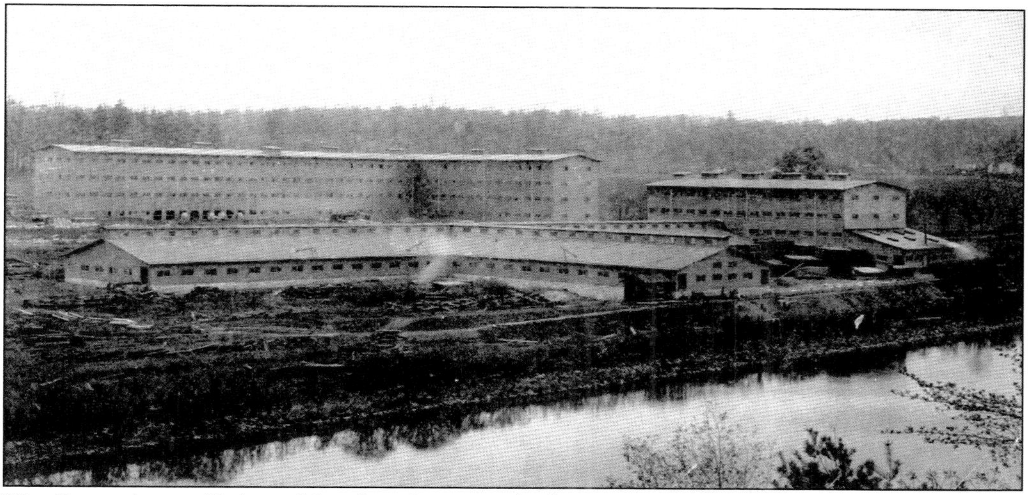

The Pennsylvania Hide and Leather Company built its tannery (above) on the former Hoover Hughes and Company sawmill lot in the early 1900s. It was damaged by fire in 1928 and sold to the Franklin Tanning Company, who partially rebuilt it. Eventually, it became Howe's Leather Company. In 1999, it still employed 140 people. Unfortunately, however, the 184-year-long tradition of Curwensville tanneries ended when the plant closed in 2003. Employees of all ages take a break to pose for the camera *c.* 1900 (below). Note the man in the front row, second from the right, with stains on the lower part of his pants. This was caused by the tannic acid used to soak the hides. (Courtesy J. Duane Test.)

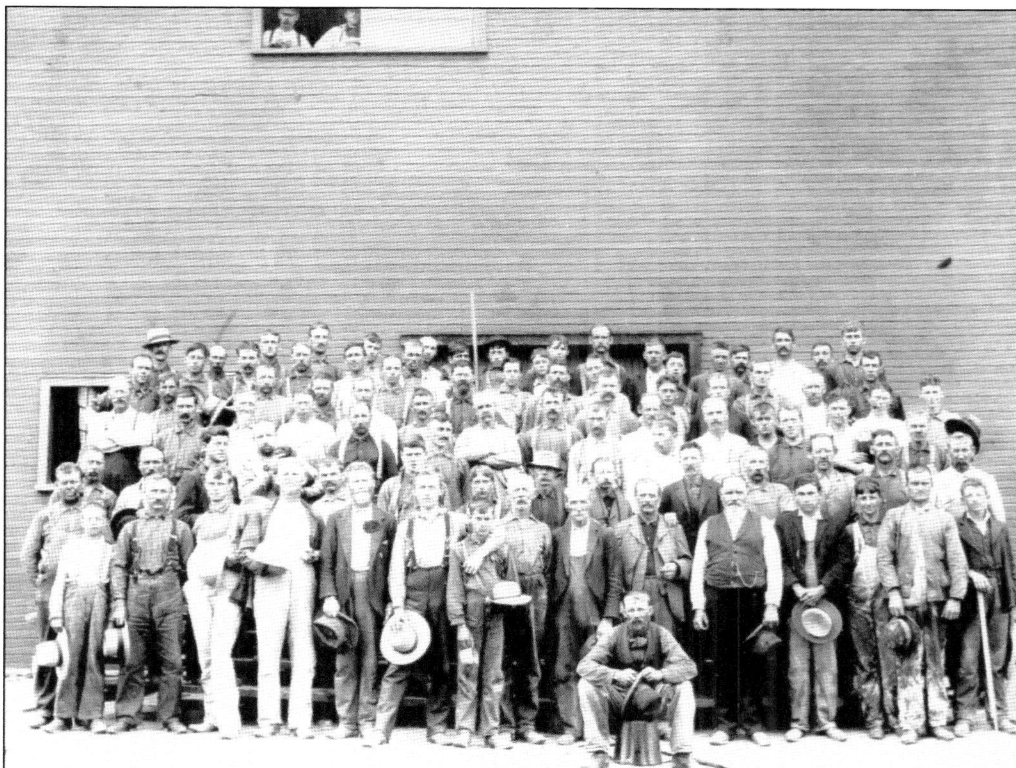

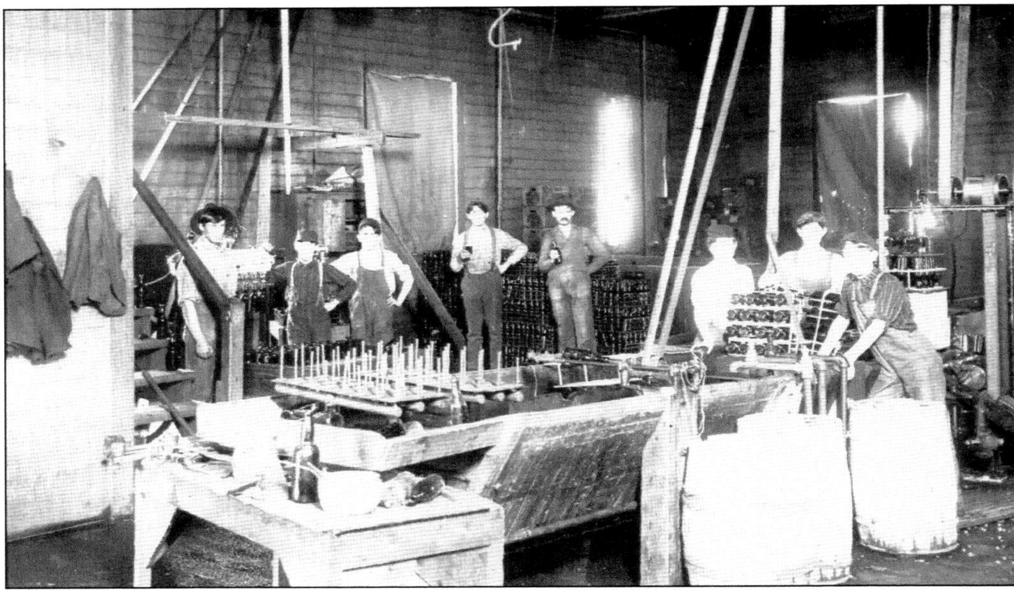

Employees of the DuBois Brewery are busy on the assembly line in this late-1890s photograph (above). The DuBois Brewery had several products, including DuBois Wurzburger, Hahne's Export (named for founder Frank Hahne Sr.), Hahne's Porter, and DuBois Budweiser. Hahne had to fight Anheuser-Busch for his right to keep the Budweiser name. At one point, the company had branches in Buffalo and Newark. Just when it was hitting its peak, the business was hurt by Prohibition. But because the company also produced ice and soda pop (DuBois cola, ginger ale, root beer, and Orange Superba), it did survive the Prohibition period, only to close in 1972. Below is a view of the entire brewery. (Courtesy DuBois Area Historical Society.)

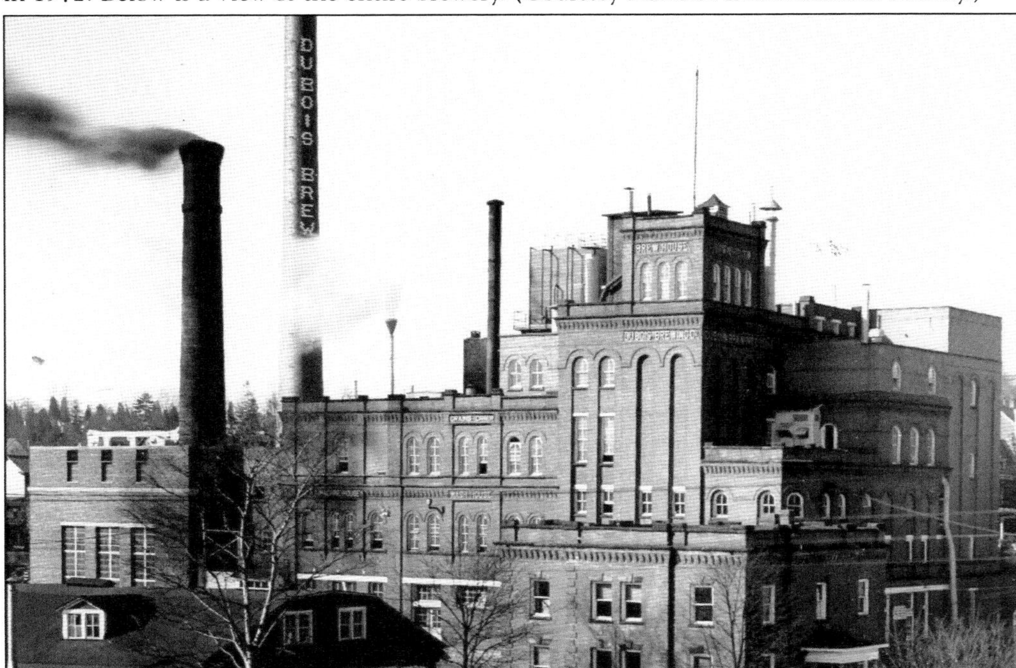

Four

LIFESTYLES AND CELEBRATIONS

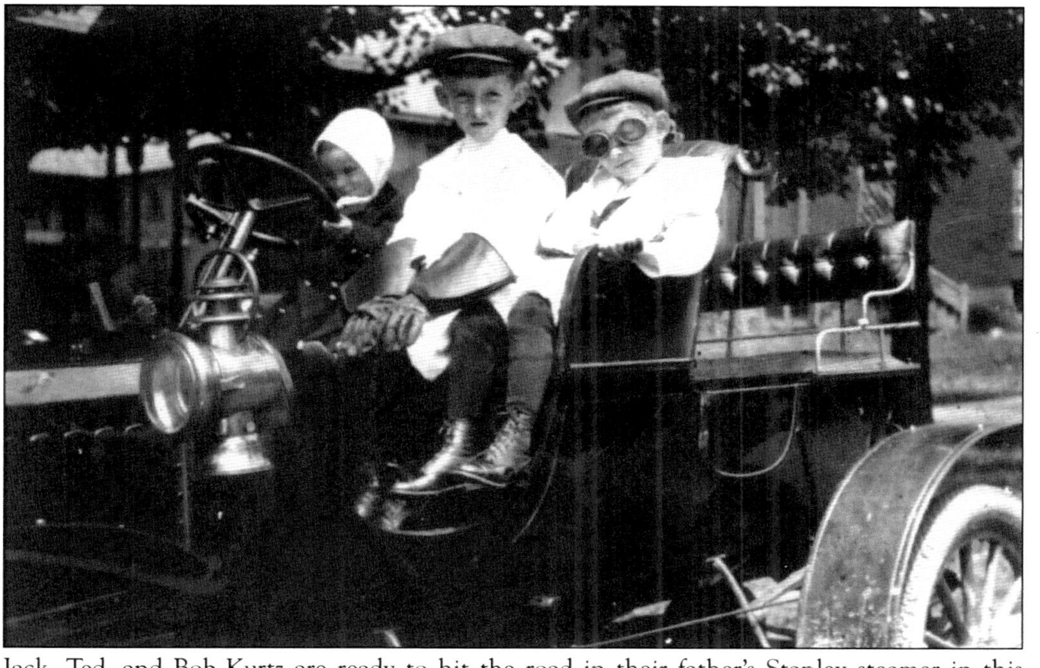

Jack, Ted, and Bob Kurtz are ready to hit the road in their father's Stanley steamer in this photograph from 1908. The boys were the sons of Kurtz Brothers founder Charles T. Kurtz and his wife, Pauline. TeBoJa, a contraction of the boys' names, was used as a trade name for Kurtz Brothers. As adults, they all were involved with the company. (Courtesy Robert M. Kurtz Jr.)

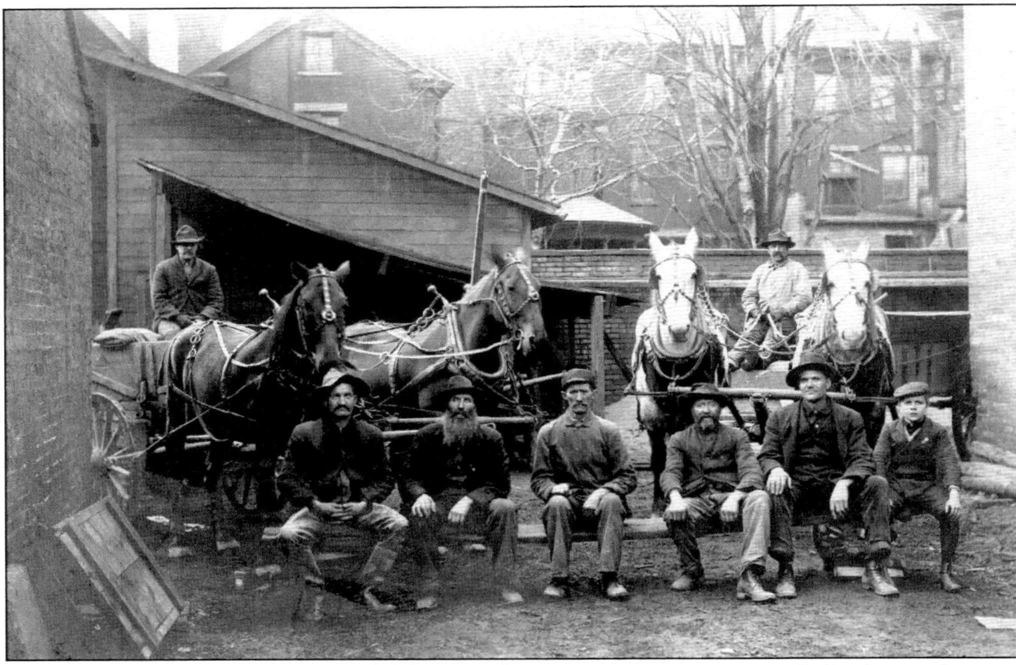

Mansfield F. Graham, the Clearfield Borough street commissioner, and the borough street crew pose in this August 1908 photograph. Graham is second from the right. Beside him is his son, Guy Graham. At this point in time, borough equipment included horses and wagons. (Clearfield County Historical Society.)

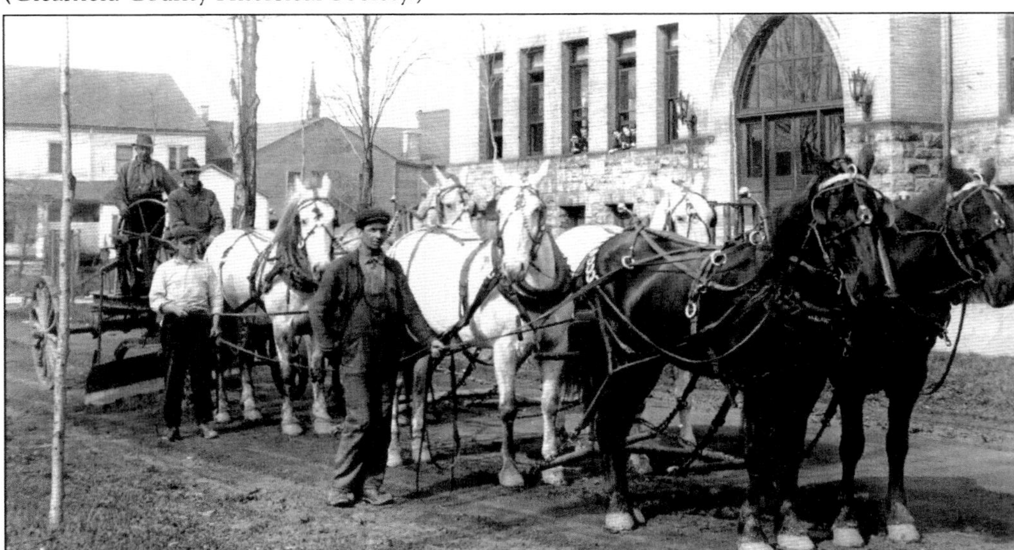

A grader passes by the Old East School building on Front Street in Clearfield as the schoolchildren watch from the windows. Riding the grader is George Washington Butler. On the far left is the Joseph and Elizabeth Shaw house; today, the property is a park. The school building was closed in 1975 and was later torn down to make way for the Clearfield Borough building. (Courtesy Clearfield County Historical Society.)

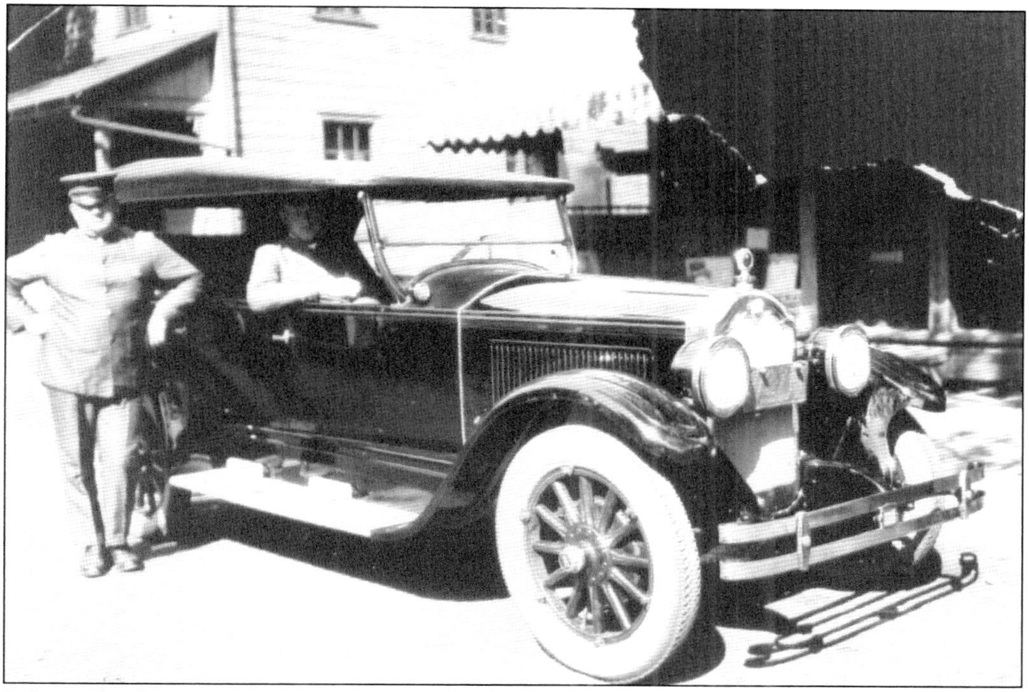

Police Chief Roy McMullen stands proudly next to Clearfield's first police car. Inside the car (a 1924 Durant) is Ernest Woolridge, the assistant chief. Both men were hired in January 1922 and served until their deaths in the 1960s. (Courtesy Clearfield County Historical Society.)

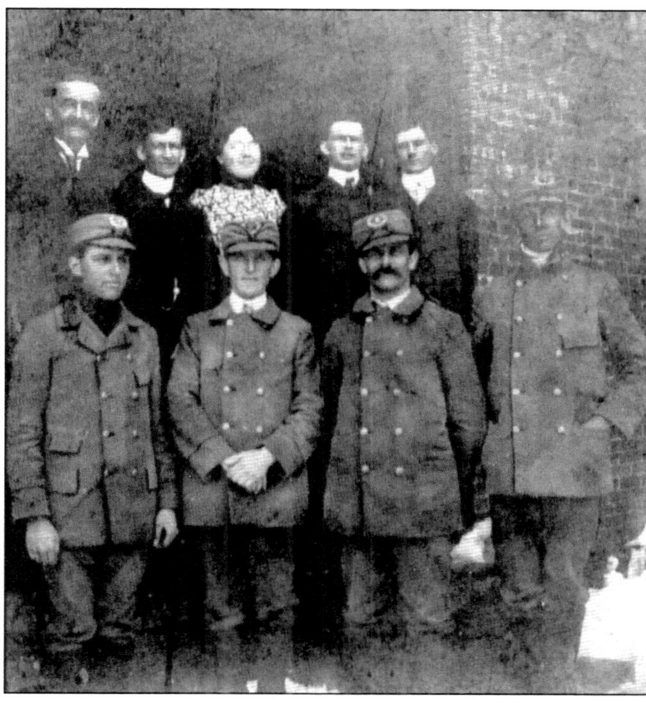

Clearfield post office workers pose in this c. 1905 photograph. At that time, the post office was located on Market Street, in the store where the B&E Coin Company does business today. The current and first permanent post office building was not constructed until 1936. (Courtesy Clearfield County Historical Society.)

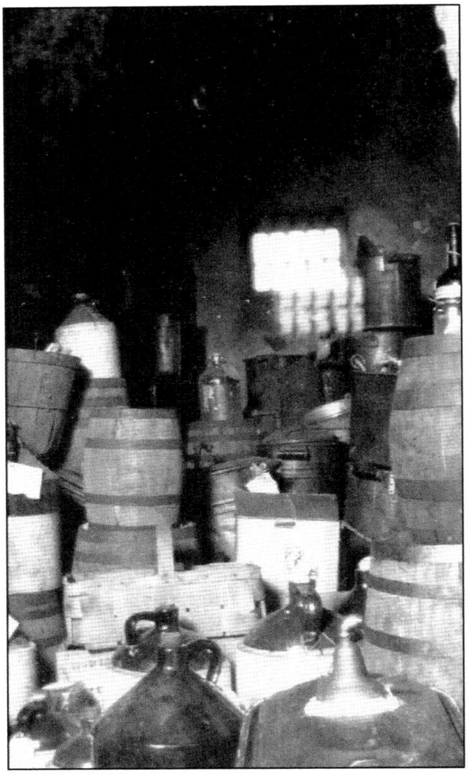

During Prohibition, confiscated alcohol found its way to the "booze cell" at the county jail. This 1924 photograph shows 400 quarts housed in various containers. (Courtesy Clearfield County Historical Society.)

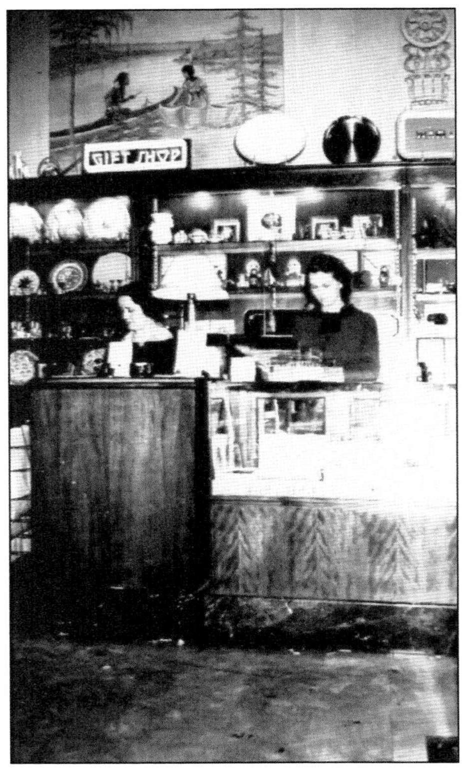

One of the landmarks of downtown Clearfield is the Dimeling Hotel, which was built in 1904 by Bezzer Brothers of Pittsburgh. This picture of the hotel's gift shop is from 1936. Eileen Smith was the manager then, and Jean Keeher was one of the clerks. (Courtesy Clearfield County Historical Society.)

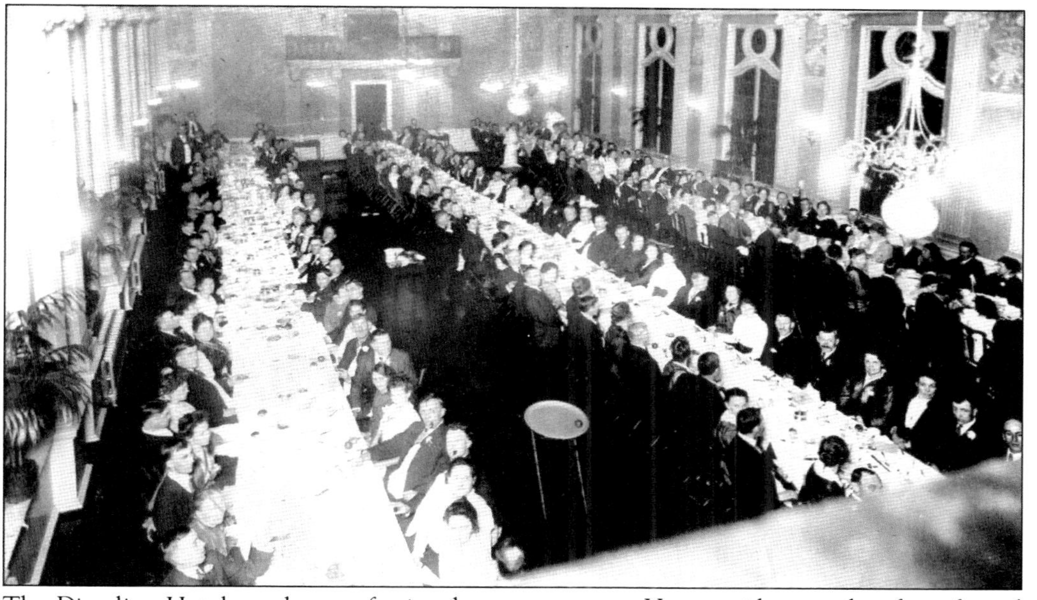

The Dimeling Hotel was known for its glamorous events. Here, residents gather for a formal dinner or perhaps a wedding reception. The ballroom covered an entire floor of the seven-story building. Unfortunately, the section of the hotel that was the ballroom was torn down when the hotel was converted into apartments. (Courtesy Clearfield County Historical Society.)

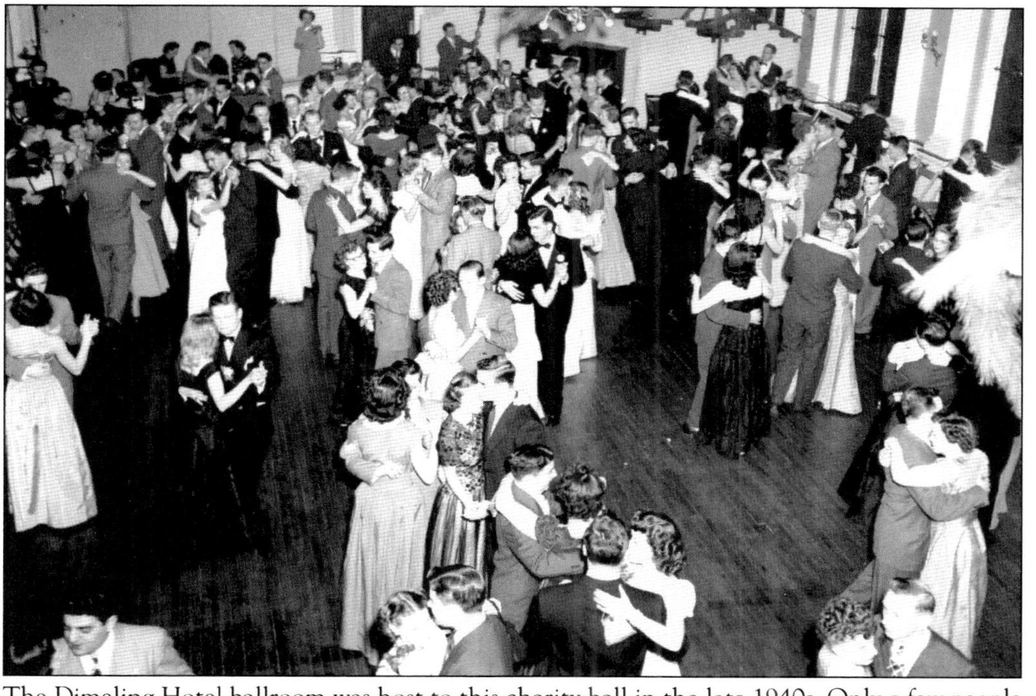

The Dimeling Hotel ballroom was host to this charity ball in the late 1940s. Only a few people have been identified in this photograph. They are Keith R. Bloom, who is in the left central area and dancing with a girl. To the right, behind him, is Helen "Honey" Axelson Smith. (Courtesy Clearfield County Historical Society.)

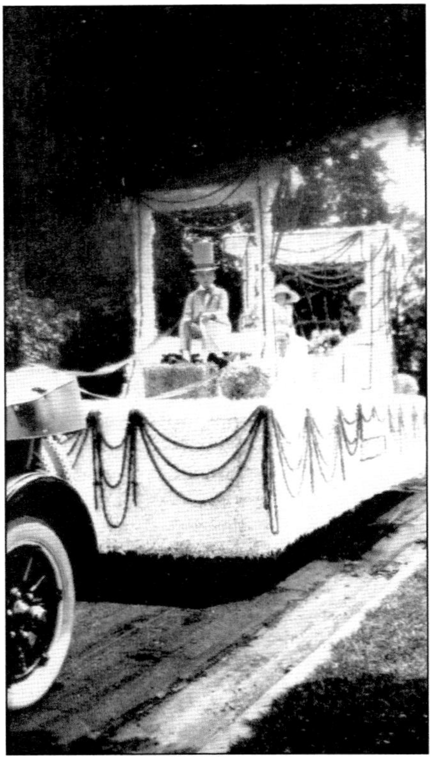

In the 1920s, an annual Fourth of July parade was held in most communities. Leitzinger Brothers and many businesses in each town made special floats for the occasion. The float to the left, from Clearfield's 1923 parade, appears to have a wedding theme. The float below, from 1927, seems to possibly be a tea party. Note the two peacocks near the back of the float. (Courtesy Jim Leitzinger.)

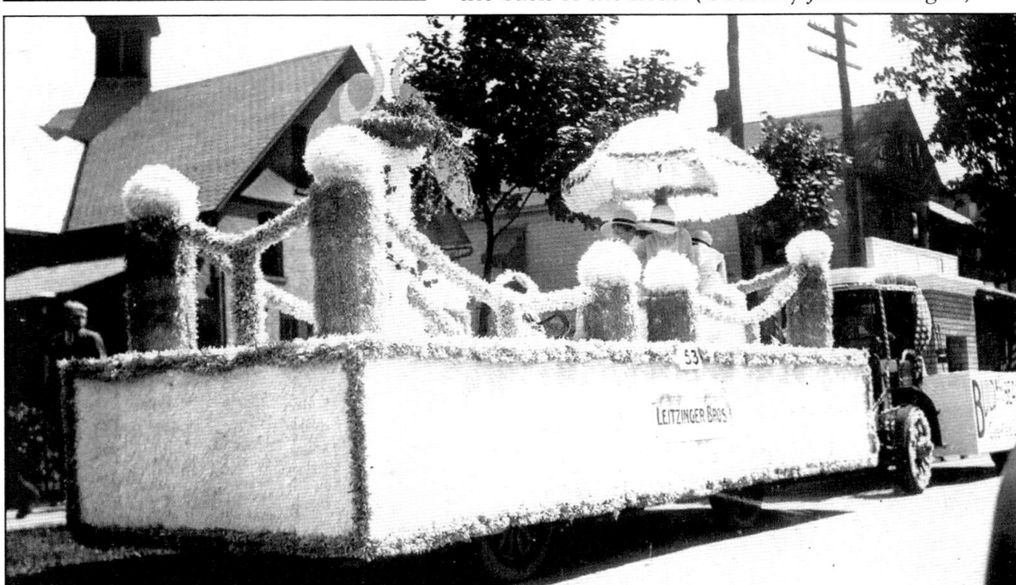

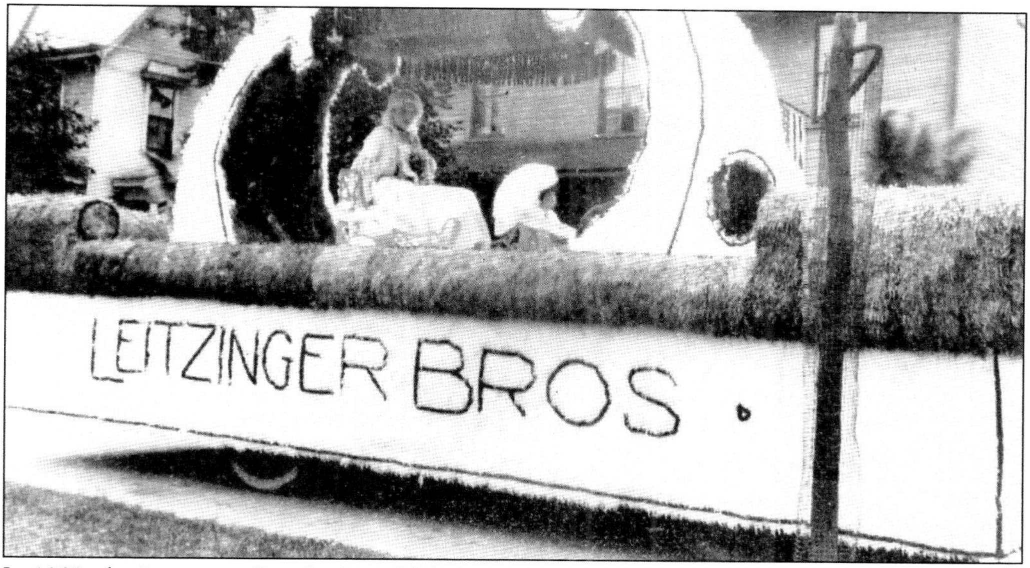

In 1928, the Leitzinger float had an old-fashioned feel, with vintage Victorian outfits. Leitzinger Brothers served the county for over 100 years, starting in 1882. The store was run by three generations of the Leitzinger family. It supplied clothing, shoes, jewelry, records, furniture, gifts, toys, and appliances. (Courtesy Jim Leitzinger.)

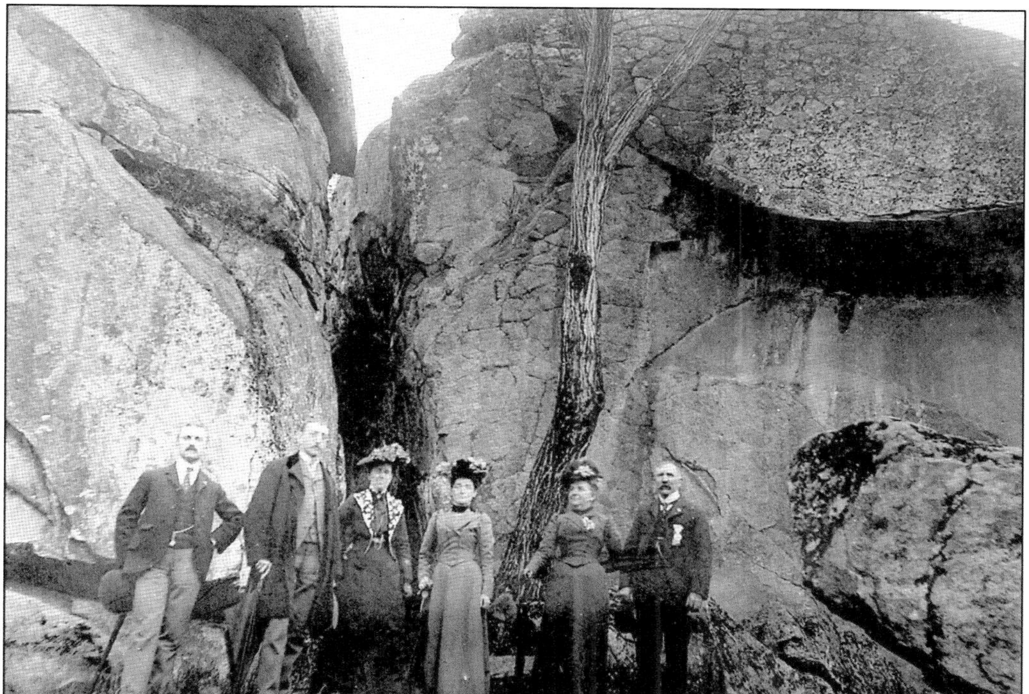

One of the most scenic places in the county is Bilger's Rocks, located just north of Grampian. Here, visitors pose in front of the spectacular rock formations. Second from the left is Charles T. Kurtz, founder of Kurtz Brothers. No one knows the exact age of the rock formation, but estimates put it between 10,000 and 25,000 years old. (Courtesy Clearfield County Historical Society.)

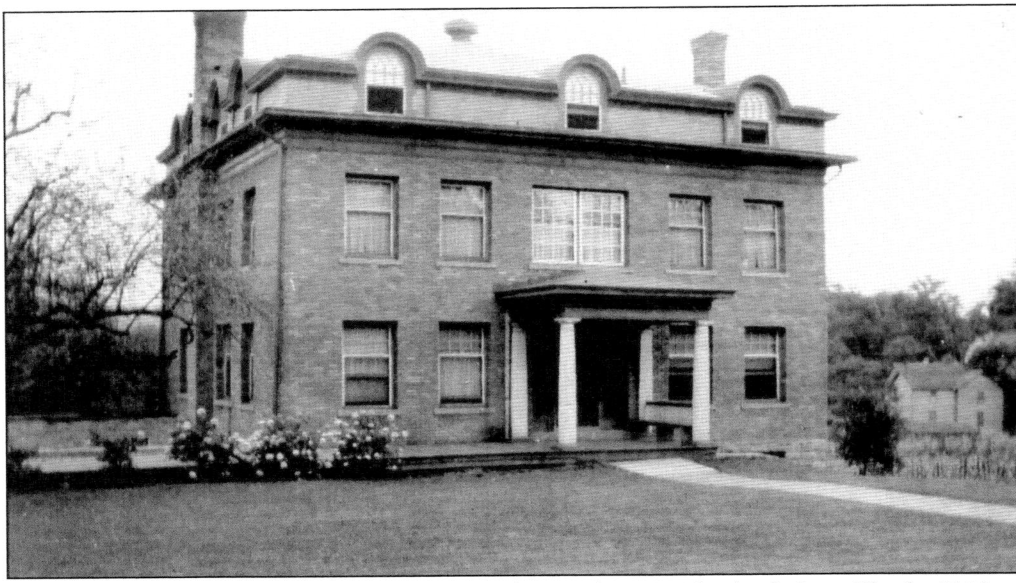

The Henry Kurtz Memorial Nurses Home was financed in 1911 by funds from Charles T. Kurtz and dedicated to the memory of his brother. The building was used for housing and classrooms for the Clearfield Hospital School of Nursing. The school started in 1907 and awarded 875 diplomas before closing in 1969. (Courtesy Clearfield County Historical Society.)

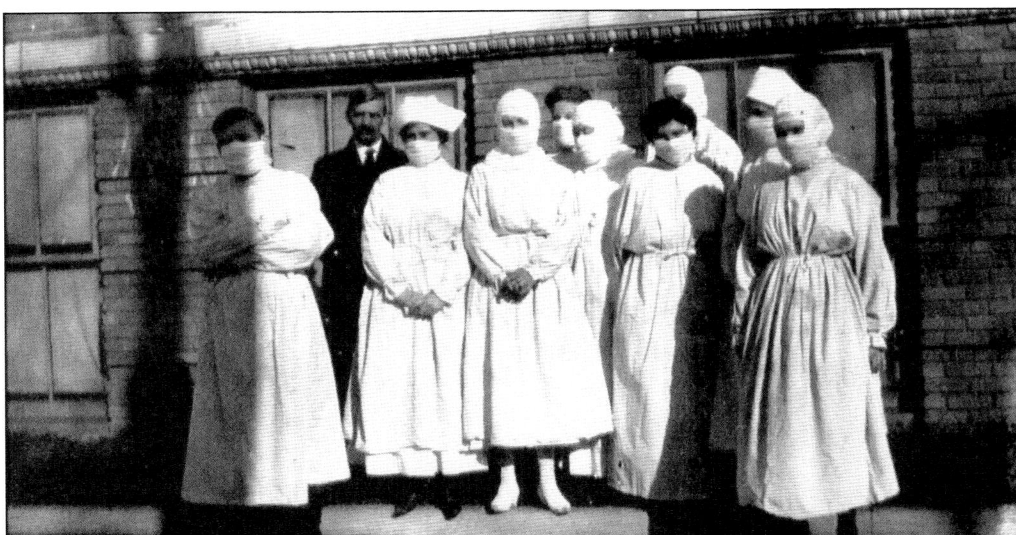

Nurses stand cautiously outside the old Clearfield High School, or West Building, on Front Street during the 1918 Spanish flu epidemic. The school and the children's home were used as additional emergency hospital space during the epidemic, which caused 500,000 deaths in the United States. At one point, 1,000 cases were reported in the Clearfield area alone. A total of 4,002 cases were documented in DuBois, along with 122 deaths. (Courtesy Clearfield County Historical Society.)

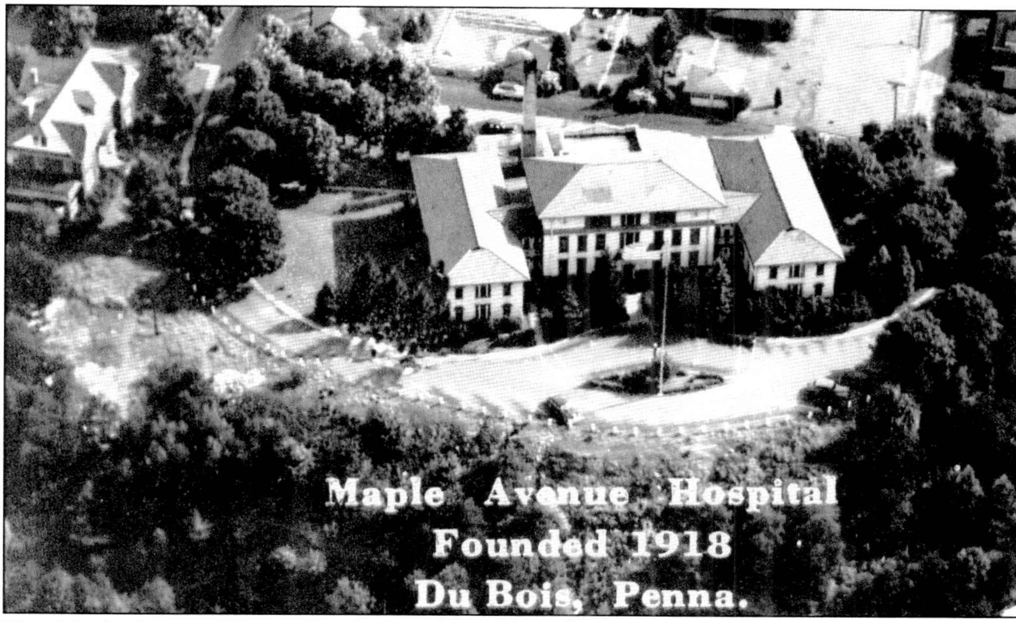

The Maple Avenue Hospital in DuBois began with $10,000 and four acres of land donated by John E. DuBois. It opened 10 days ahead of its planned October 8, 1918, date because of the Spanish flu epidemic. The hospital merged with the DuBois Hospital in 1985 to become the DuBois Regional Medical Center. (Courtesy Autumn Watson.)

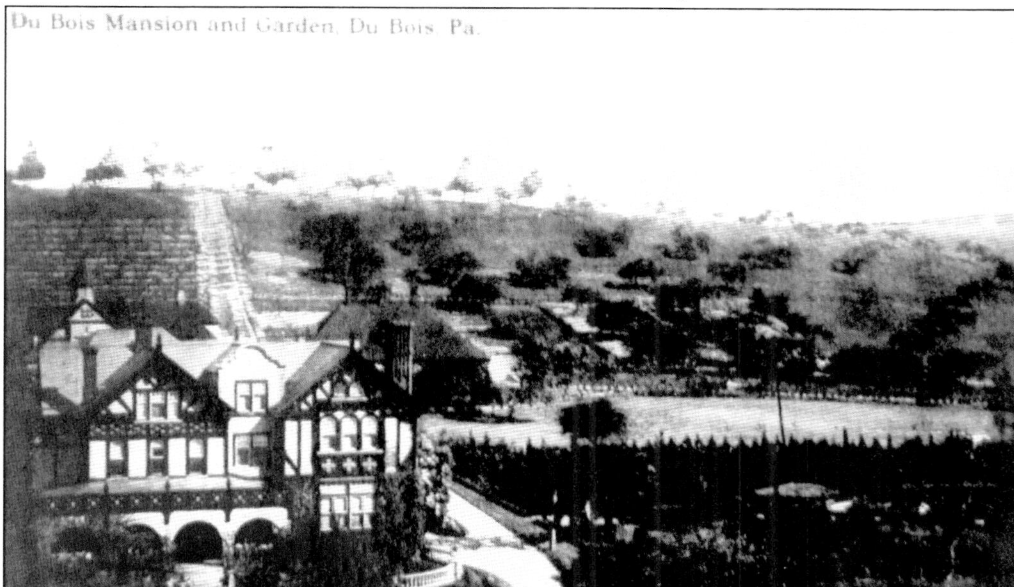

The DuBois mansion was renovated and expanded after John E. DuBois married Willie Gamble in 1897. It was redone in the English Tudor style, as shown in this postcard. The home was the site of many glamorous events, including one in which opera star Enrico Caruso sang. To the right of the home are the spacious mansion gardens, and behind the home is the carriage house. (Courtesy Autumn Watson.)

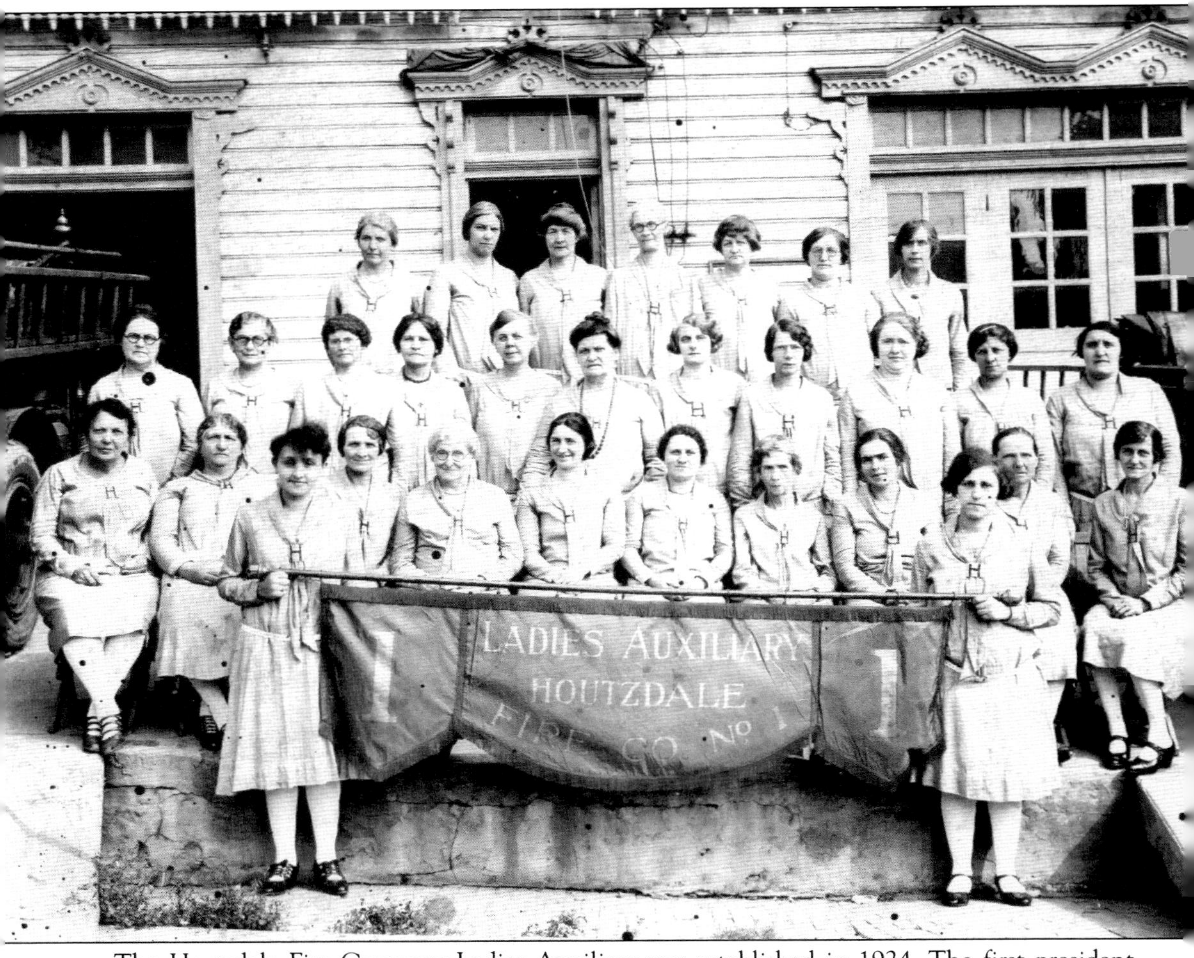

The Houtzdale Fire Company Ladies Auxiliary was established in 1924. The first president was Lillie Madigan (front row, center). The group was a favorite at local parades and once won an award for the largest and best appearing ladies organization at a fireman's convention. The banner ladies are Theressa Huber (left) and ? Huber (right). Also seen here are, from left to right, the following: (front row) unidentified, Mrs. Fred Sherkel, unidentified, Mrs. Frank Saupp, Lillie Madigan, Mrs. Charles Elllis, Mary McMahon, Annie Brady, unidentified, and Mary Godin McHenry; (middle row) Bridget Zeigler, ? Feldman, Effie Cartwright, ? McQuillan, Louise Dale (a registered nurse), ? Reardan, unidentified, Becky Swanson, Mary Malloy Gallagher, Sadie Tompkins, and Annie Hubler; (back row) unidentified, Margaret Love, ? Griffith, ? McKenzie, ? Benson, Mrs. Albert Kasubick, and unidentified. (Courtesy Clearfield County Historical Society.)

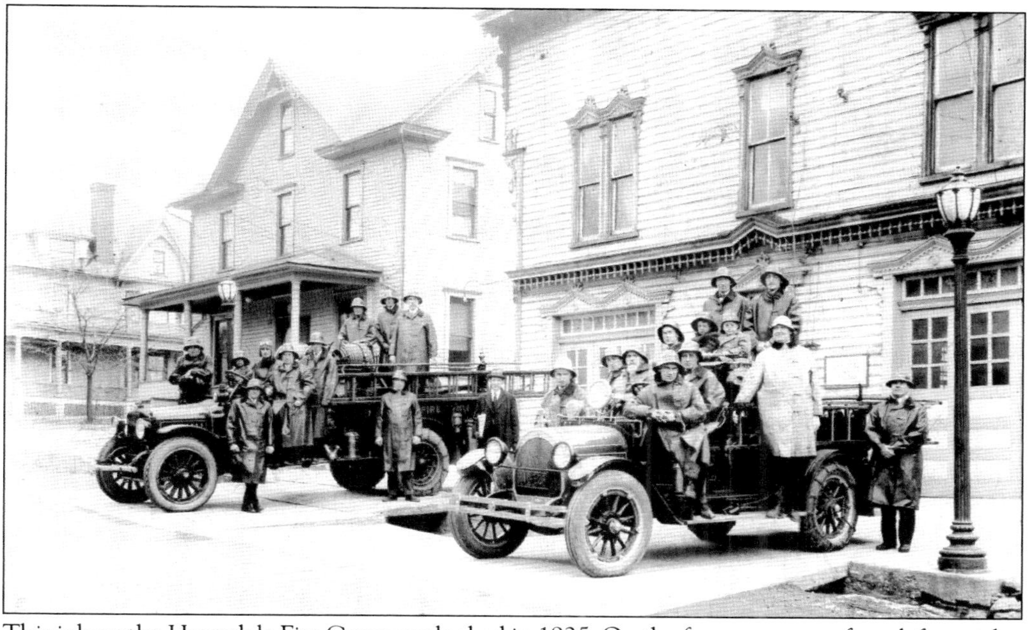

This is how the Houtzdale Fire Company looked in 1925. On the far pumper are, from left to right, Ray Brady, an unidentified child, Kurt Houser, Charles Saupp, John Mills, Tony Rodgers, Harry Tompkins, John Love, Jake Arnold, and John Markowitz. The man between the trucks, holding a newspaper, is Fred Hiller. On the other pumper are, from left to right, Jim Brady, Leo McDermott, Dave Litz, Ben Ellis, Ambrose O'Connor, Jack Arnold, Jack Archer, Albin Benson, William Lewis, Karl Huber, and Charlie Arnold. (Courtesy Clearfield County Historical Society.)

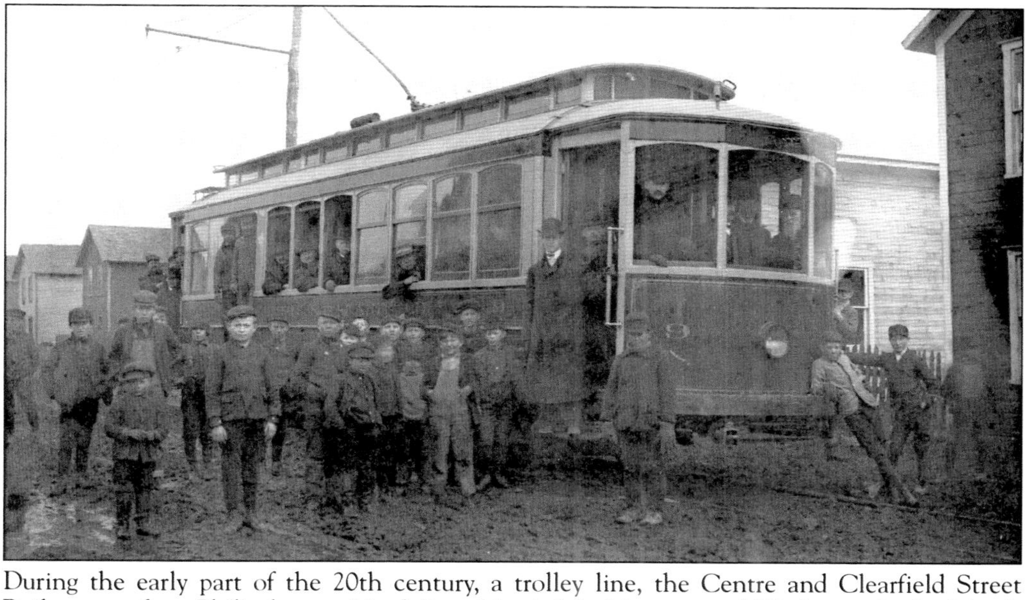

During the early part of the 20th century, a trolley line, the Centre and Clearfield Street Railway, ran from Philipsburg to Hawk Run, Morrisdale, Munson, and Winburne. In this March 1904 photograph, the car arrives at the end of the line in Winburne. DuBois also had a short trolley line that ran from 1891 to 1926. (Courtesy Clearfield County Historical Society.)

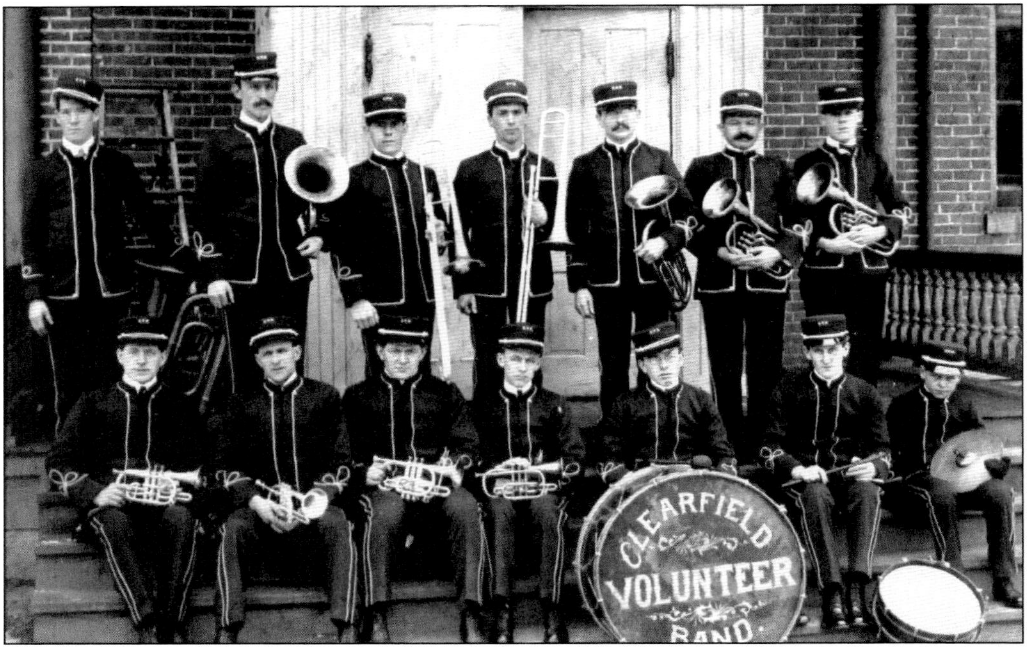

The Clearfield Volunteer Band was organized in 1902 and led the centennial parade in 1904. This photograph, taken in 1903, is in front of the Fourth Ward School. Seen here are, from left to right, the following: (seated) Wright Turner, Charles Williams, Leslie Hopfer, Paul Flaharty, Orvis Bender, Tom Stalcup, and Harry Carlson; (standing) John Lloyd, George I. Thurston, Pat Turner, Allen Parker, Harry Ward, Fred Schurig Sr., and Clarence DeArmitt. (Courtesy Clearfield County Historical Society.)

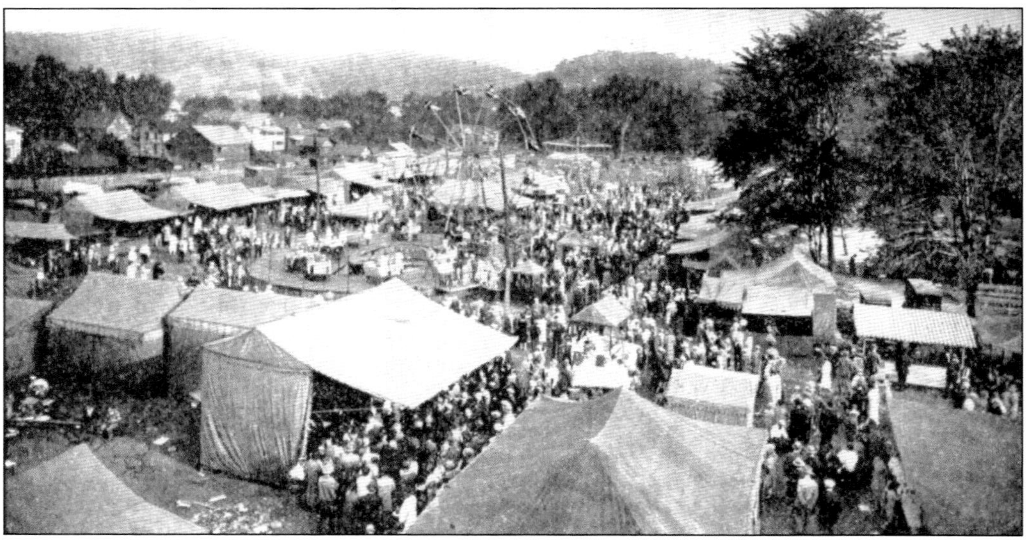

This is a familiar sight to most residents of Clearfield County even though this is a c. 1925 photograph. The Clearfield County Fair started in 1852. It moved to its current Driving Park home in the 1870s, although the 1895 and 1896 fairs were held in Grampian. Originally run by the Clearfield County Agricultural Society, the fair was taken over by the Clearfield Volunteer Fire Department in 1938. (Courtesy Clearfield County Historical Society.)

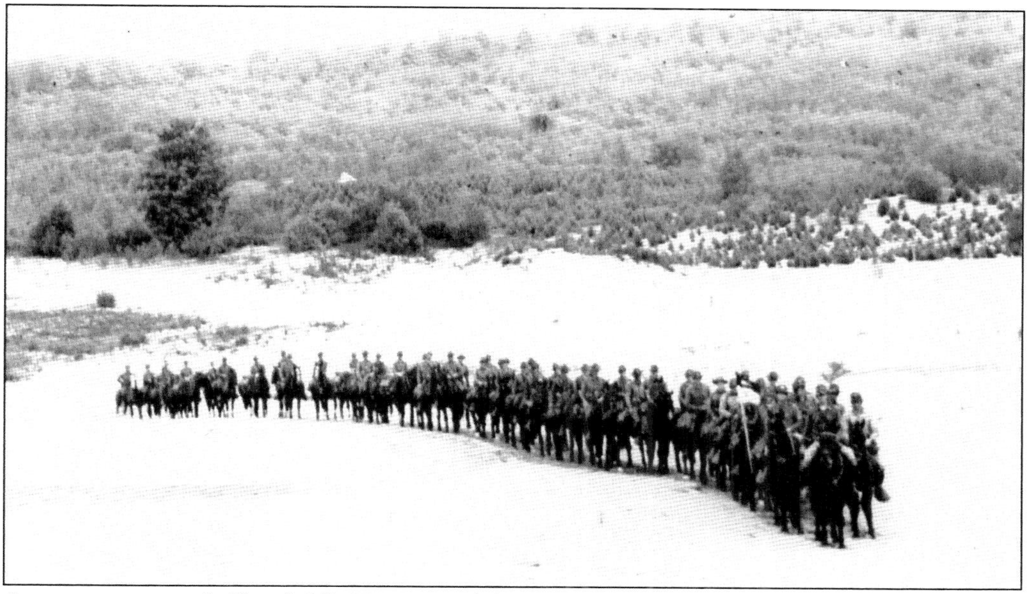

A camera captured Clearfield's Troop A of the 104th Calvary of the Pennsylvania National Guard during this training drill. The troop, when founded in 1927, consisted of 56 men and 2 officers, Capt. Harry Fred Bigler Jr. and Lt. William A.E. Leitzinger. It was eventually replaced by the more modern Battery A of the 190th Field Artillery Battalion, which served in World War II. (Courtesy Clearfield County Historical Society.)

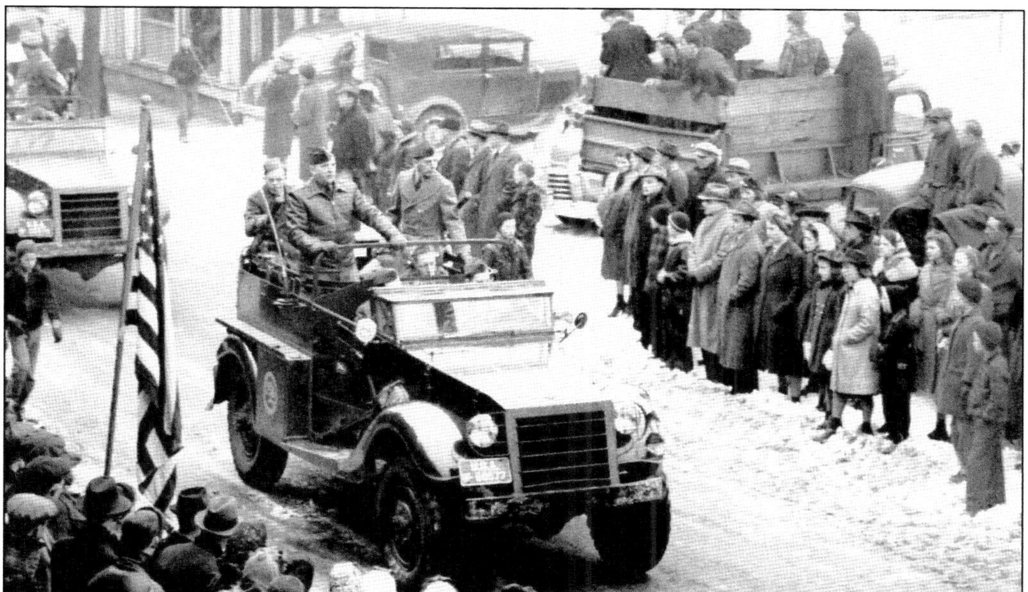

In January 1941, Troop A, now Battery A, was mobilized for active duty. The community held many dinners and special events to honor the troop. In February, a parade in honor of the group was led by the American Legion Band and Major Leitzinger's cavalry headquarters troop in scout cars. Major Leitzinger is on the left, standing up in the Jeep. (Courtesy Clearfield County Historical Society.)

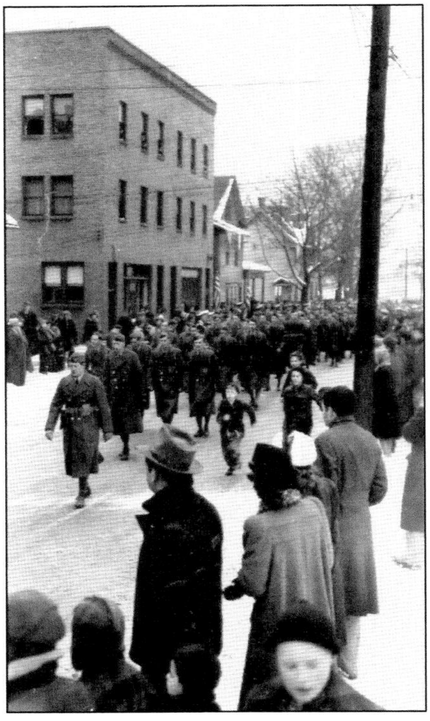

The Clearfield Volunteer Fire Department, in uniform, followed the cars. Then the Citizen's Band and the rest of the troop entered, marching complete with their packs. The parade ended at the Third Street train station, where their train awaited. (Courtesy Clearfield County Historical Society.)

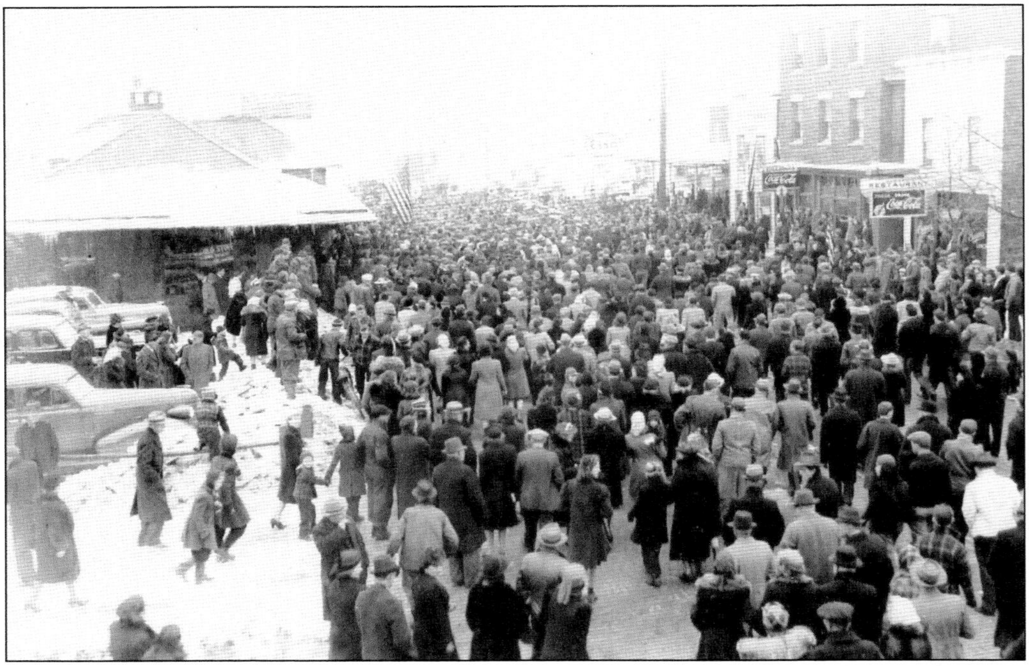

Despite the cold February weather, the parade drew thousands, many of whom gathered at the Third Street train station. Here, speeches were made and many tears were shed as the community sent their men off to fight in the war in Europe. (Courtesy Clearfield County Historical Society.)

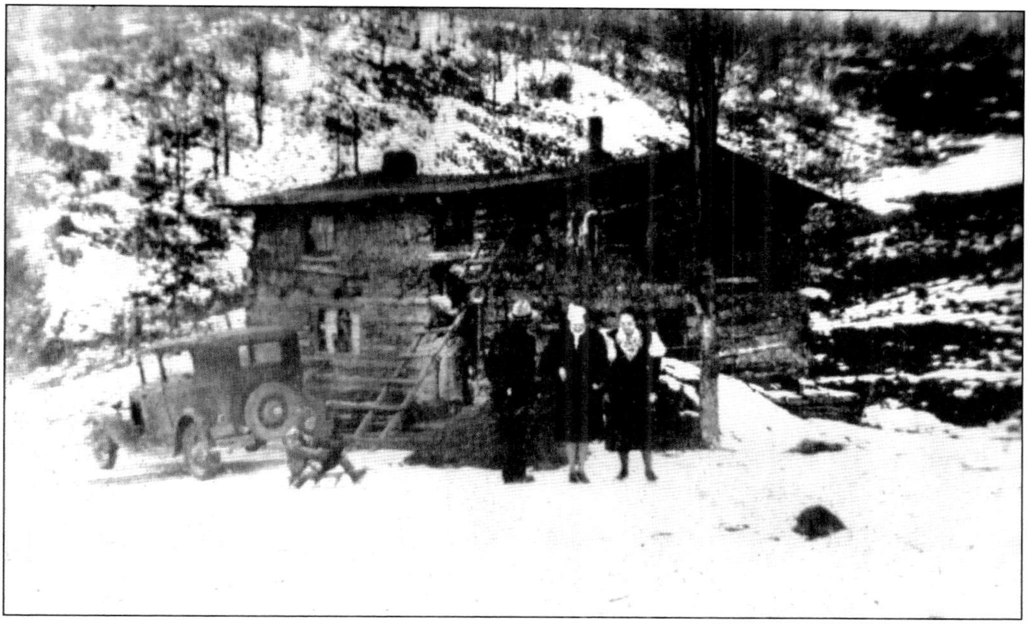

James Burkett, his sister Hazel Vittotow, and his mother Ella Burkett visit outside their Penfield cabin in this picture *c.* 1935. On the ladder is his daughter, Ella Jane Burkett, and on the sled is his son, James. (Courtesy Autumn Watson.)

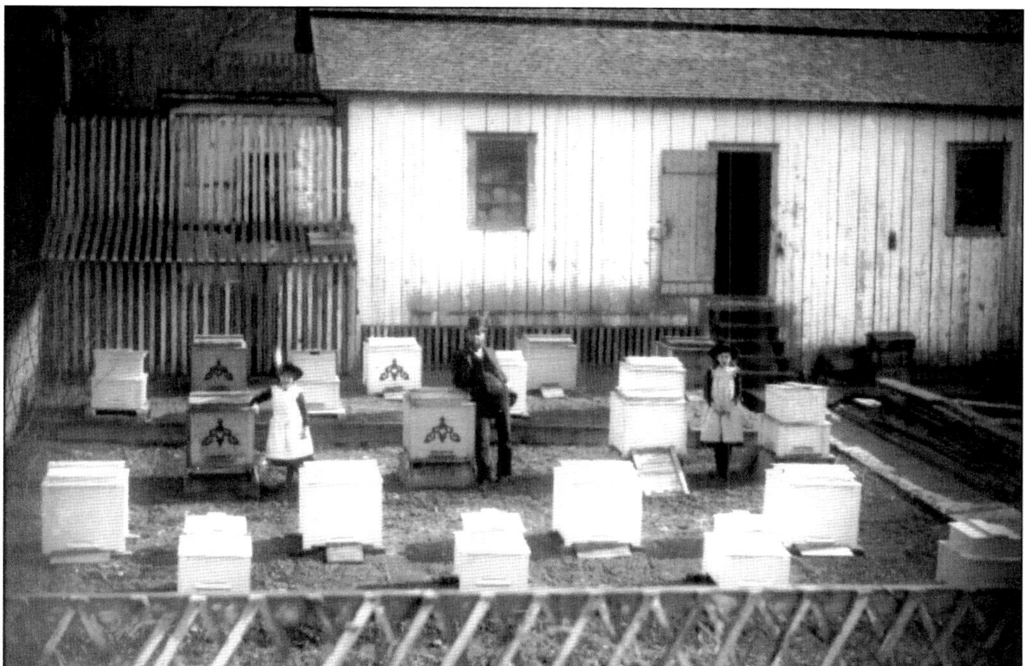

A man poses with his family outside a business where several beehives are on display in this undated photograph from Curwensville. In the early 20th century, beekeeping was so common that there was a County Bee Keepers Association. The manufacturer of these beehives was possibly named Sweeney. (Courtesy Curwensville-Pike Township Historical Society.)

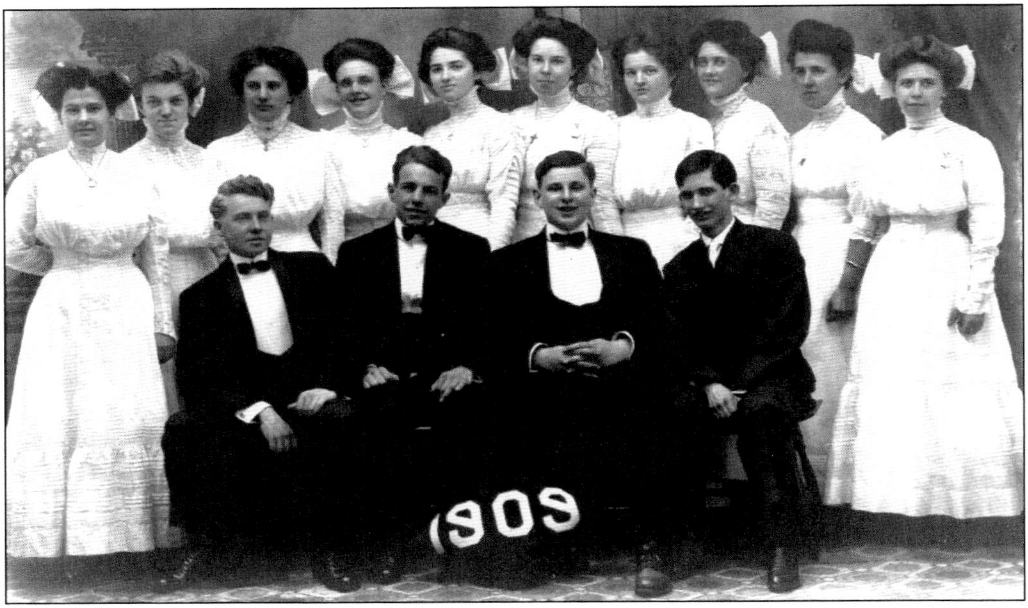

The Curwensville High School graduates of 1909 pose for their class photograph. These students attended the Patton School on State Street, which opened in 1885. The third woman from the right is Marie Addleman, who later married Jay W. Murphy of Murphy's Drug Store. (Courtesy Pat Murphy.)

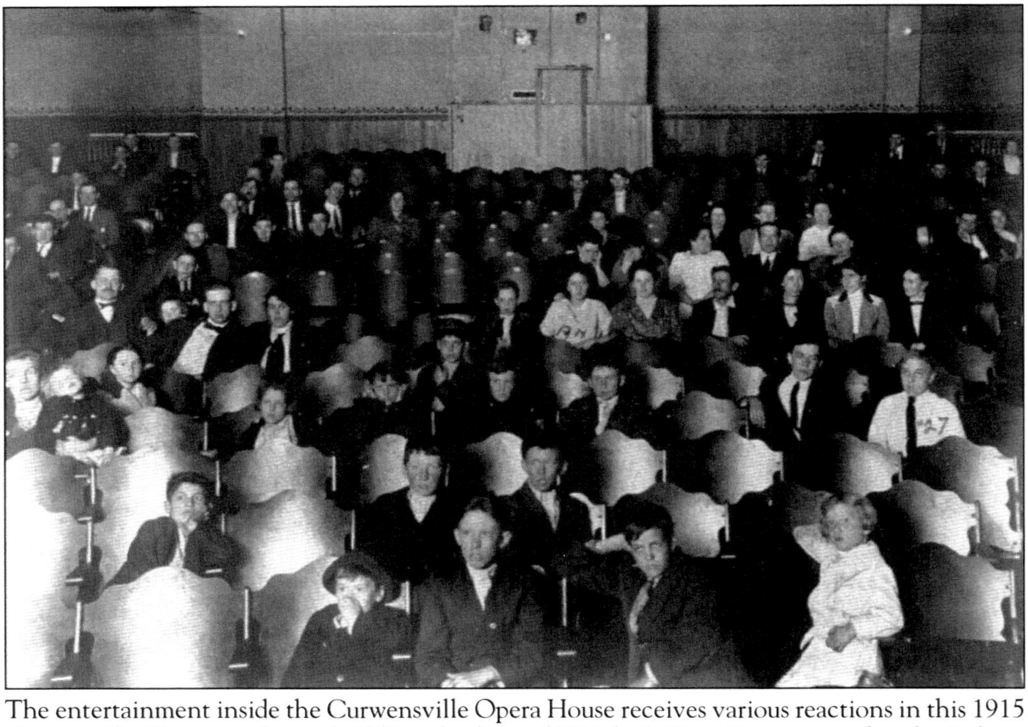

The entertainment inside the Curwensville Opera House receives various reactions in this 1915 photograph. The opera house building also housed Wrigley's Drug Store, a watchmaker's shop, and the W.F. Patton Academy of Music. It was torn down in 1946. (Courtesy Pat Murphy.)

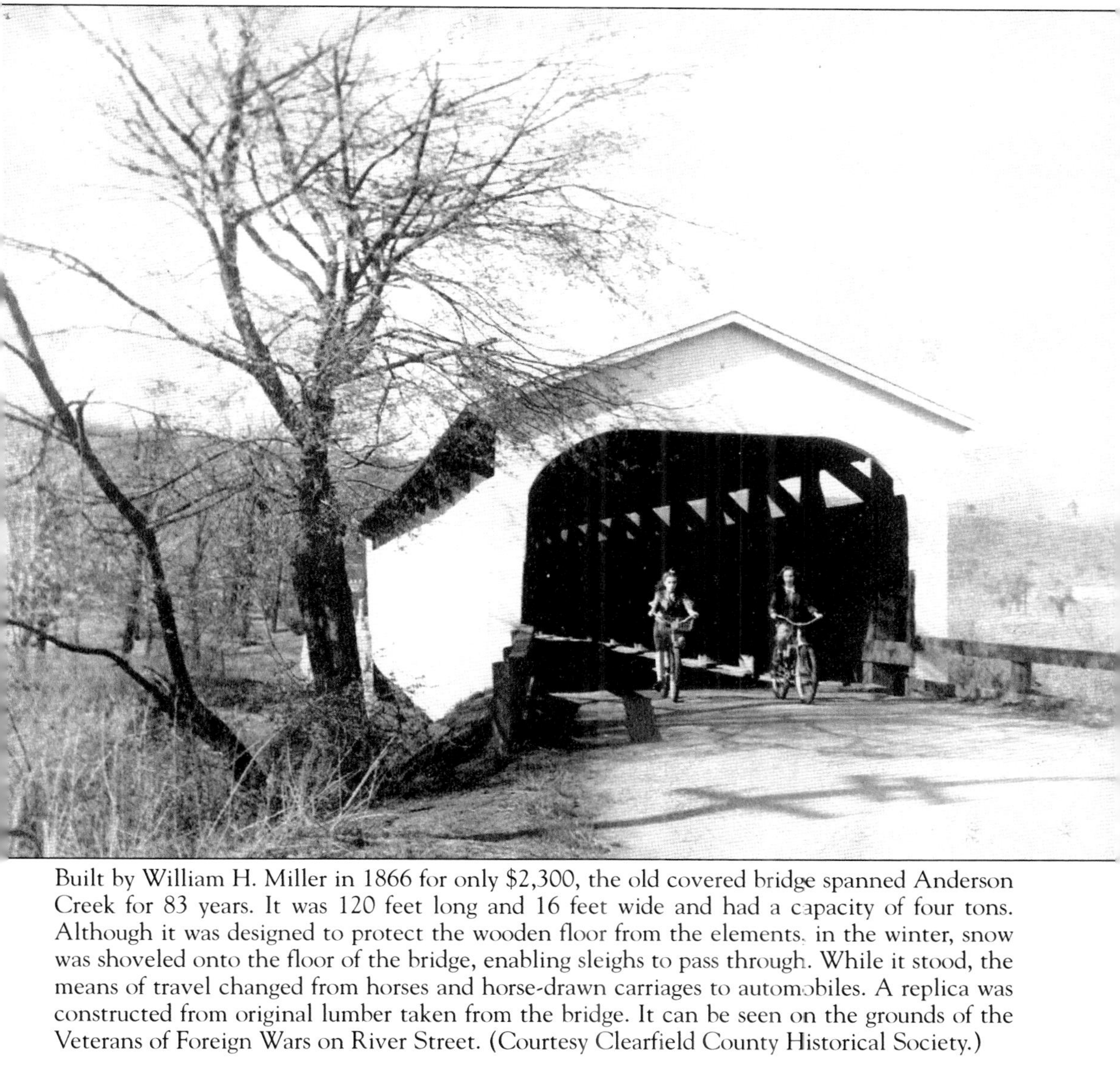

Built by William H. Miller in 1866 for only $2,300, the old covered bridge spanned Anderson Creek for 83 years. It was 120 feet long and 16 feet wide and had a capacity of four tons. Although it was designed to protect the wooden floor from the elements, in the winter, snow was shoveled onto the floor of the bridge, enabling sleighs to pass through. While it stood, the means of travel changed from horses and horse-drawn carriages to automobiles. A replica was constructed from original lumber taken from the bridge. It can be seen on the grounds of the Veterans of Foreign Wars on River Street. (Courtesy Clearfield County Historical Society.)

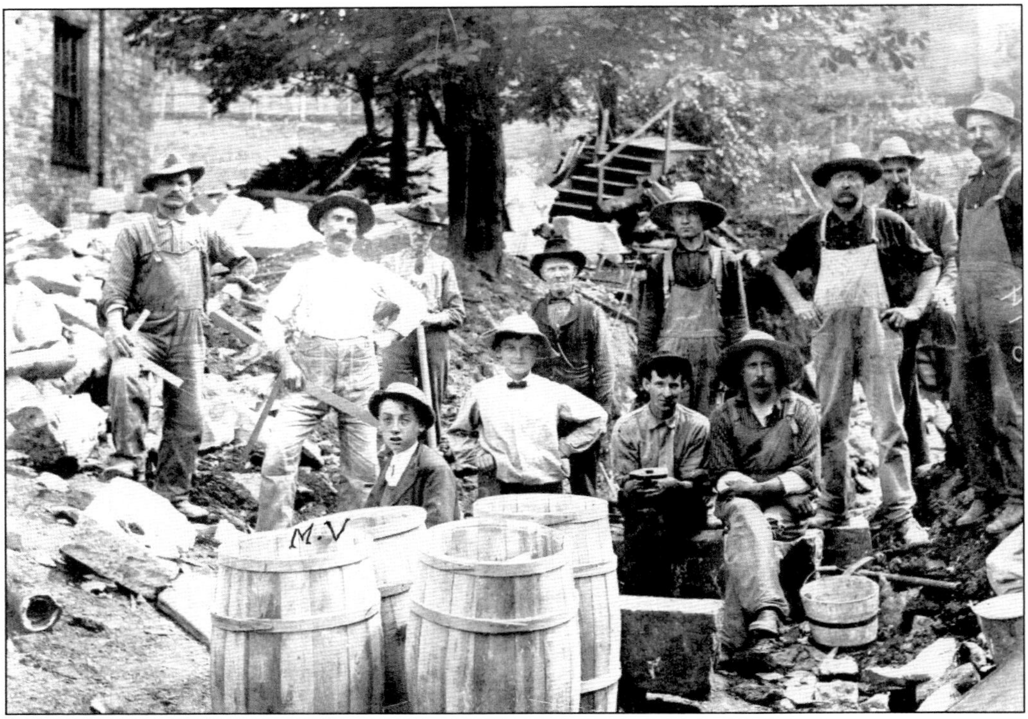

These two undated photographs illustrate life in Curwensville *c.* 1900. Above, construction workers take a break. The man second from the left is Michael Volpe. Below, a large band fills the street during a patriotic ceremony or parade. Curwensville is one of the oldest towns in the county, having been established in 1799, before Clearfield became a county. Curwensville was named for an Englishman, John Curwen, who owned the land there. (Courtesy J. Duane Test.)

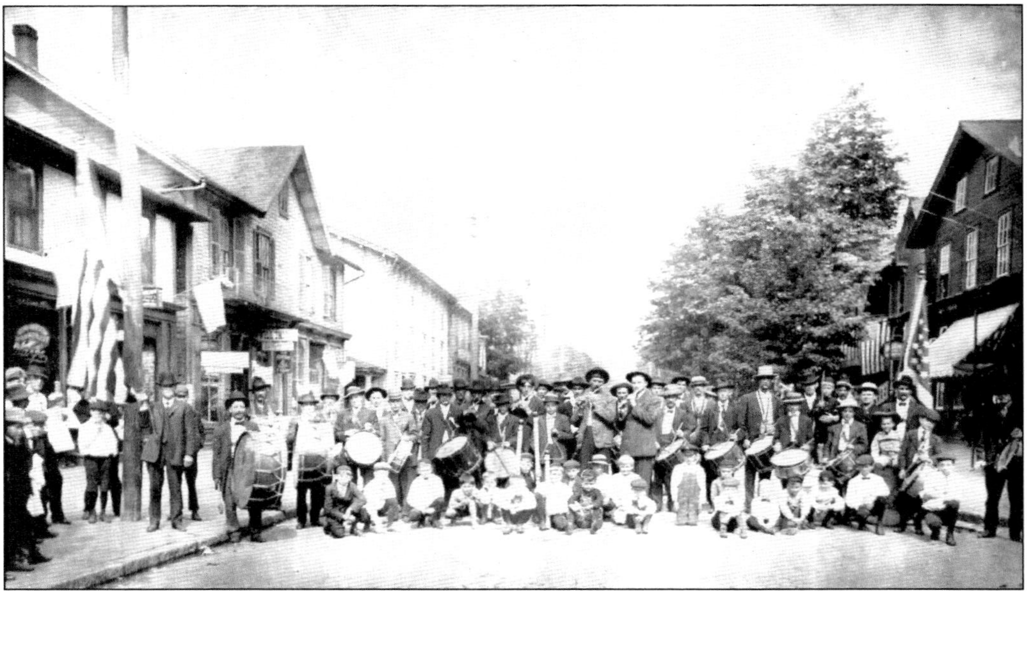

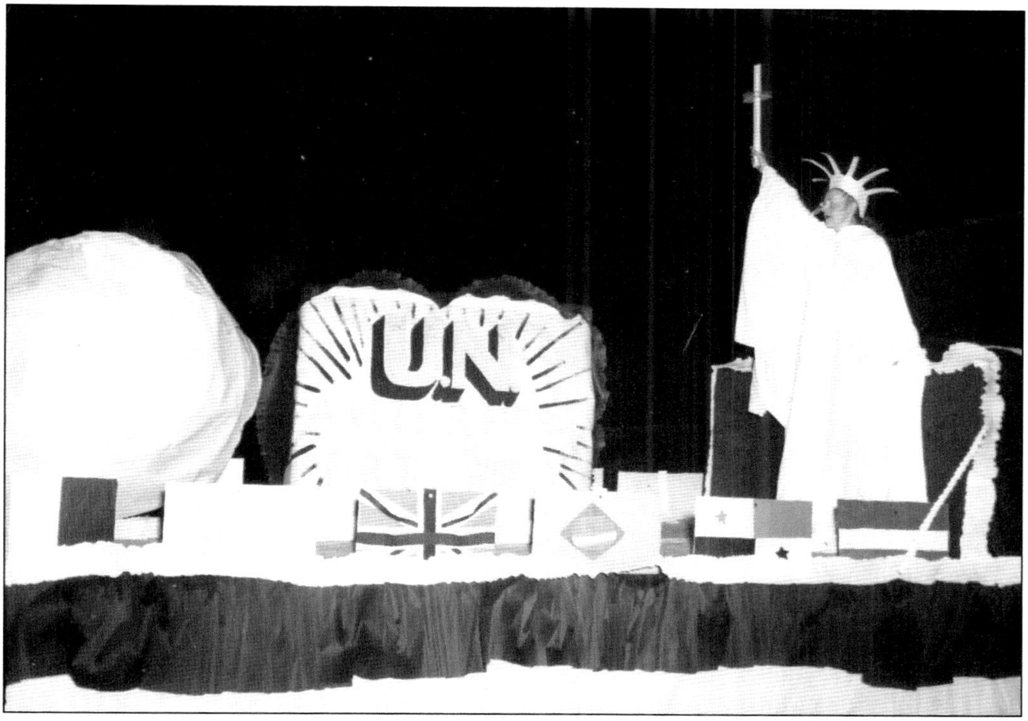

The prize-winning float in Curwensville's 1948 Halloween parade was this entry from the Woman's Club of Curwensville. "Liberty" celebrated the new organization established in 1945 as the United Nations. The Woman's Club, an integral part of the community since 1936, also sponsored the parade. (Courtesy Curwensville Public Library.)

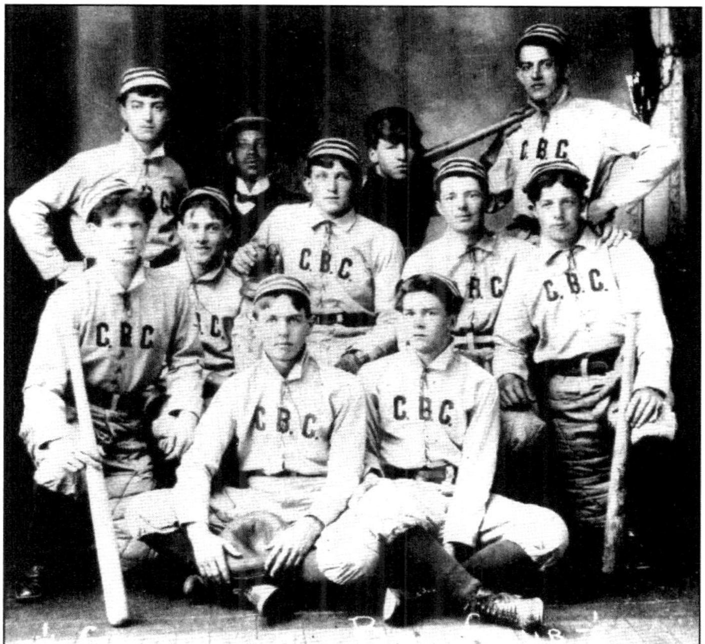

In the latter part of the 1800s and the early 1900s, watching local baseball teams play was a popular pastime. Each town had its own team that competed in various local leagues. Competition became so fierce that some towns paid dearly for the better players to join their teams. This was Curwensville's baseball team in 1901. (Courtesy J. Duane Test.)

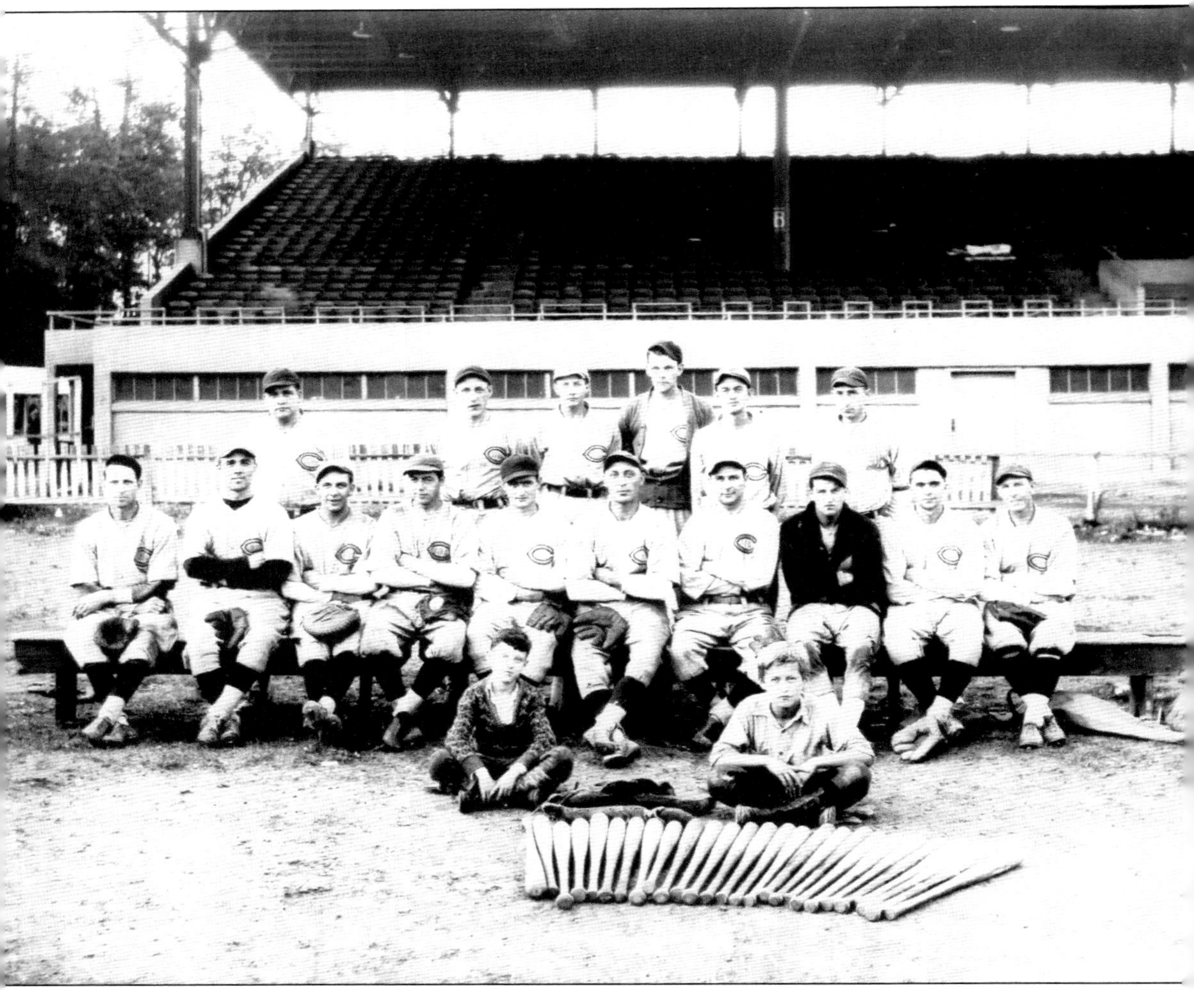

The Clearfield-Centre Baseball League, featuring local players only, began in 1924 and ended in 1940. There were teams in Clearfield, Philipsburg, Osceola Mills, and DuBois. This Clearfield team won the championship in 1930. The members are, from left to right, as follows: (front row) Frank "Spike" Buck Jr. and Myron Merrey, bat boys; (middle row) Emory "Slugger" Rowles, first baseman; Lloyd "Moon" Mullen, outfielder; Clair High, catcher; Abe Bailey, center fielder; Ben Bodle, infielder; Rex Fauver, pitcher; Sol Robinson, shortstop; Jimmy Sughrue, catcher; Droze "Diz" Rowles, pitcher and third baseman; and Carl Peterson, second baseman; (back row) Paul Smith, pitcher and manager; Bill Bauver, shortstop and third baseman; Lefty Helt, outfielder; Nile Mellott, pitcher; Sparky Braid, pitcher; and Bill Malone, utility player. (Courtesy Clearfield County Historical Society.)

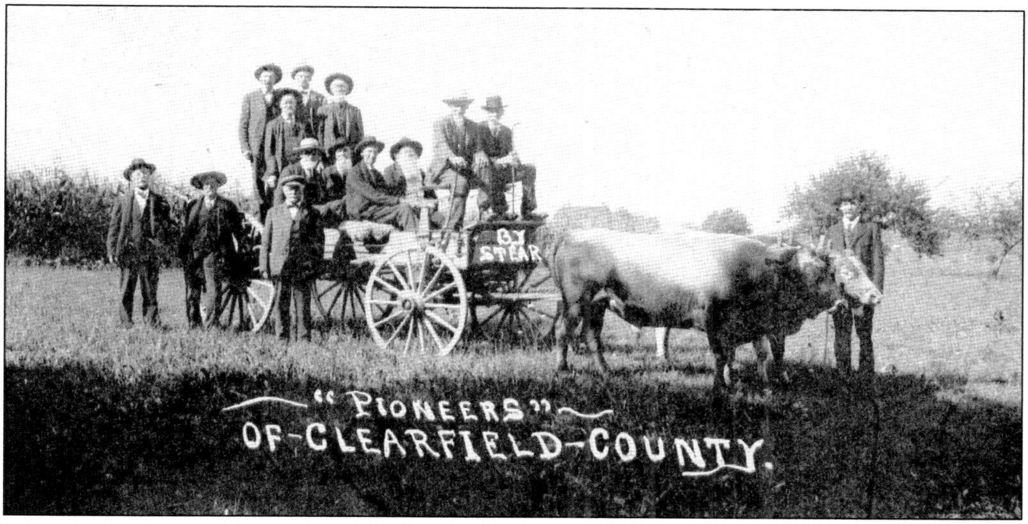

John R. Dunlap and his wife of Turkey Hill celebrated their golden wedding anniversary in 1906 with a large party at their home. Entertainment included wagon rides provided by Fred Dunlap and his bull team. Standing beside the wagon are John R. Caldwell, D.R.P. Rowles, and Philip A. Long. The men in the wagon are John Owens, Conrad Baker, A.P. Bloom, Benjamin Bloom, Reuben Caldwell, Joseph H. Rowles, John F. Read, Joseph Alexander, and John R. Dunlap. (Courtesy Clearfield County Historical Society.)

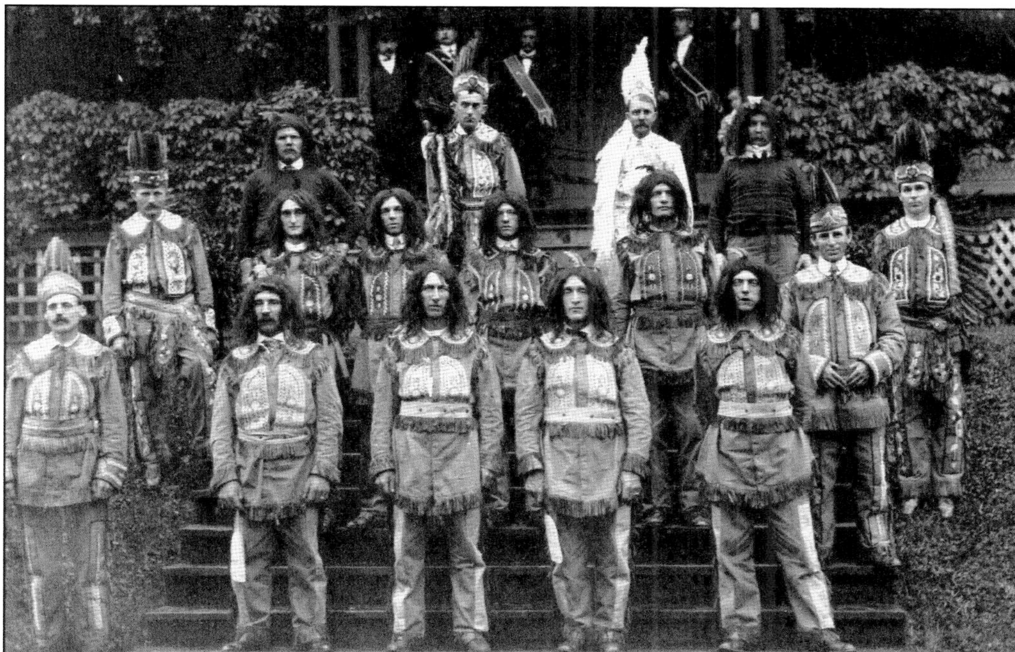

This undated photograph shows Curwensville's Order of Red Men in ceremonial dress. In this national organization, men dressed as Native Americans. An assembly of Philadelphia men started the order during the War of 1812. Although today the group seems to be politically incorrect, the group's principals were positive ones, including freedom, brotherhood, friendship, and charity. (Courtesy J. Duane Test.)

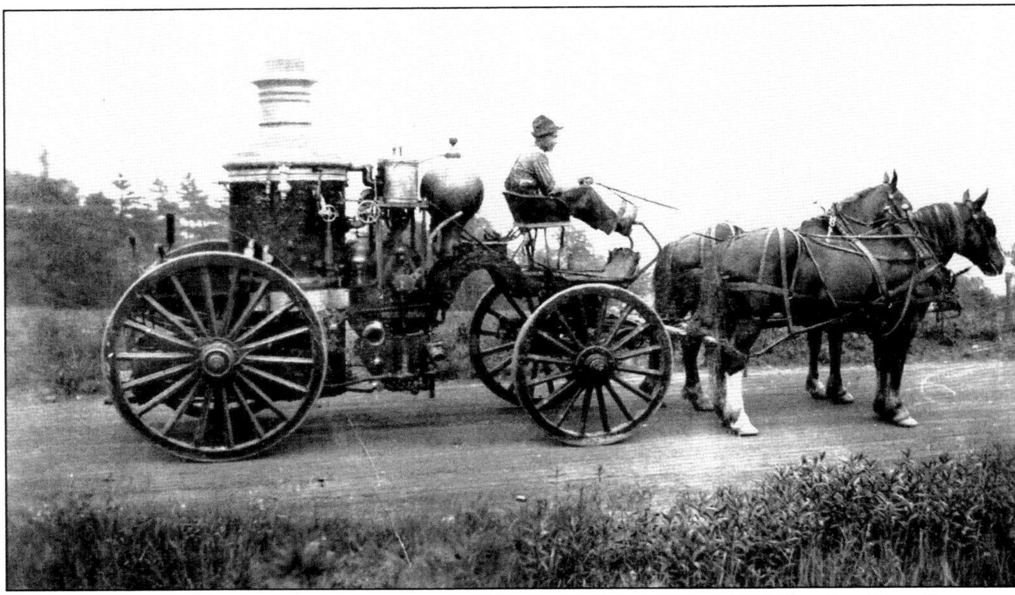

This fire truck was seen around Osceola Mills in 1925. The town's Columbia Fire Company No. 1 was organized several years earlier, in 1889. Osceola was in need of fire protection after 1875, when a fire destroyed most of the town, leaving 1,200 people homeless. Another fire (in 1913) destroyed many businesses. (Courtesy Osceola Mills Public Library.)

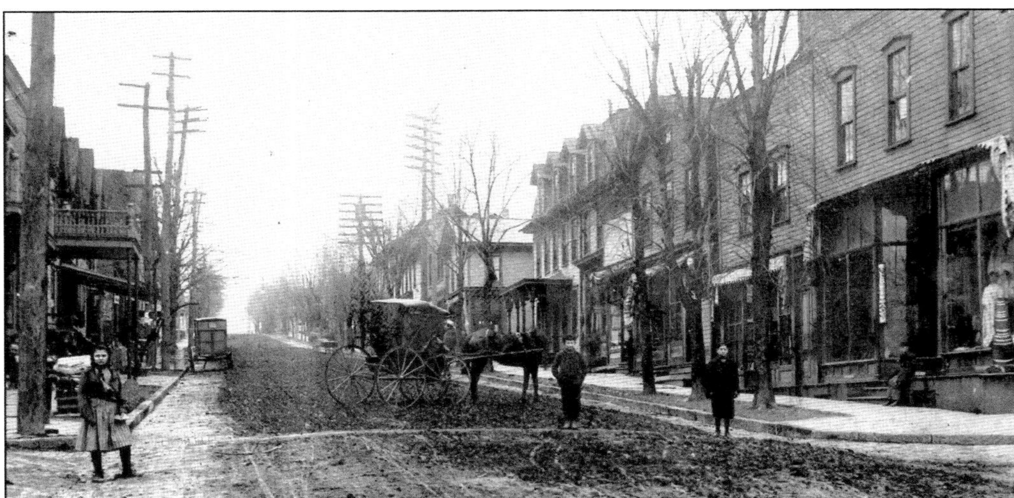

This postcard shows Curtain Street in Osceola Mills c. 1900. The streets are still brick and wagons are the means of transportation, but there are telephone and electric poles. Electricity came to Osceola in 1887, and by 1889, 36 streetlights were installed. They had a telephone in the train station in 1878, and in 1881, there were 27 phones in town. (Courtesy Osceola Mills Public Library.)

Five

SCHOOLS

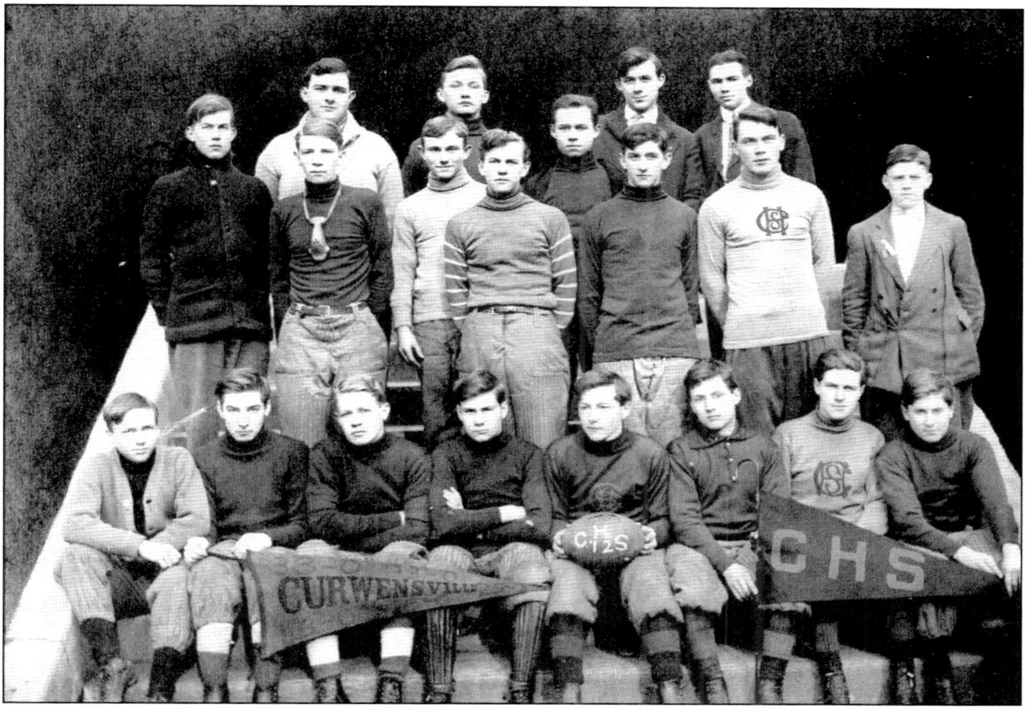

Curwensville's first high school football team took the field in 1912. Seen here are, from left to right, the following: (front row) Frederick Kittelberger, Paul Gardlock, Leslie Kline, Harold Daugherty, Lex Bailey, Victor Kirk, Dan Bailey, and Maurice Dale; (middle row) Booty Smith, Fred Sawtell, Malvin McClure, James Murphy, Ted Ake, Abner Bloom, Commodore Everett, and Scott Ammerman; (back row) Douglas Dunsmore, James Hile, Prof. Charles H. Miller (coach), and Natt Charnas (assistant coach). (Courtesy Curwensville-Pike Township Historical Society.)

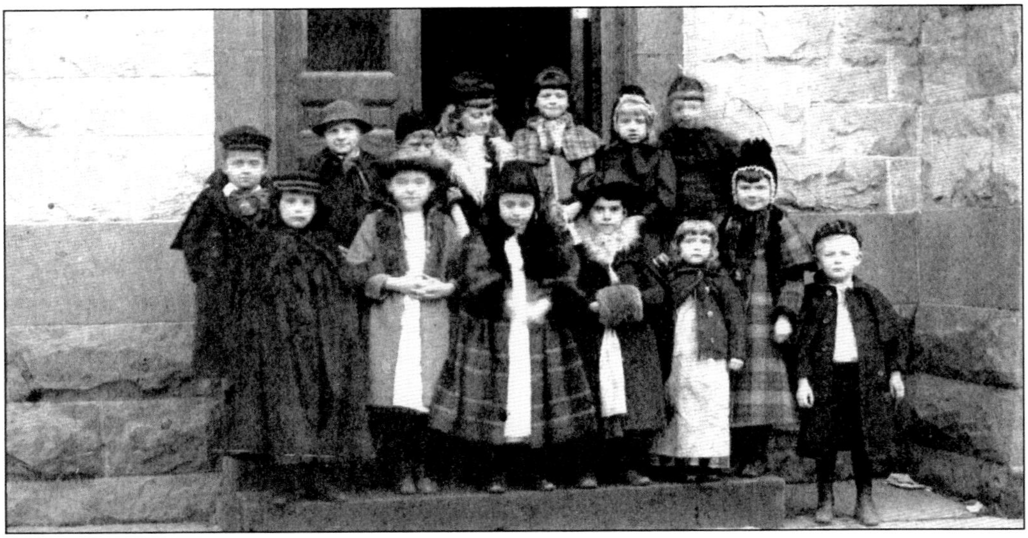

These cute kids attended Miss James's kindergarten class held in the County National Bank building *c.* 1890. Seen here are, from left to right, the following: (front row) Sue Savage, Letha Moore, Edith Dill, Margaret Biddle, Margaret Powell, Isabel Powell, and Enrmott Harder; (back row) Henry Powell, Letha Moore's cousin, Guy McKinley, Mary Lee, Alice Bigler, Margaretta Powell, and Amelia Bigler. (Courtesy Clearfield County Historical Society.)

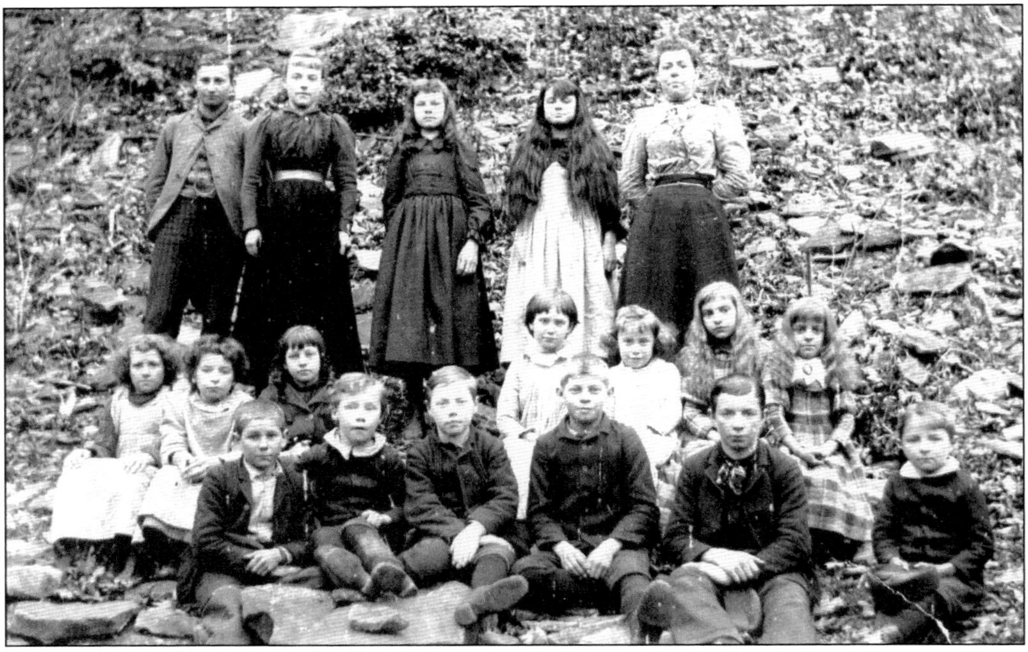

Students from the Driftwood School pose *c.* 1890. From left to right are the following: (front row) ? Bloom, Dean Bloom, Harry Spackman, Sam Stephens, Bill Stephens, and Howard Dunlap; (middle row) Tressa Schrot, Mary Schrot, Eda Stephens, Myrtle Dunlap, Ada Spackman, Nettie Bloom, and Ella Thompson; (back row) Joe Winters, Turzah Stephens, Tina Stephens, Pearl Henry, and Gertrude Redibaugh Rienier (teacher). (Courtesy Clearfield County Historical Society.)

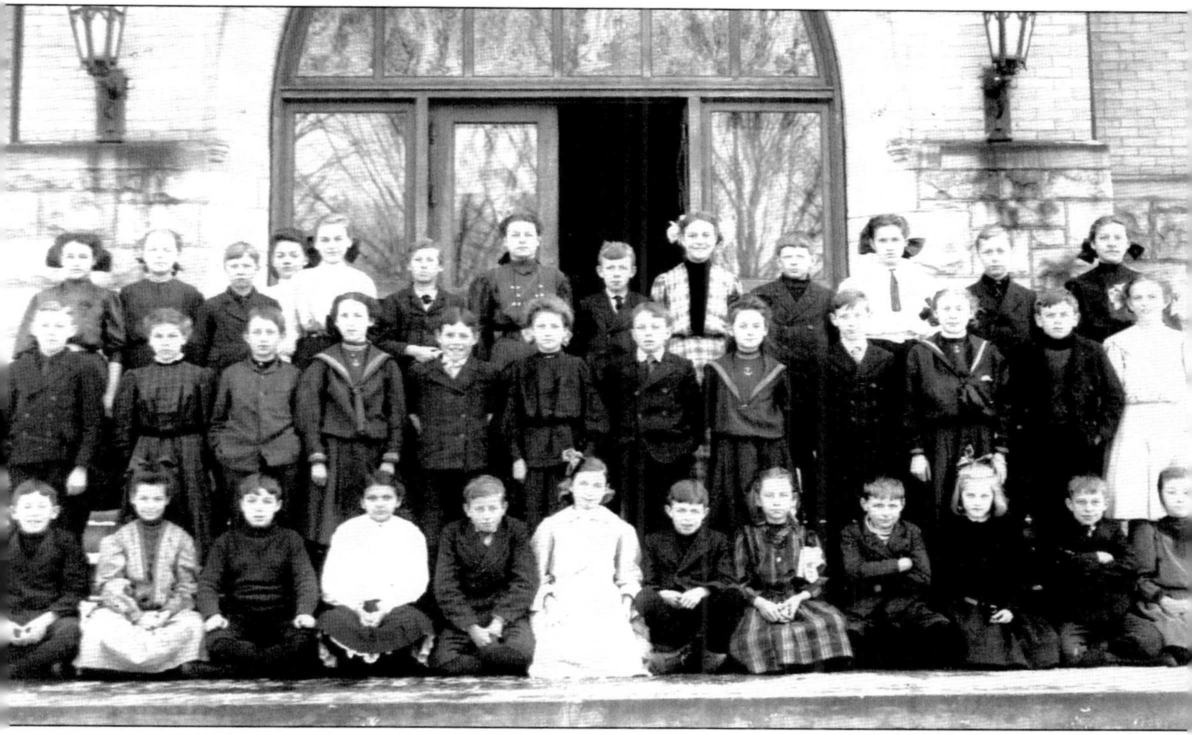

Posing in this photograph are Clearfield sixth-grade students from the 1906–1907 school year. From left to right are the following: (front row) Marl Weimer, Elizabeth Dufton, William Stephens, Mary Brenize, Austin Kline, Elsie Bailey, George Adams, Lida Stage, Philander Reed, Rebekah Smith, William Wallace, and Erma Bush; (middle row) Veryl Cowder, Nancy Rhine, ? Smith, Mary Bateman, Hayes Wilson, Orpha Stalcup, Willard Barratt, Elizabeth MacBlain, Stayman Reed, Dorothy Woodward, William Apgar, and Gussie Thorn; (back row) Ruth Gearhart, Jean Carlson, Wayne Wrigley, Bessie Green, Nora Carlson, Raymond Helsel, Sarah Goss, Boyd McCullough, Anna Shoff, Huston Hartswick, Esther Ross, George Johnson, and Eva Fauver. Their teacher was Augusta Connelly. (Courtesy Clearfield County Historical Society.)

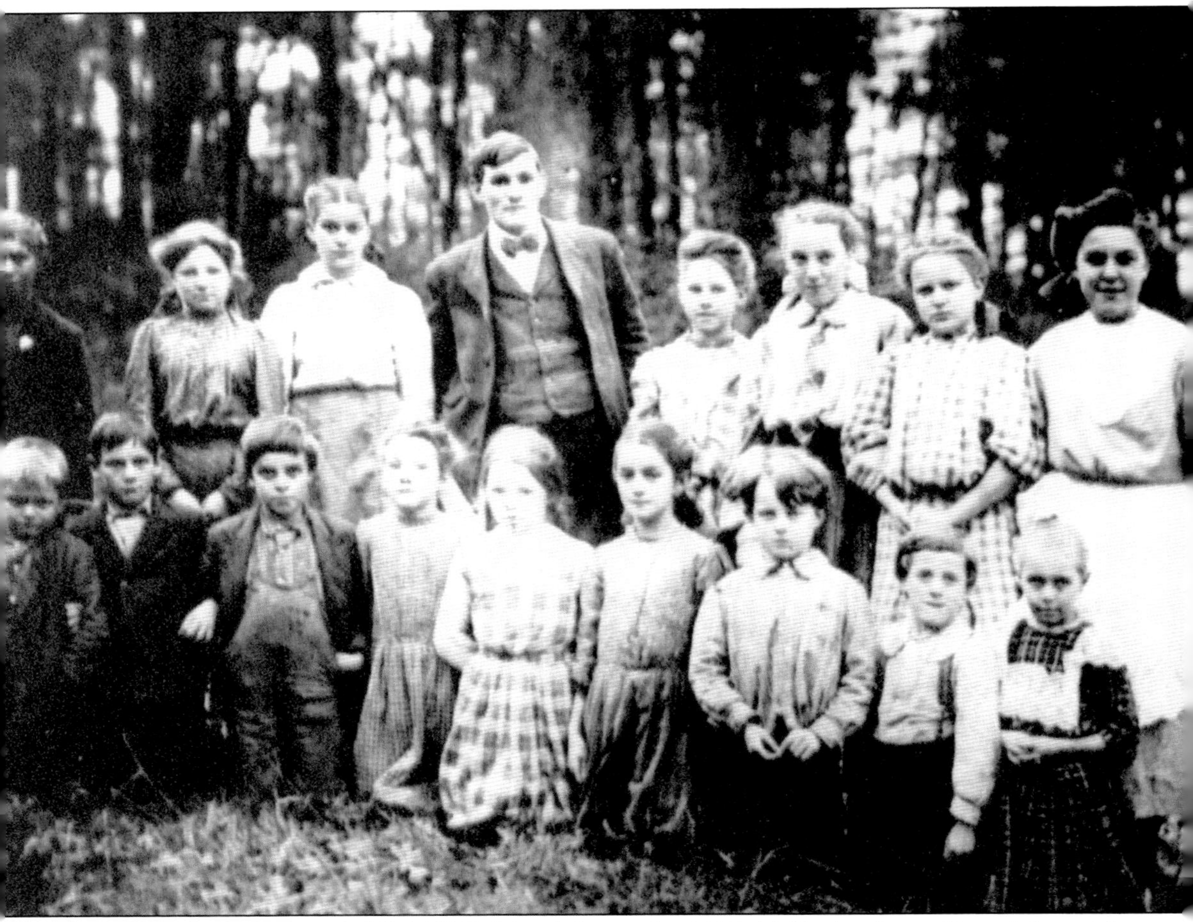

These students attended Bald Hill School during the 1907–1908 school year. From left to right are the following: (kneeling) Kyle Luzier, Merwin Bumbarger, Kyle Graham, Maida Condon, Delia Luzier (Jury), Beatrice Falls, Walter Murray, Bowman Graham, and Margaret Graham (Hausen); (standing) Charlie Falls, Anna Luzier (Shugarts), Ada Falls, George Knepp (teacher), Lena Murray, Letha Graham, Olive Murray (Brinton), and Eva Graham (Ogden). The school was located in the southwest part of Girard Township. Its name came from the nearby Bald Hills. Cornelia Kincade taught at the first school in Girard Township. The residents built that first schoolhouse at Congress Hill near LeContes Mills. It was simple log structure. (Courtesy Clearfield County Historical Society.)

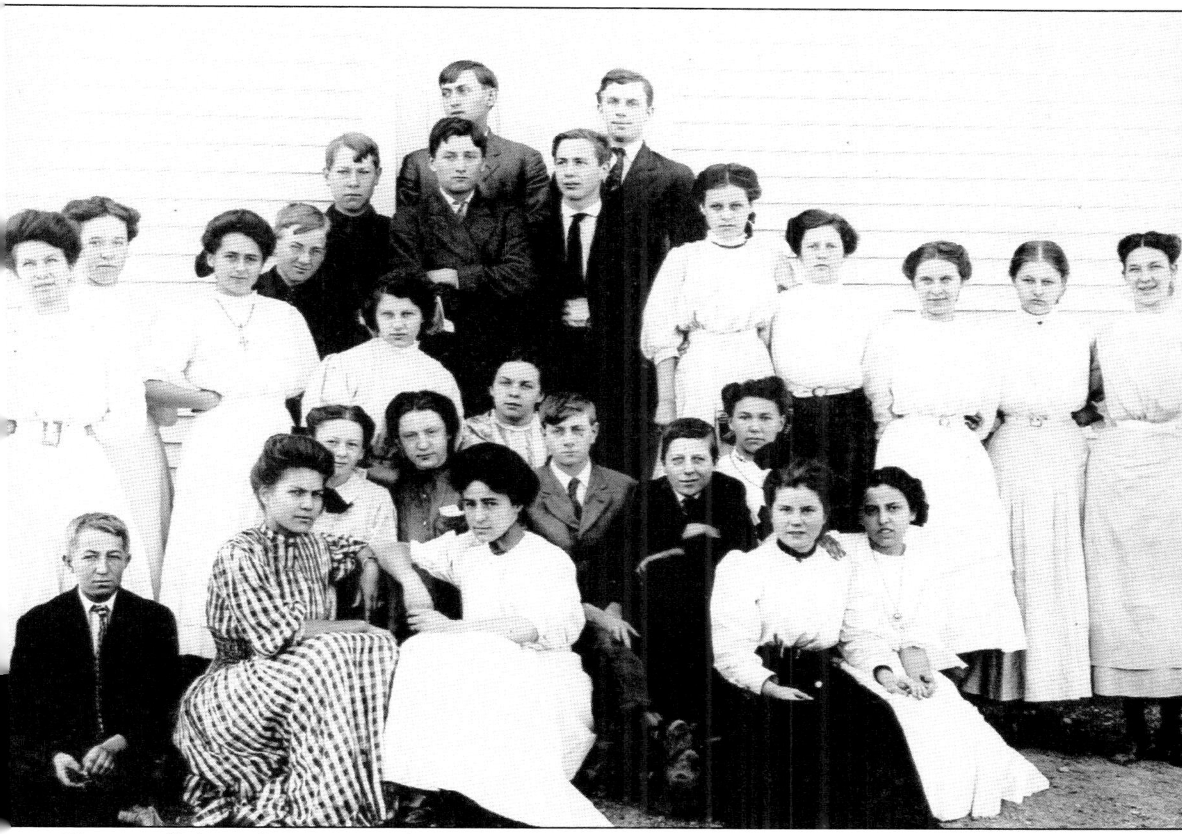

These well-dressed young people are students of the Brady Township High School c. 1908. From left to right are the following: (first row) Harvey Moose, Bessie Mehrwein, Lillian Pentz, Hazel Woods, and Ethel Hamilton; (second row) Lucille Lines, Pat Murphy, Jesse Arnold, and Malcolm Knarr; (third row) Lulu Smith, Effie Kriner, Lillian Weisgerber, Lillian Kirk, Betty Campbell, and Sarah Seyler; (fourth row) Harry Kriner, Jesse Kriner, Art McGaughey, Leland Edinger, Eva Ellinger, Rosie Seyler, Bertha Smith, Muriel Hayes, and Joe Lines; (fifth row) John Hayes and Walter M. Tobias (the high school principal). The first school in Brady Township was held in Lebbeus Luther's barroom in Luthersburg. The barroom was also used for church services by Reverend Anderson starting in 1822 or 1823. (Courtesy Clearfield County Historical Society.)

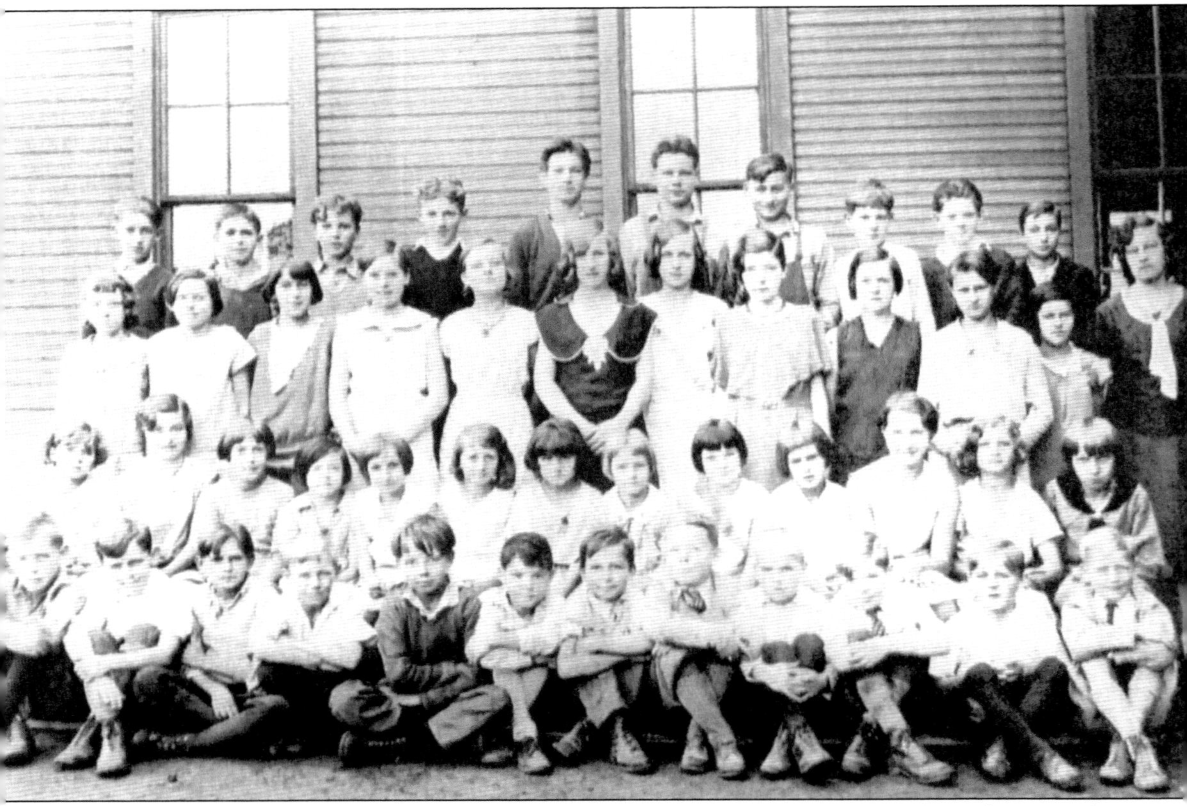

This 1928 photograph shows Blain City's students in the third and seventh grades, according to information found with the picture. From left to right are the following: (first row) Andy Sinclair, Don Wilkinson, Tom Collins, Marshall Tyler, Charles Mayes, Bob Hooper, Fred Evanchuck, Dick Sinclair, Tony Labonawski, George Sinclair, Gayle Thomas, and Matt Sinclair; (second row) unidentified, Anita Zweiner, Sophia Cherish, Edine Sincox, Adaline Knotts, Helen Good, unidentified, Harriet Kerchensky, Anna Mae Warrender, Dorothy Collins, Evelyn Lesher, Helen Skebeck, and Esther Schenley; (third row) unidentified, Rose Rahocki, Dotty Sinclair, Grace Nevling, Liz Galla, Betty Jenkins, Sara Peno, Dolly Conrad, Mame Sinclair, Sophie Banko, and Dora Hewitt; (fourth row) Lynn Hoffman, Bill "Rip" Collins, John Goralsky, Andy Turchick, two unidentified students, Raymond Spade, Cliff Nevling, Henry Swasing, Raymond Knotts, and Margaret Irvin (teacher). (Courtesy Coalport Area Coal Museum.)

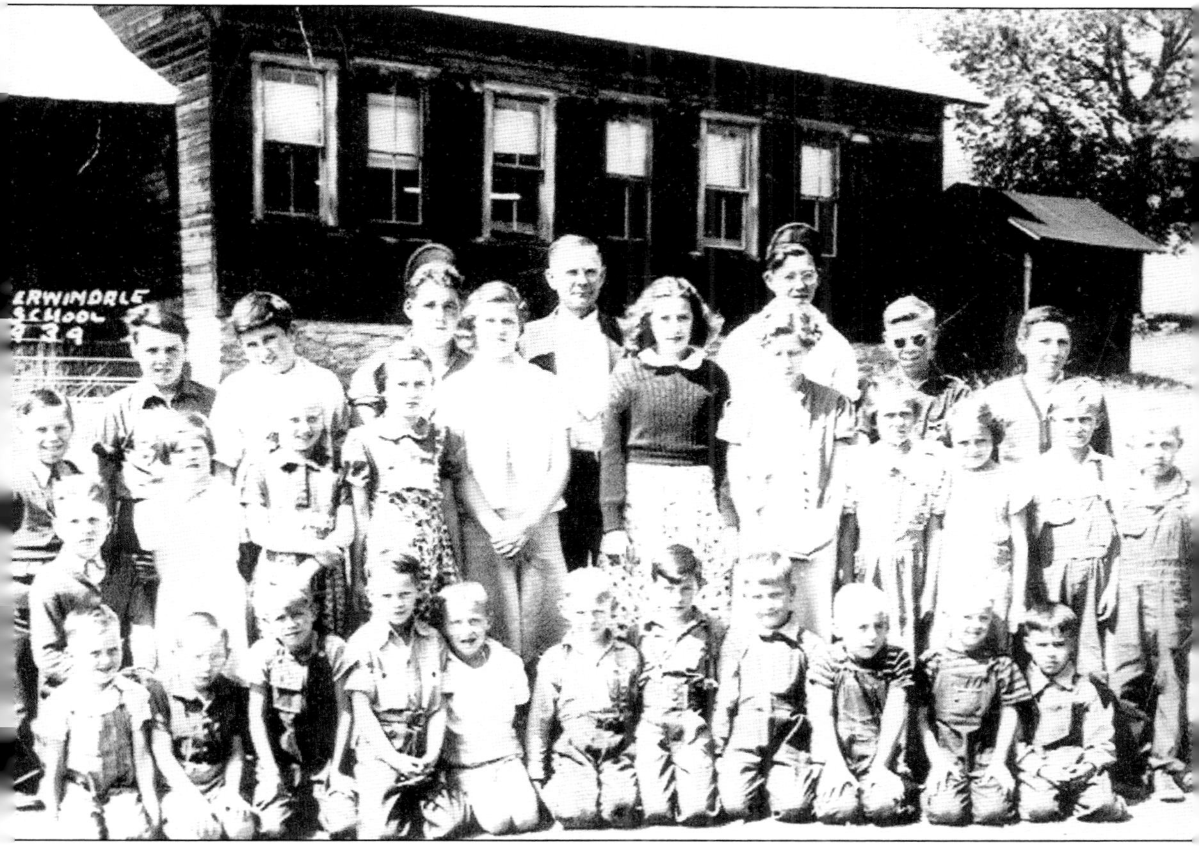

This photograph is from the Berwinsdale School in 1934. From left to right are the following: (front row) Jim Pearce, Bill Irvine, Harold Swan, Bob Witherow, two unidentified students, Carl Bishop, Harvey Clark, Paul Strong, Allen Hunter, and Art Clark; (middle row) Junior Pearce, "Cookie" Witherow, Jean Brink, Gerry Bishop, Eleanor Swan, Vida Gill, Betty Witherow, Katy Swan, Mabel Jean Hunter, Jim Davies, and Raymond Witherite; (back row) John C. "Bud" Witherow, Al Smith, Joe Smith, Bill Davies, Steward Straw, George Smith, Fred Davies, and Ed Smith. The Berwinsdale School was a one-room schoolhouse for grades one through eight. After that, students had to pass a test to qualify to go to the Coalport-Irvona High School. (Courtesy Clearfield County Historical Society.)

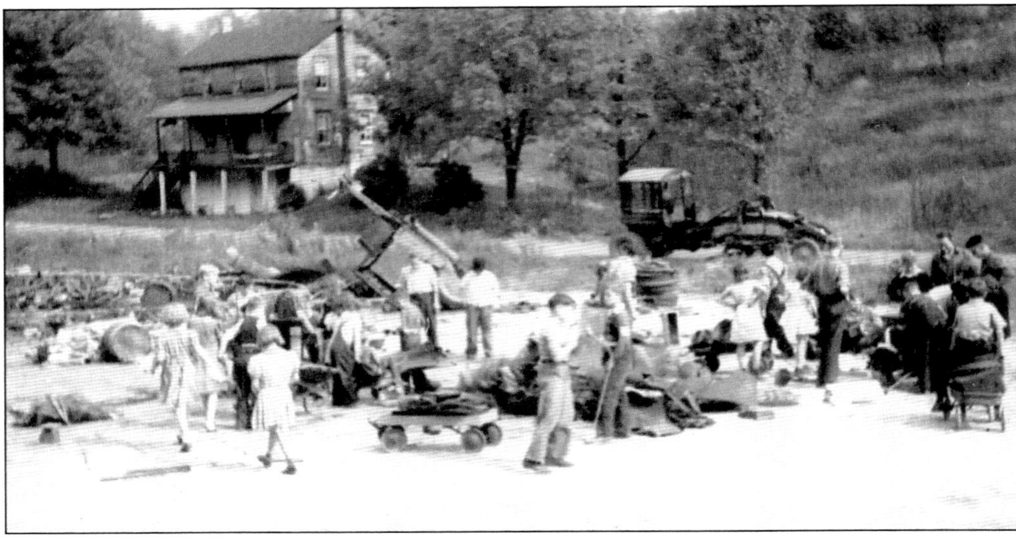

In 1942, some 180 students from the Glen Richey Elementary School gathered 29,722 pounds of scrap metal, which they sold for $141.91. This represented 165 pounds per pupil. In the above photograph, students sort through a junkyard. One hundred twelve of the students lived in remote areas, which means that they left for school between 6:30 a.m. and 7:00 a.m. and returned home after dark. In order to achieve their goal, they worked and gathered many of the items in the dark. (Courtesy Paul Rishell.)

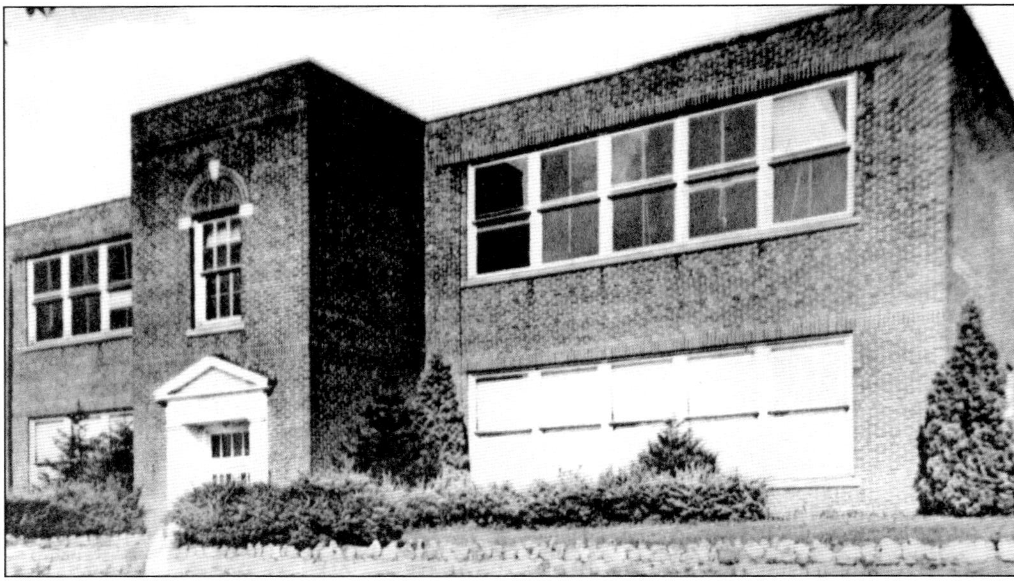

This was the Beccaria Township High School in the mid-1900s. The building was originally a Catholic school. At this point, the Beccaria Township High School was on Main Street in Coalport, but students who lived in Coalport went to the Coalport-Irvona High School, which was in Beccaria Township. (Courtesy Coalport Area Coal Museum.)

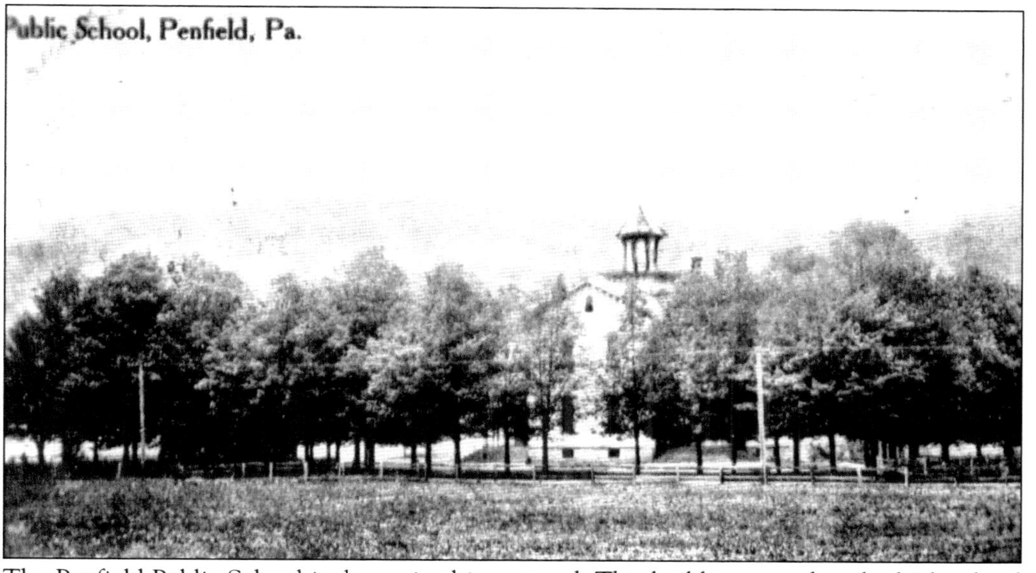

The Penfield Public School is shown in this postcard. This building served as the high school until it burned down in the 1940s. During the early years of Penfield schools, teachers were boarded locally and paid $12 to $15 a month. (Courtesy Autumn Watson.)

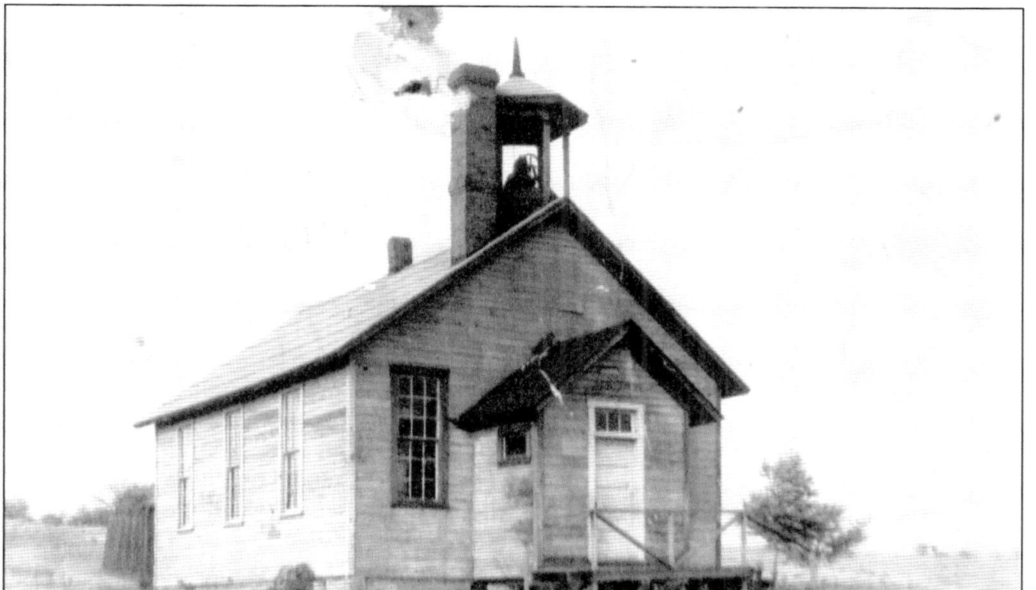

This photograph of the Mount Pleasant School was taken c. 1916. John Wilhelm was one of the teachers in this one-room schoolhouse. The building closed in the 1930s, and the students were sent to the Penfield school. (Courtesy Autumn Watson.)

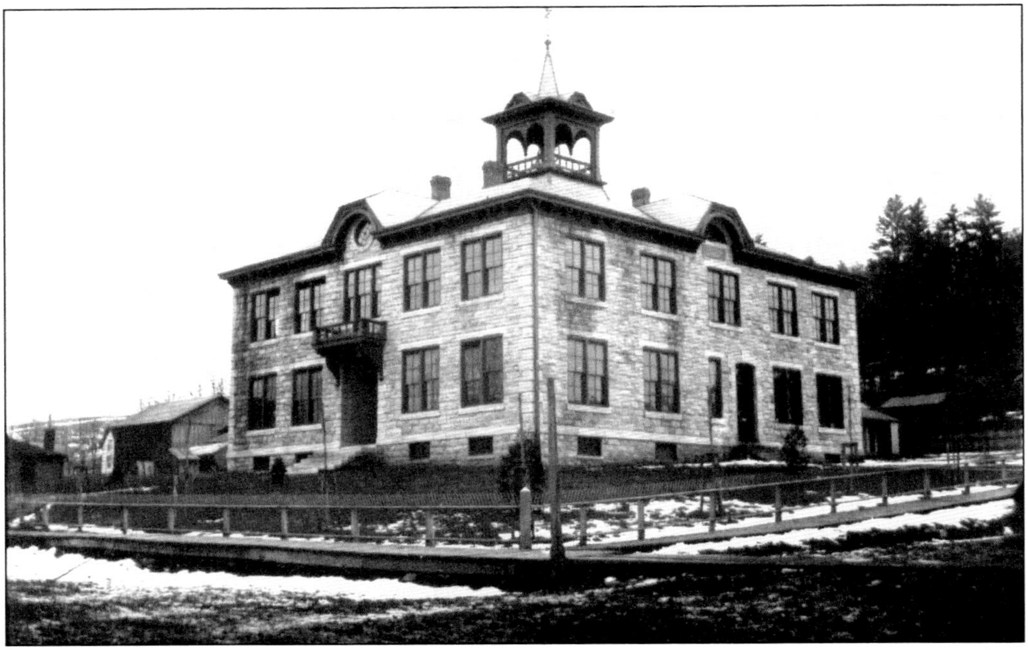

Citizens of Curwensville celebrated the dedication of the Patton Graded Public School in 1885. The school was named for John Patton, who donated $10,000 toward the construction of the building. Patton, who did not have much of a traditional education, wanted every child in Curwensville to have the opportunity to learn. (Courtesy Curwensville-Pike Township Historical Society.)

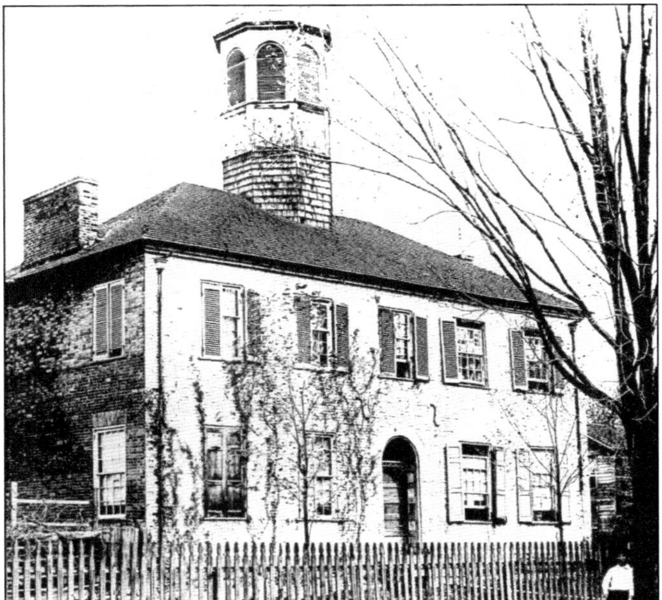

The Clearfield Academy was located on the site of the current Clearfield Borough building in downtown Clearfield. It opened in 1830, with A.T. Schriver as the principal. After Clearfield incorporated in 1840, it was used for the common schools of the borough. The Clearfield Academy was torn down in 1901, and a new high school, which eventually became the junior high, or East Building, was built in its place. (Courtesy Clearfield County Historical Society.)

Six

Floods and Other Disasters

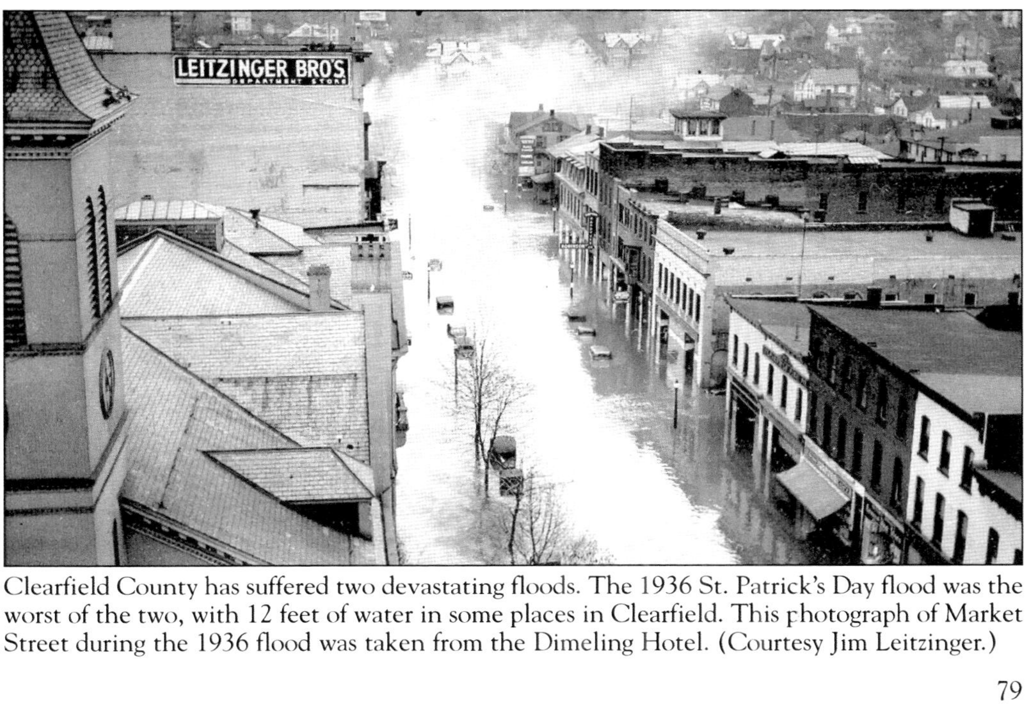

Clearfield County has suffered two devastating floods. The 1936 St. Patrick's Day flood was the worst of the two, with 12 feet of water in some places in Clearfield. This photograph of Market Street during the 1936 flood was taken from the Dimeling Hotel. (Courtesy Jim Leitzinger.)

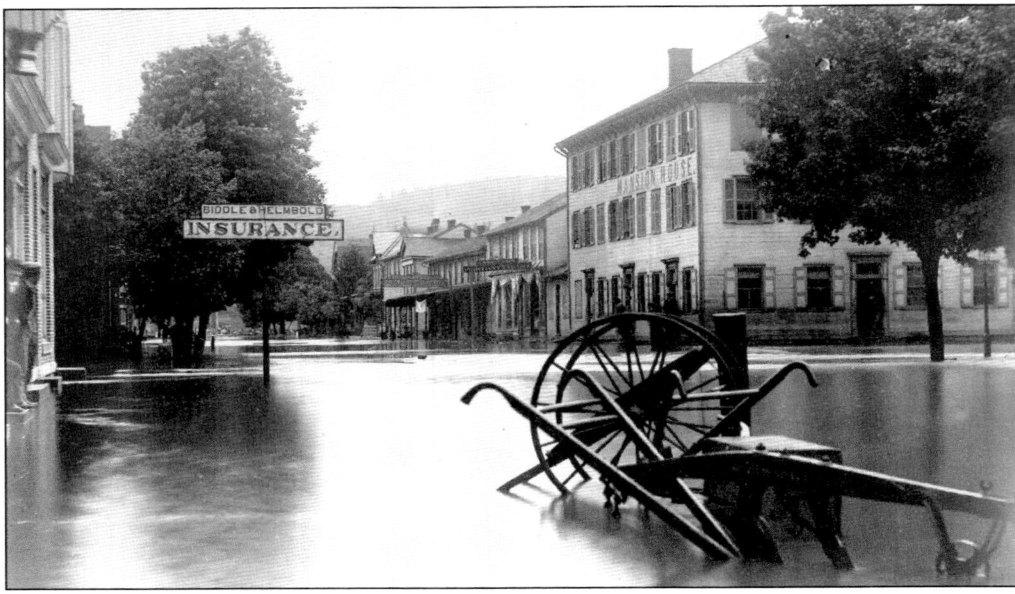

Water fills Clearfield's Market Street in this photograph from the 1889 flood. On the left is Biddle and Hembold Insurance. On the right is the Mansion House, which was the last place in town to flood. The Mansion House was located on the corner of Second and Market Streets, where the Dimeling Hotel is now. Next to the Mansion House are Henry Bridge and Son, Merchant Tailors, and Andrew Harwick, a saddler and harness maker. (Courtesy Clearfield County Historical Society.)

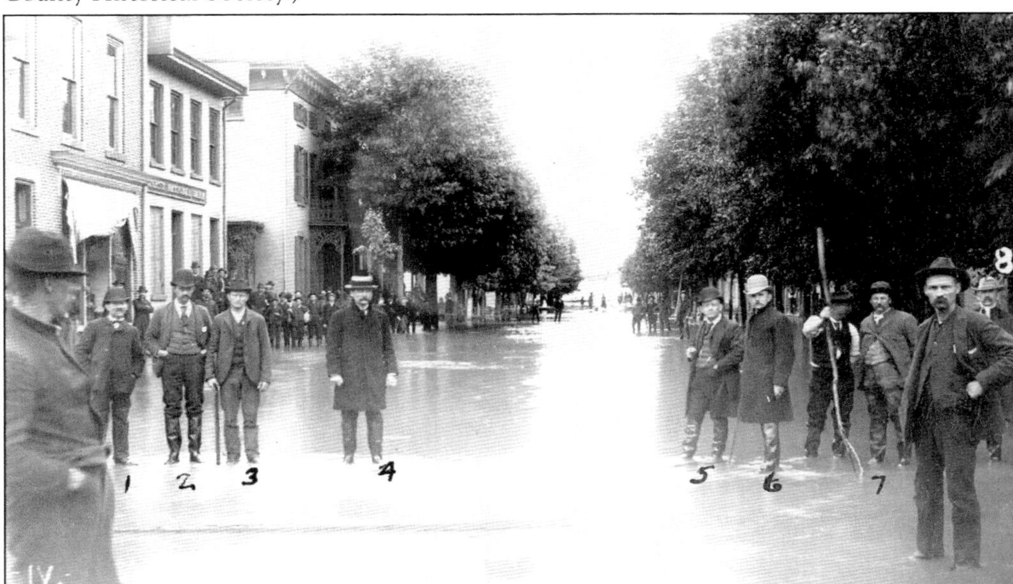

People gather on Second Street in Clearfield as the waters recede from the 1889 flood. The view looks south from Market Street. On the left are the First National Bank and the home of Jonathan Boynton. The numbered men are Richard Duckett (1), Fred Martin (2), Bill Turner (3), Jack Lytle (4), Fred Mossop (5), Dr. J.L.R. Herchold (6), Jack Schriver (7), and Dr. Samuel Stewart (8). (Courtesy Clearfield County Historical Society.)

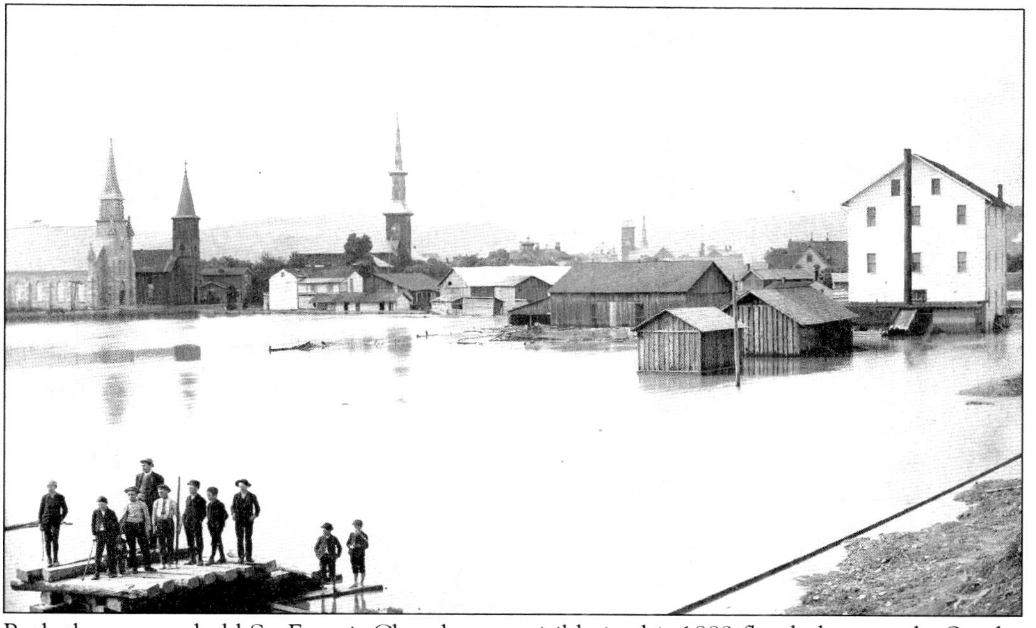

Both the new and old St. Francis Churches are visible in this 1889 flood photograph. On the left are the current St. Francis Church and the Trinity Methodist Church, and in the center of the photograph, with the tallest steeple, is the old St. Francis Church. Smith Mill, which later became Mitchell Milling, is on the right. (Courtesy Clearfield County Historical Society.)

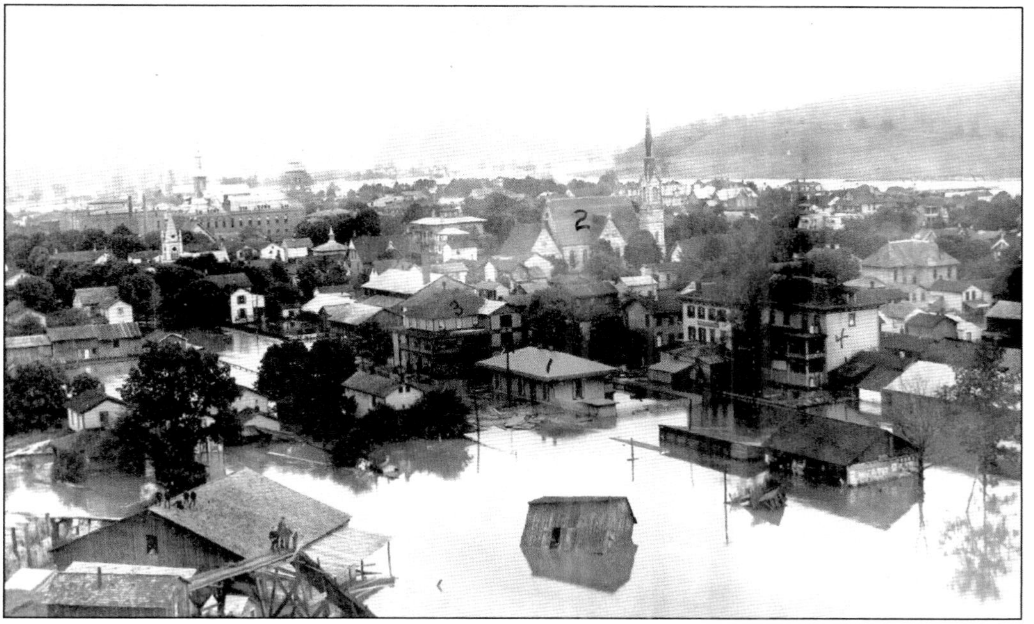

This view of the 1889 flood in Clearfield is from Brewery Hill. Marked as No. 1 in the photograph is the Pennsylvania Railroad station, and next to it is the St. Charles Hotel. No. 2 is the Presbyterian church, and No. 4 is the Leonard house. The flood had one casualty, Ada Tate, who drowned after the boat that was rescuing her capsized. (Courtesy Clearfield County Historical Society.)

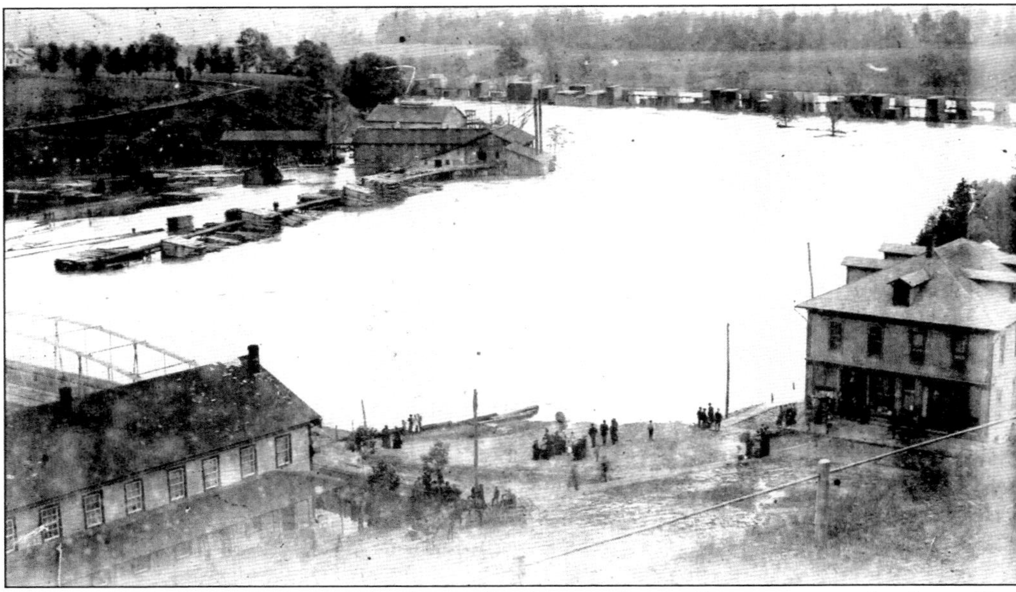

The 1889 flood hit Curwensville hard as well. The river has well overgrown its banks and has taken over the Big Mill, which was at the bottom of Irvin Hill. To the left is the iron bridge that leads to Irvin Hill and the Susquehanna House. To the right is the corner store, a building that still stands today. (Courtesy Curwensville-Pike Township Historical Society.)

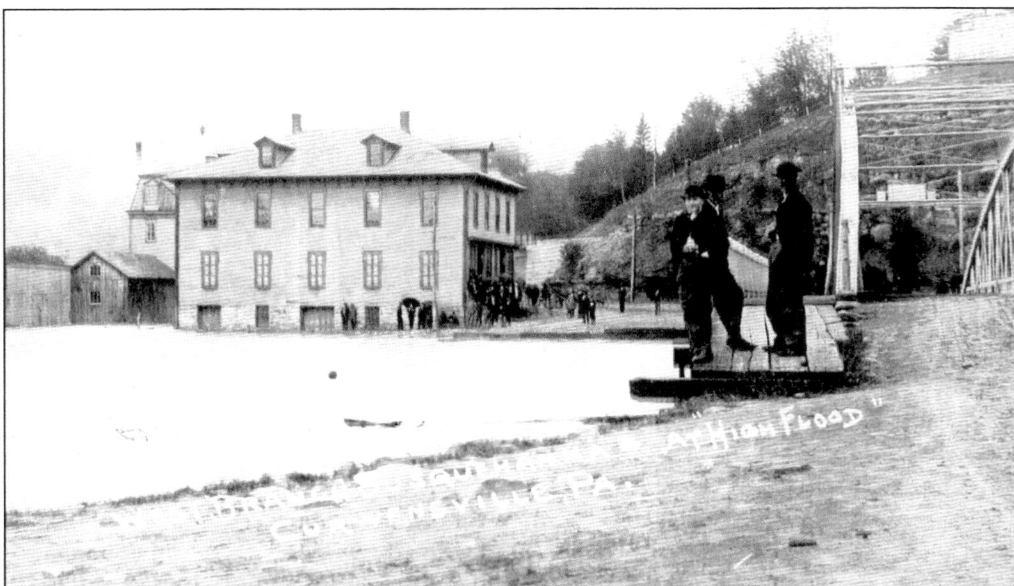

Men watch the river rise from the other side of the Irvin Hill Bridge in this photograph. On the left is the corner store. The bridge on Anderson Creek below Walnut Street was destroyed and swept into the Filbert Street Bridge, damaging it. But a Pennsylvania Railroad bridge held, which saved the covered bridge and the bridge in this photograph. The damage totaled thousands of dollars. (Courtesy J. Duane Test.)

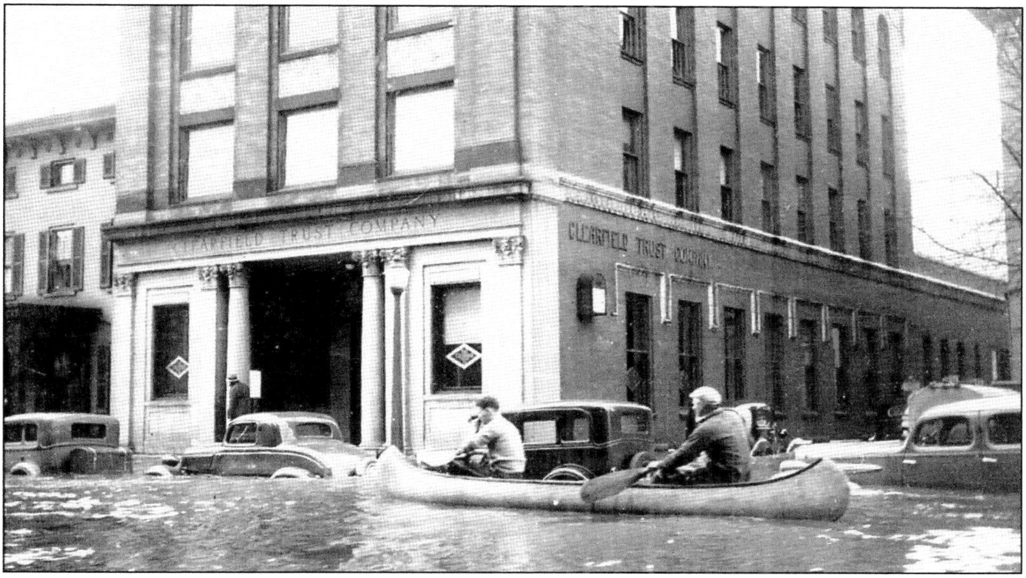

Canoes were a practical way to travel down Second Street in Clearfield, as seen in this photograph from the 1936 flood. The men are paddling past the Clearfield Trust Company, which is now known as Clearfield Bank and Trust Company. The photograph was taken from across the street, at the Dimeling Hotel. (Courtesy Clearfield County Historical Society.)

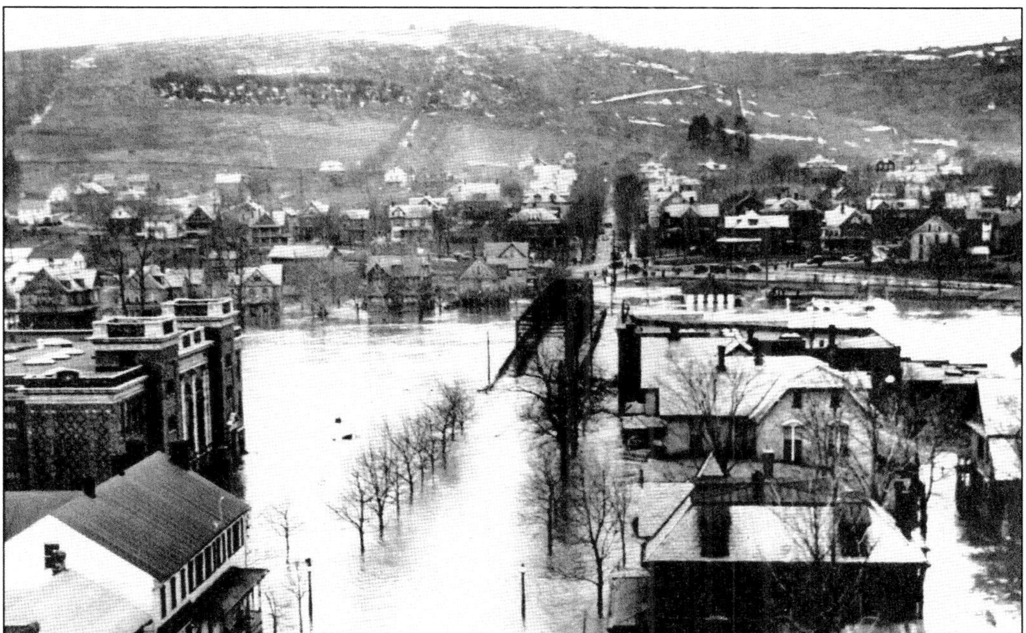

Market Street was clearly underwater, as shown in this picture taken from the top of the Dimeling Hotel. The bottom of the Market Street Bridge is barely visible. It closed at 6:00 p.m. that day. On the left is the old high school. Above the town on the hill can be seen the Clearfield sign, which was erected by a Boy Scout troop in 1930. (Courtesy Clearfield County Historical Society.)

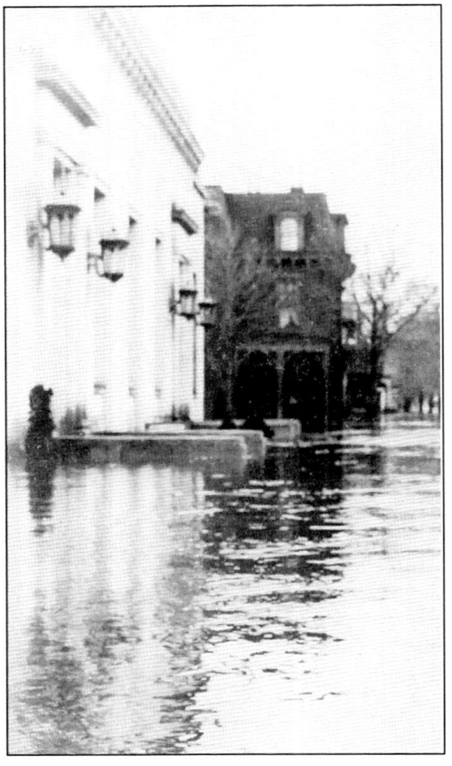

This photograph illustrates just how high the water was during the 1936 flood. The water completely engulfed the steps of the Clearfield post office on Second Street. Today, the old county jail has a high-water mark on its side for both the 1936 and 1889 floods. (Courtesy Clearfield County Historical Society.)

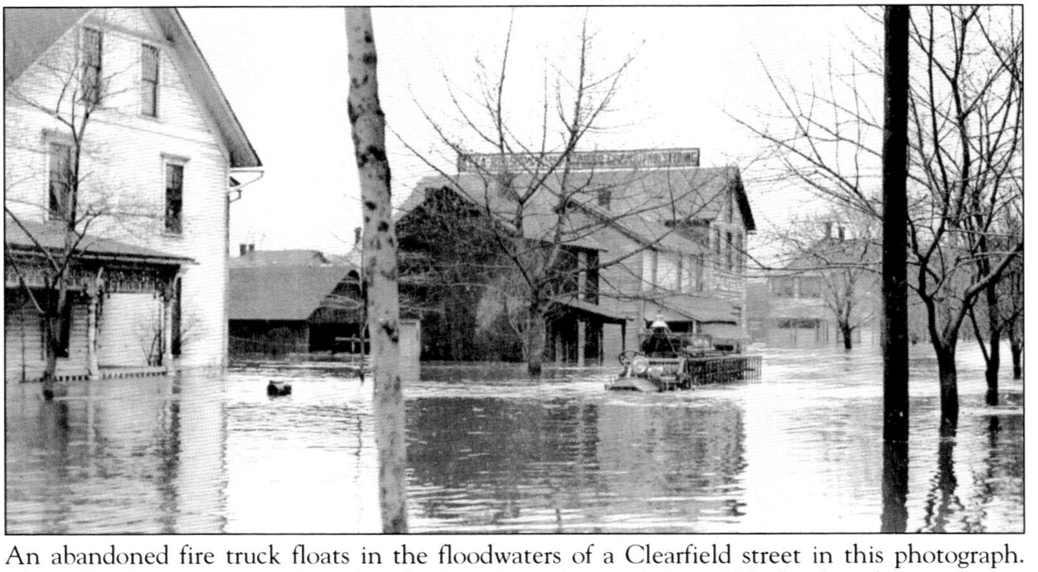

An abandoned fire truck floats in the floodwaters of a Clearfield street in this photograph. These floodwaters were 18 inches higher than those of the 1889 flood and caused over $1 million in damage. The 1936 flood is known as the St. Patrick's Day flood, since it occurred on March 17. (Courtesy Tina Shadduck.)

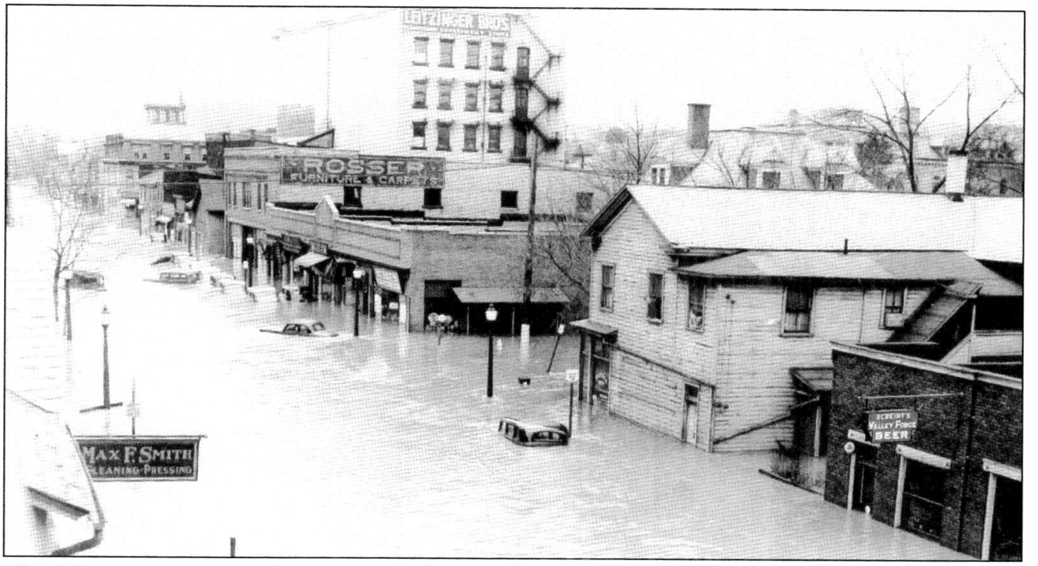

Third Street is a river with many parked cars still on the sides. Valley Forge Beer is on the right, and the Max F. Smith cleaning and pressing shop is on the left. Farther down on the left is the sign for the Lyric Theater. Note the people looking out of the second-story windows in the light-colored building on the right. (Courtesy Tina Shadduck.)

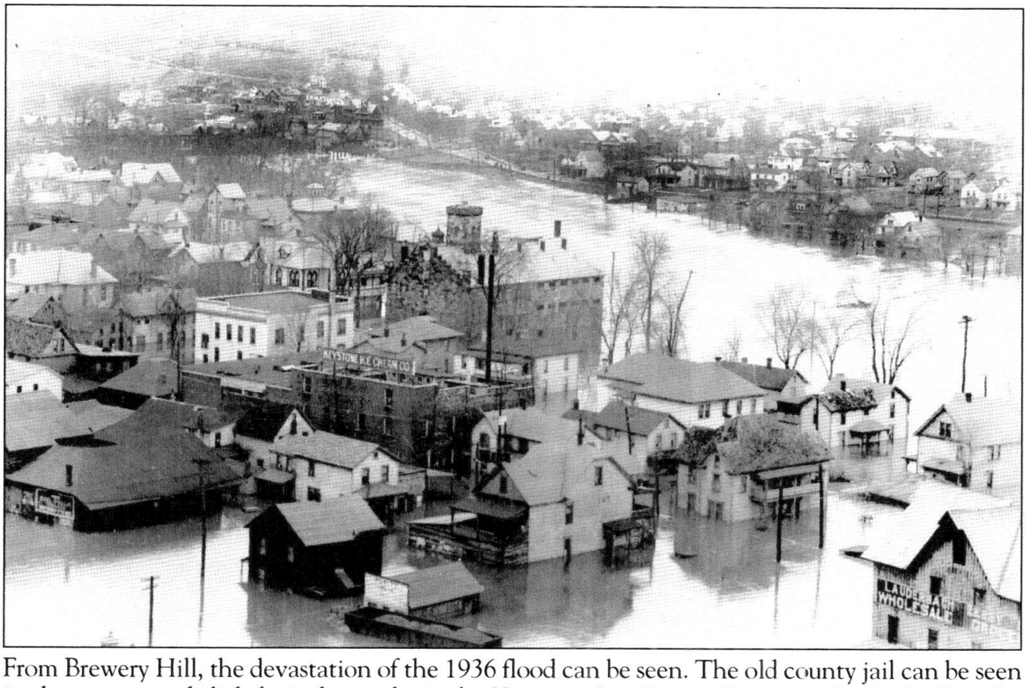

From Brewery Hill, the devastation of the 1936 flood can be seen. The old county jail can be seen in the center, and slightly in front of it is the Keystone Ice Cream Company. Lauderbach Zerby Company, wholesale grocers, is in the bottom right-hand corner. (Courtesy Tina Shadduck.)

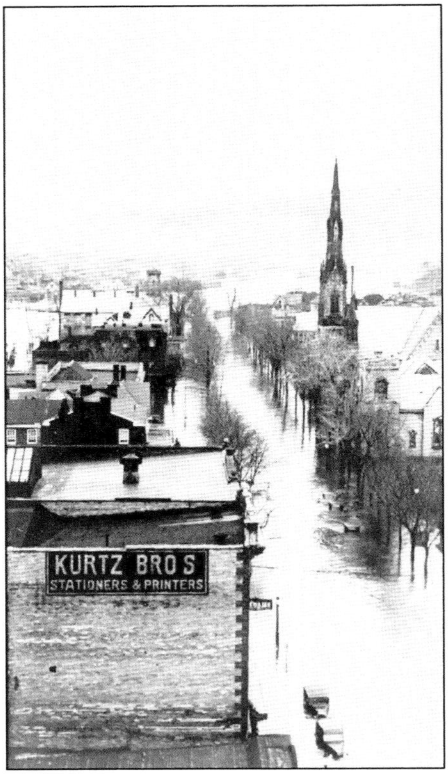

This photograph, another from the top of the Dimeling Hotel, shows Second Street and the cars that were left there. The 150-foot steeple of the Presbyterian church can be seen on the right, and the Kurtz Brothers building is on the left. Many people were stranded in Clearfield and were forced to stay at the Dimeling Hotel, the county courthouse, and the YMCA. (Courtesy Clearfield County Historical Society.)

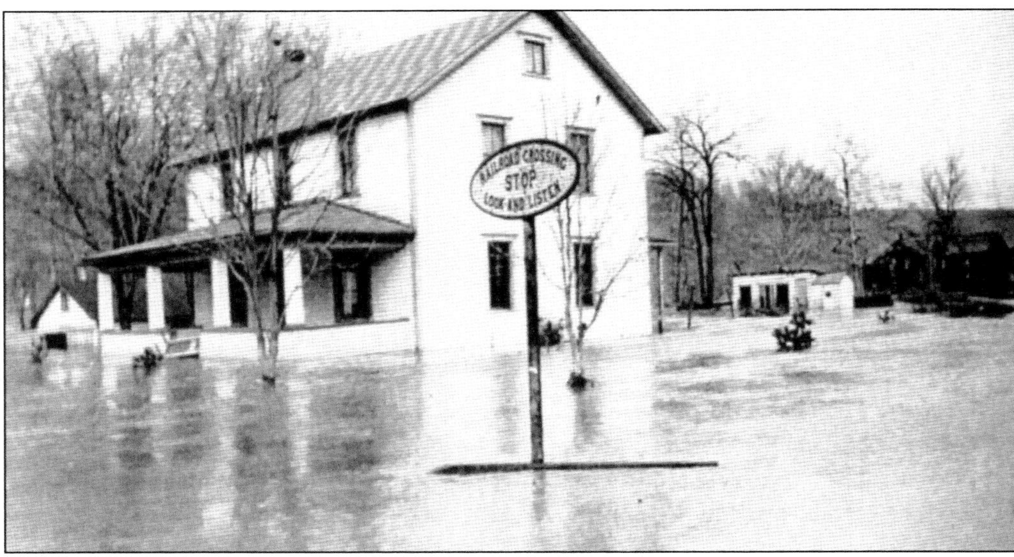

The 1936 flood affected many parts of the county. The flood followed a difficult winter, during which snow fell heavily. In March, the huge piles of snow began to melt. The heavy rain that began on March 16 and continued into the next day combined with the melting snow to cause the flood. Here, we see Coalport's railroad crossing engulfed by water. (Courtesy Coalport Area Coal Museum.)

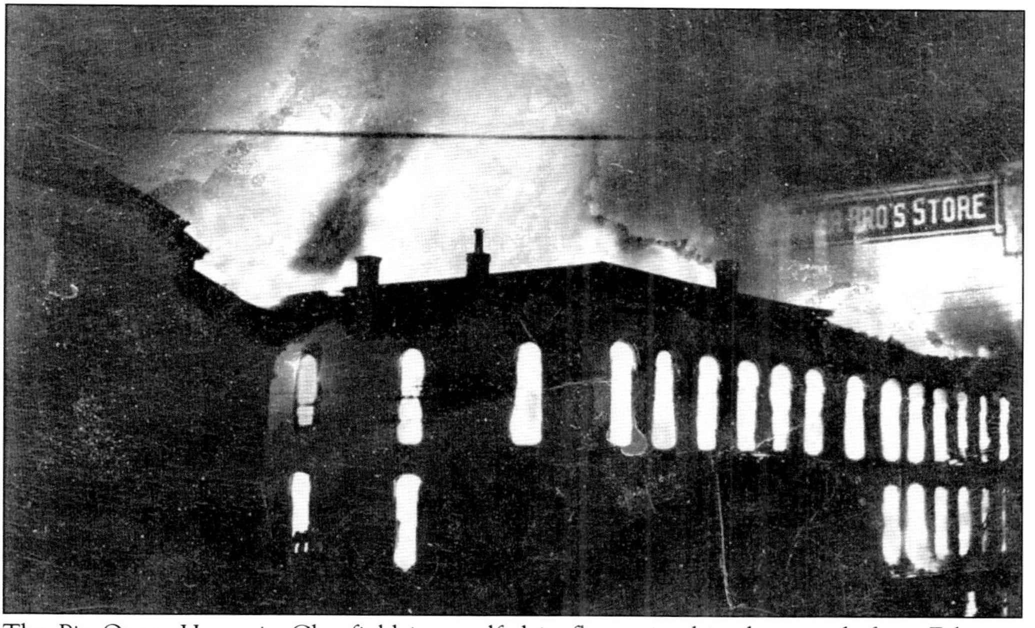

The Pie Opera House in Clearfield is engulfed in flames in this photograph from February 27, 1917. The building caught fire early in the morning and burned rapidly. Even though the firefighters responded quickly, the building was beyond saving. Built in 1873, it also housed several businesses, including the Regal Five and Dime store and several law offices. (Courtesy Jim Leitzinger.)

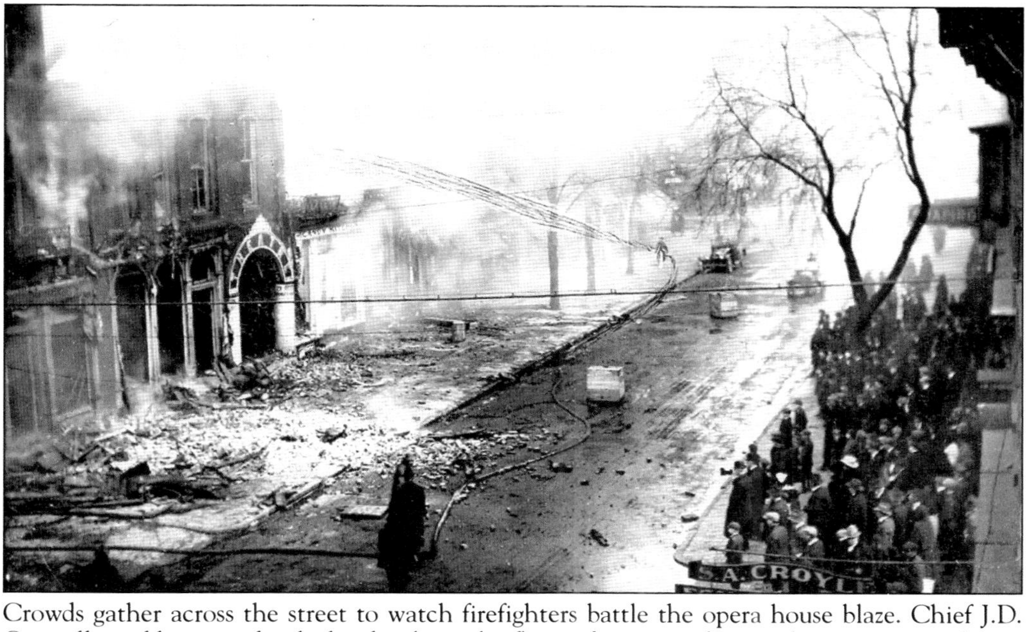

Crowds gather across the street to watch firefighters battle the opera house blaze. Chief J.D. Connelly and his crew fought hard to keep the flames from spreading to the county courthouse and the Leitzinger Brothers store. Chief Connelly directed the attack from an iron catwalk that attached the opera house to the courthouse. (Courtesy Jim Leitzinger.)

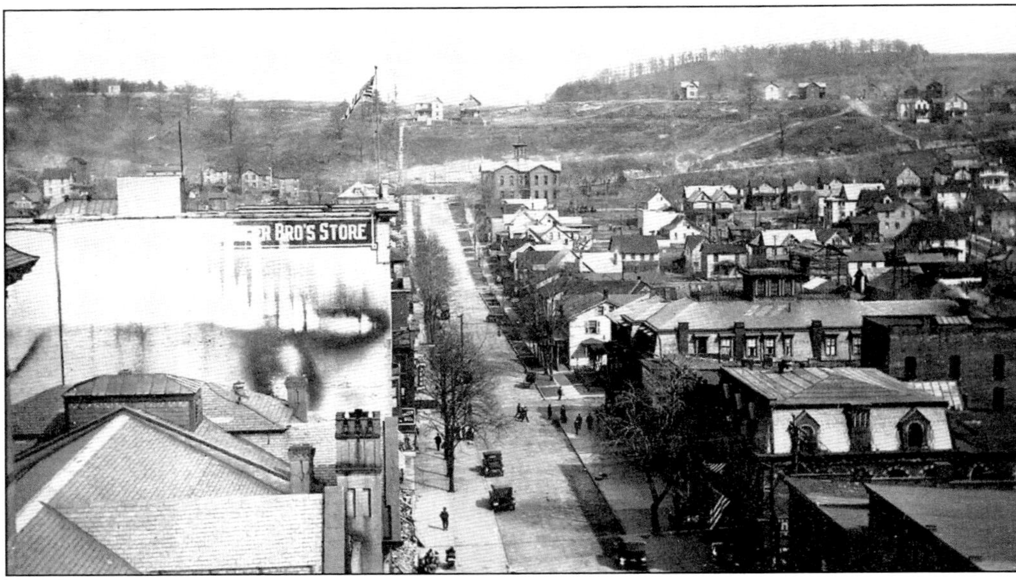

This is an aerial view of Market Street in downtown Clearfield after the opera house fire. Note the scorch marks on the side of the Leitzinger building. This building was saved because a newly installed sprinkler system misted water along the outside wall of the store. The cause of the fire was never discovered. (Courtesy Jim Leitzinger.)

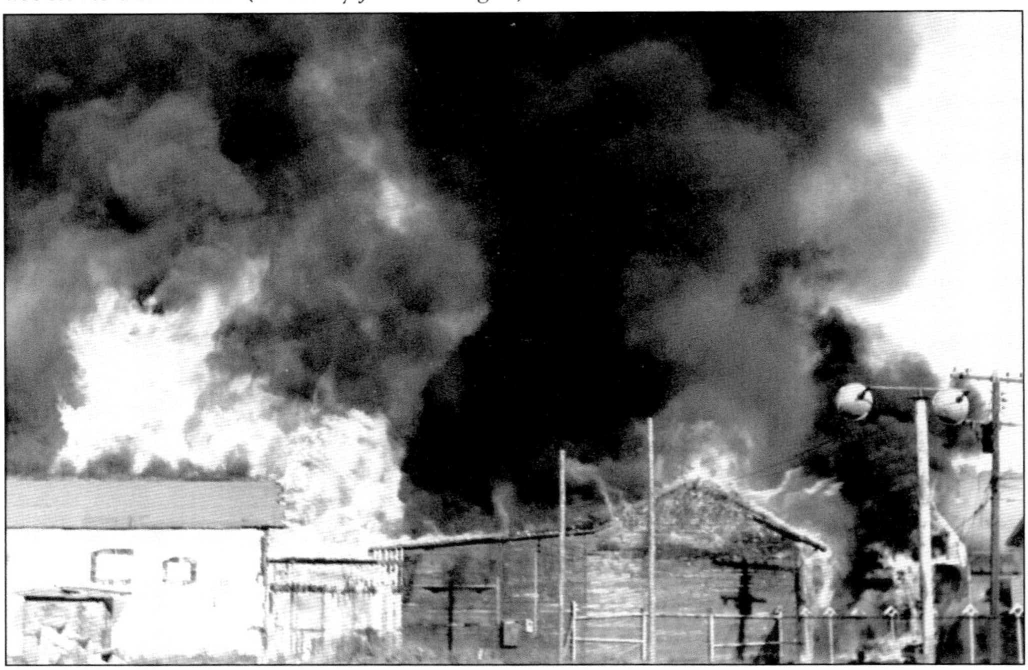

The Soult Lumber Company caught fire on September 14, 1959. The block-long plant, located on Williams Street between Merrill and Fulton Streets in Clearfield, burned for over 18 hours and caused $1 million in damage. Faulty outside wiring was listed as the cause of this blaze, which also destroyed two nearby homes and damaged three others. (Courtesy Clearfield County Historical Society.)

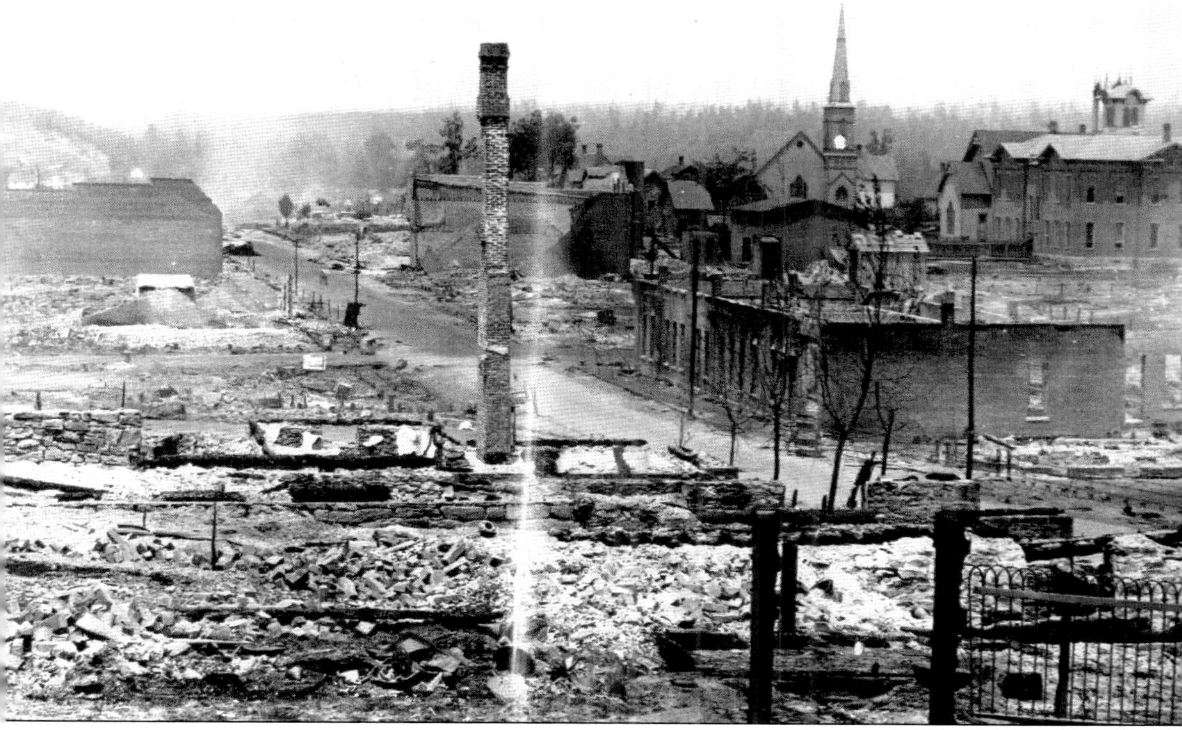

In June 1888, DuBois suffered a devastating fire that practically destroyed the entire town, which was built from lumber. The blaze stared at the Barker's Hotel, and with the help of shifting winds, it spread quickly through the town. Five fire hydrants produced no water, so the fire was fought with water from wells and the creek. In the end, the fire wiped out 14 blocks. Only 6 of 166 businesses survived, and at least 500 people were homeless. This photograph shows the ruins. The unharmed Central School can be seen in the upper central part of the picture. The First Presbyterian church and the Reformed church are on the left. The lone chimney belonged to the Commercial Hotel. One report claims a Philadelphia committee reviewed the situation to assess whether funds would be available to help rebuild. They decided this young lumber town was not worth investing in. Luckily for DuBois, John E. DuBois and other local businessmen felt differently, and the town was quickly rebuilt. (Courtesy DuBois Area Historical Society.)

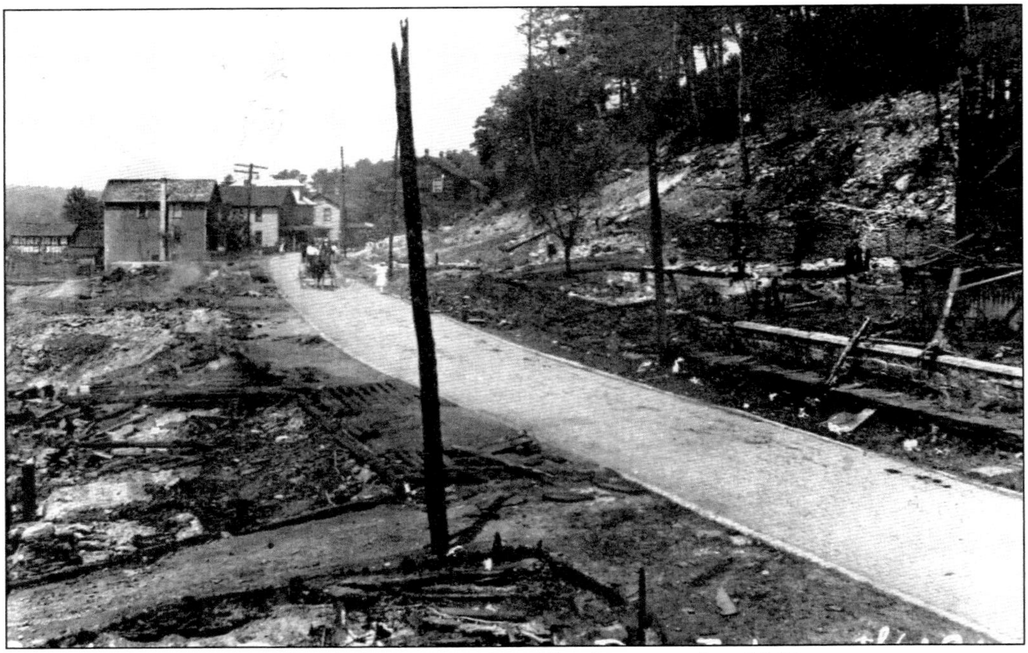

In July 1914, it was Woodland that was on fire. The fire started at 10:50 p.m. at a restaurant owned by James Merritt of Clearfield. The flames quickly engulfed the town, as locals had no way to fight it. A fire company from Harbison-Walker Refractories helped save one home by using chemicals. Clearfield's fire department was called but was delayed because their steam pumper was too heavy for the horses to pull to Woodland. A special train was set up with a flatcar for transporting the pumper. They arrived after 1:00 a.m., and a half-hour later, they had the fire under control. These photographs show the damage, which was estimated to be $35,000. (Courtesy Clearfield County Historical Society.)

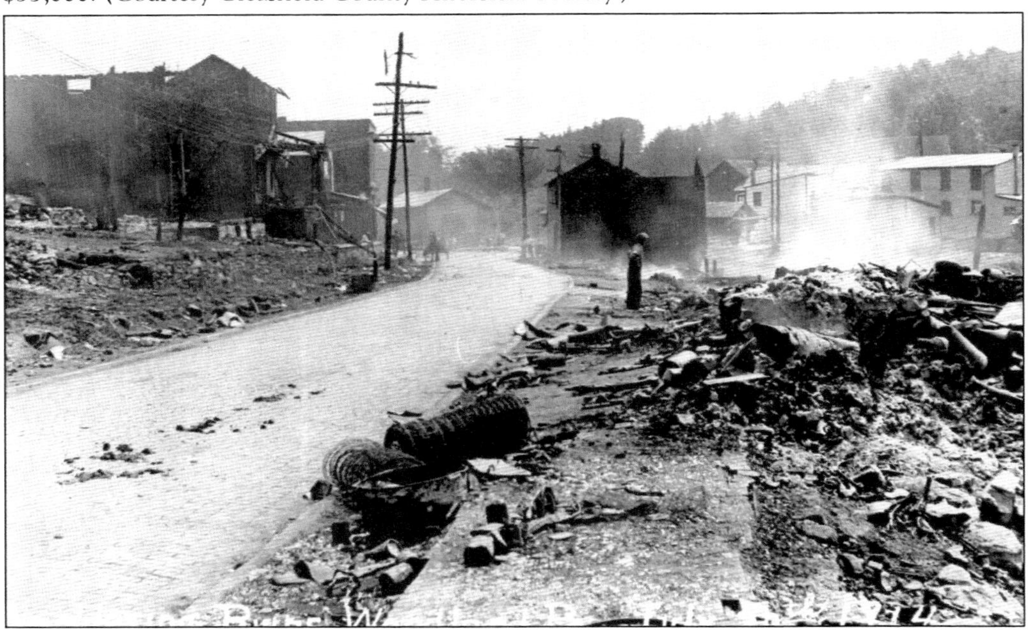

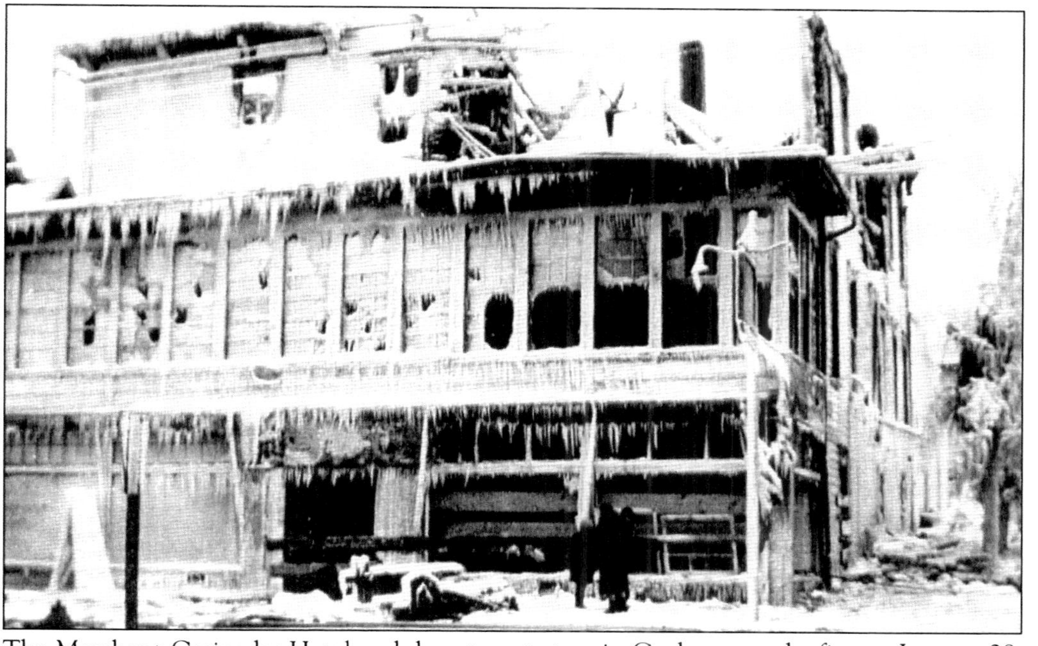

The Merchant-Greinader Hotel and department store in Coalport caught fire on January 28, 1934. The fire spread quickly due to high winds. Cresson, Philipsburg, Madera, and Houtzdale fire companies were called to help. The firefighters braved the cold temperature (around zero degrees), but the structure was a complete ruin in a short time. The above photograph shows ice forming on the remains of the building, which was owned by Edward Greinader. (Courtesy Coalport Area Coal Museum.)

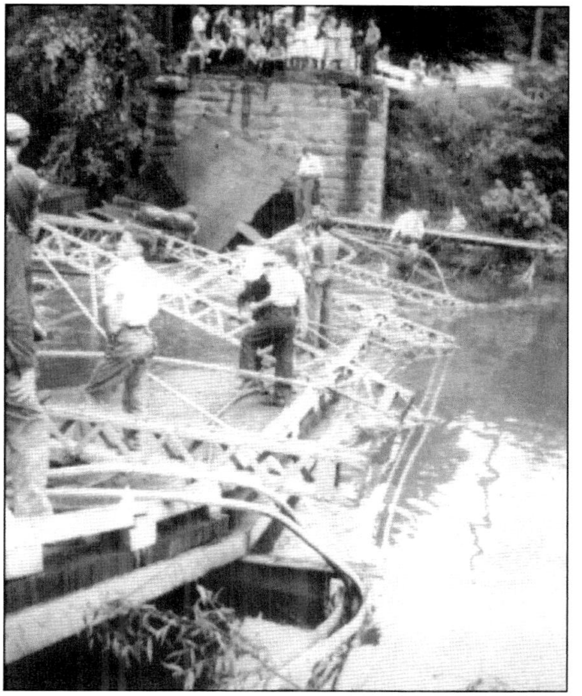

The Irvona Bridge over Clearfield Creek on Route 53 collapsed, as shown in this 1939 photograph. Reports indicate that a truck struck the end of the bridge and knocked it off balance. There were no injuries, but a truck and a car both fell into the water. The bridge was rebuilt the following year. (Courtesy Coalport Area Coal Museum.)

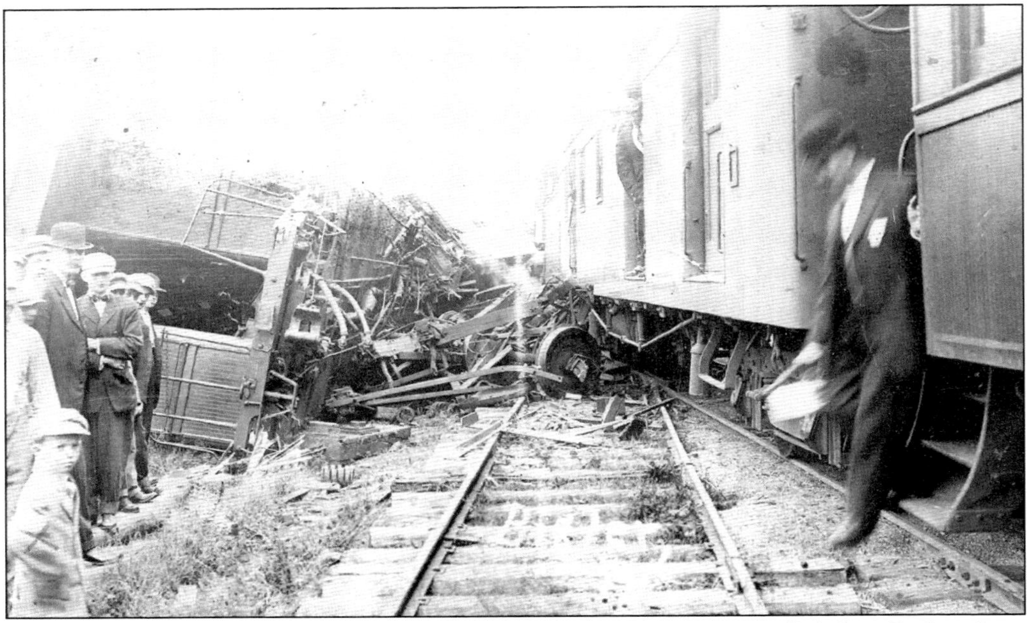

Onlookers survey the aftermath of a train wreck. The two trains collided at Bigler along Route 322 on August 20, 1911. One of the trains was en route to a camp meeting. Trains were a regular sight in Bigler then, as four passenger trains stopped at each station daily. (Courtesy Clearfield County Historical Society.)

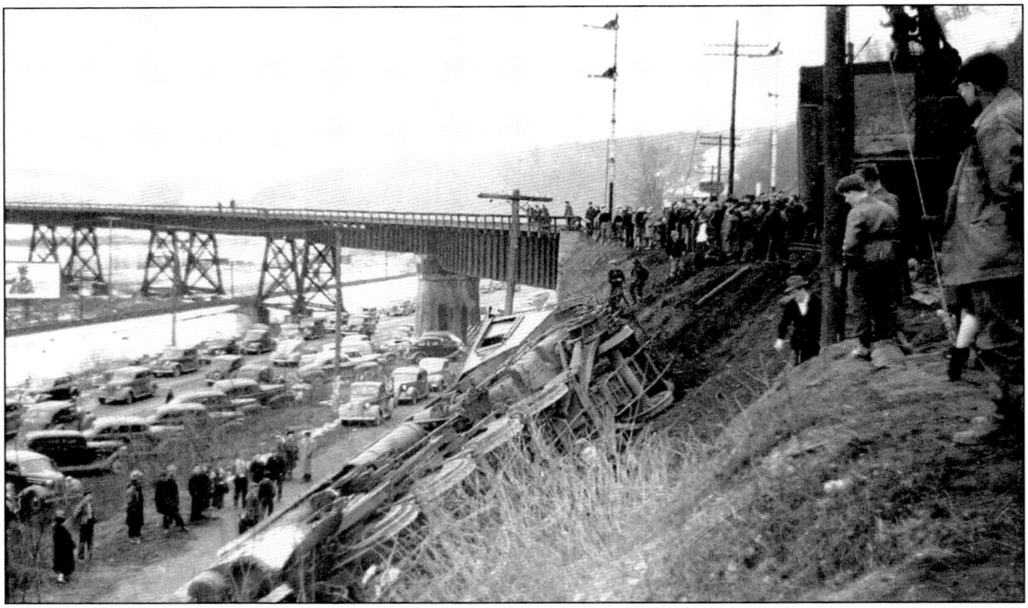

This train wreck occurred at Arnoldtown, on Route 879 near Curwensville, in 1941. It was part of the New York Central Railroad, which was incorporated in 1914. The company then was a consolidation of 11 companies. The New York Central Railroad first came to this area in the 1880s. (Courtesy Clearfield County Historical Society.)

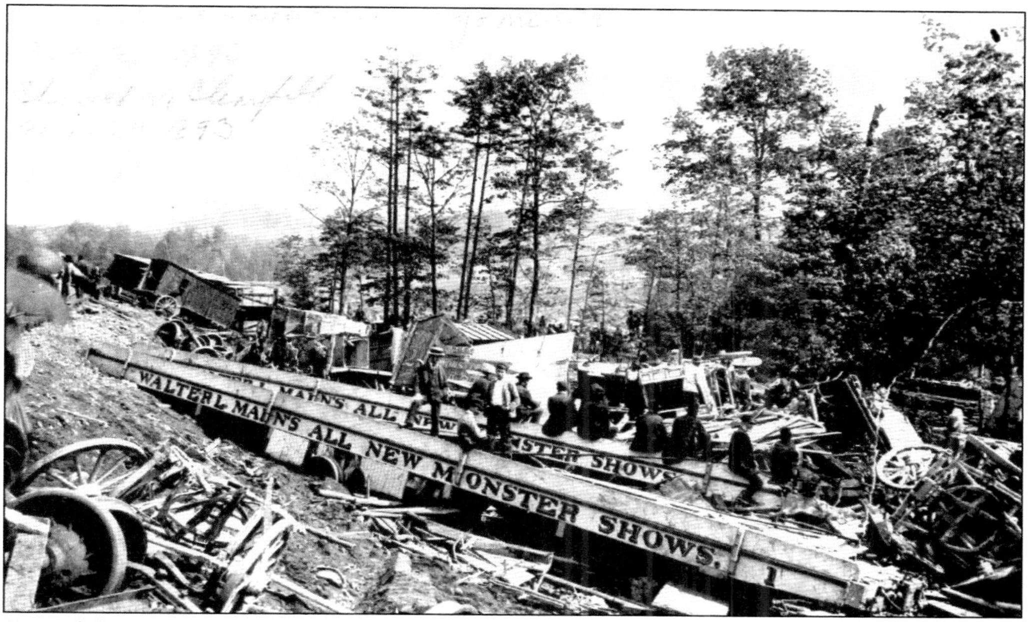

One of the most infamous train wrecks that occurred in the area, although not in Clearfield County, was the circus train wreck that happened in May 1893. The train left after a performance in Houtzdale and traveled to Osceola Mills to the junction of the Tyrone-Clearfield Railroad. There, a request was put in for an additional engine to increase the braking power. This request was denied, and the train began its ill-fated trip. This route involved traveling down a mountain with several twists and turns. The train was going around a horseshoe curve when it lost control. Six people and 52 horses and other animals were killed. There were numerous other injuries. Many of the animals were free, and a few escaped. Although most of the escaped creatures were either captured or killed, legend says some of their descendants are still living in the mountains. Seen above are the wrecked circus cars, and below, some of the dead animals are laid out. (Courtesy Clearfield County Historical Society.)

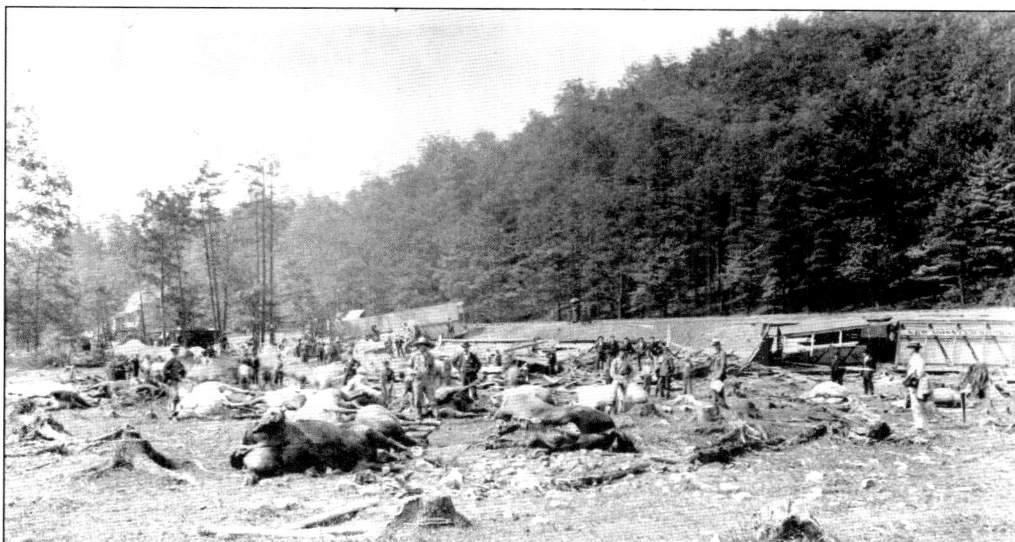

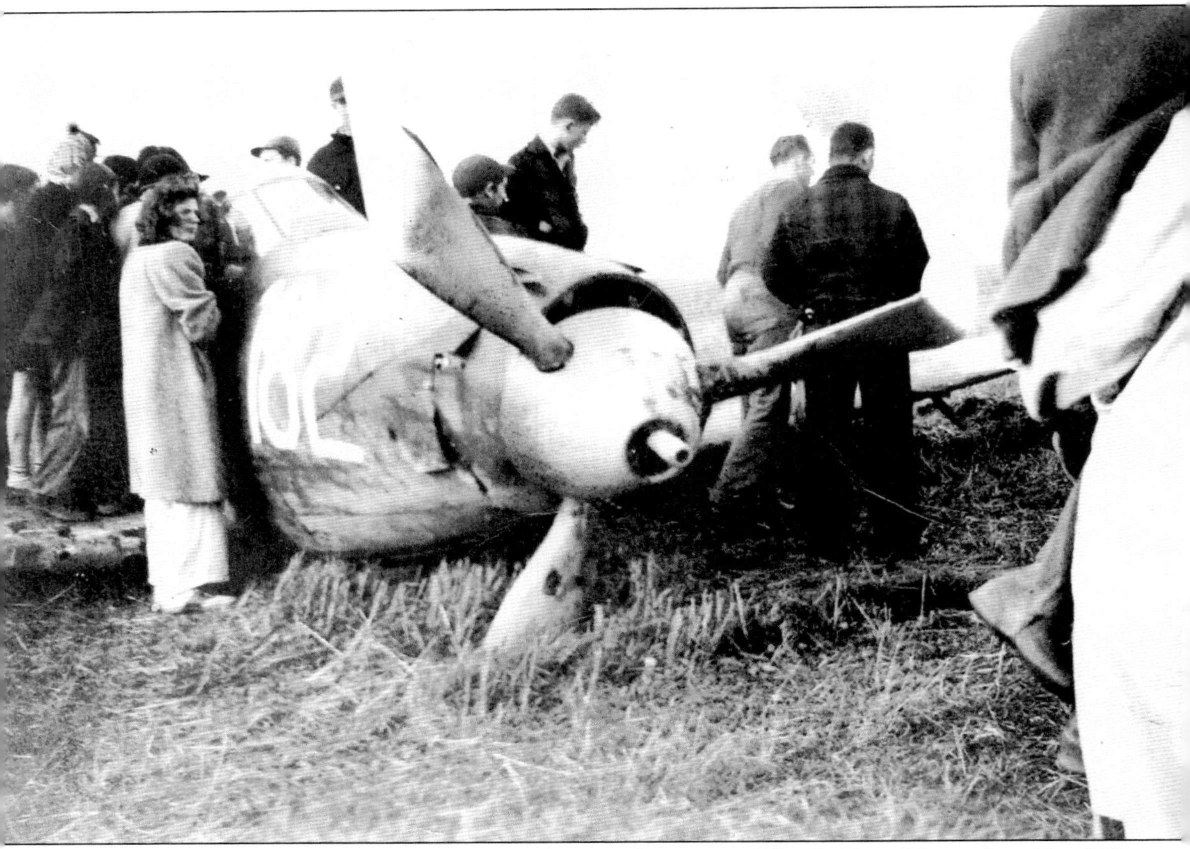

An army pilot, Lt. Harold W. Freemantle, was flying over Clearfield on November 12, 1942, when he had trouble with his plane, a Bell P-39D. Freemantle said his engine began to vibrate and he could not maintain altitude. He was forced to attempt a landing when his engine cut out completely. He crashed at Thompson Cemetery near Glen Richey. According to eyewitnesses, the plane circled for quite a while before attempting to land. H.H. Owens, the owner of the field, reported that there was approximately $100 damage to his newly seeded wheat and hay fields from the crash and from people trampling through the area. In this photograph taken by Allen Rowles just minutes after the crash, curious neighbors brave the cold to look over the wreckage. Once the army arrived, the area was roped off and guarded. (Courtesy Duane Rowles.)

Seven

Coal Towns

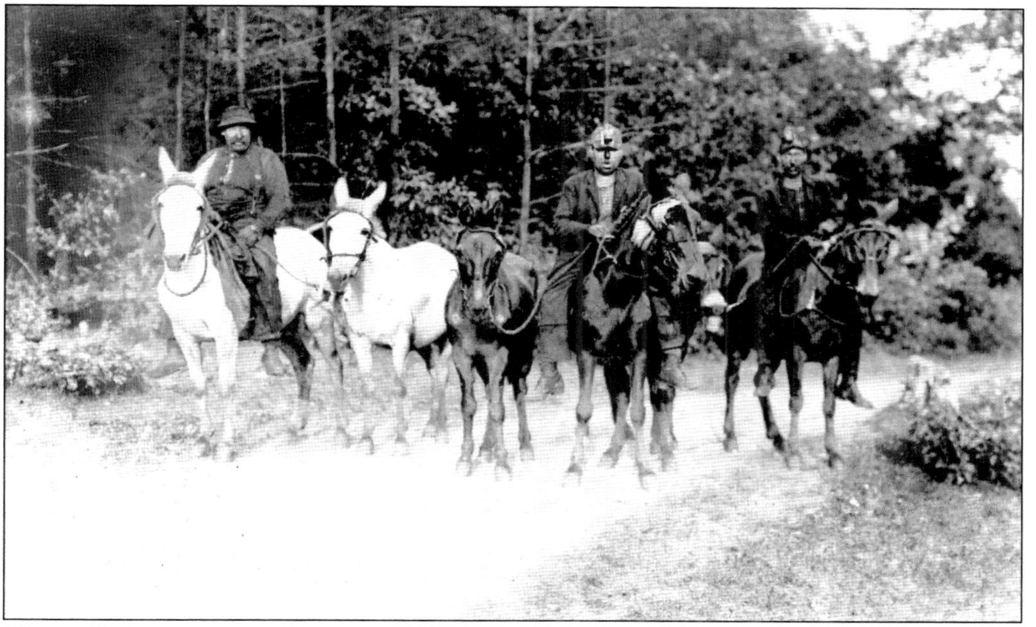

Clearfield County was well known for its coal. During the early part of the 1900s, many little coal or company towns sprang up. Each had stores, theaters, churches, and schools. After the mines were empty, so were many of the towns. The men in the above photograph were working at the Potter and Bigler mines. (Courtesy Clearfield County Historical Society.)

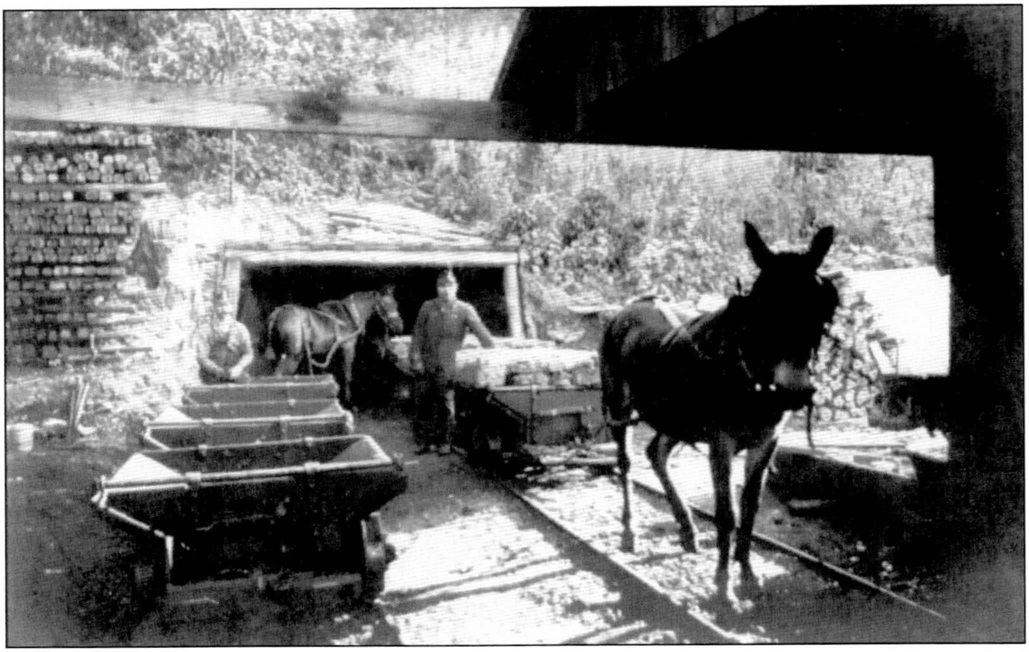

Just outside Curwensville were the Bickford coal mines. Mules and horses were standard equipment for mining when this photograph was taken. The abundance of coal was an incentive to the railroad companies, and most coal towns had access to trains. (Courtesy Curwensville-Pike Township Historical Society.)

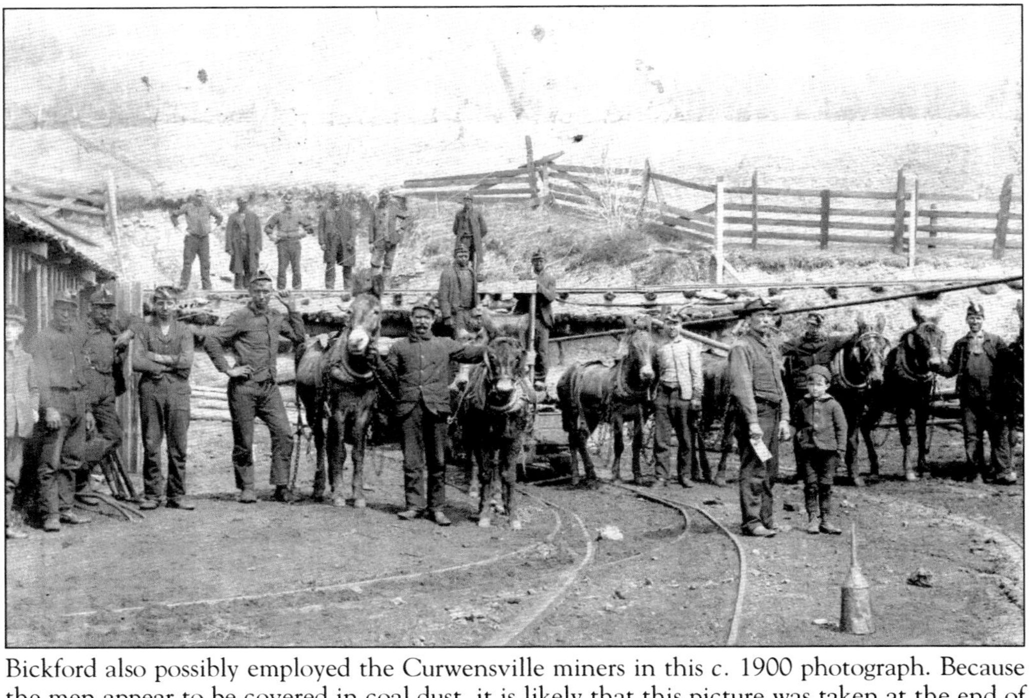

Bickford also possibly employed the Curwensville miners in this *c.* 1900 photograph. Because the men appear to be covered in coal dust, it is likely that this picture was taken at the end of the workday. (Courtesy J. Duane Test.)

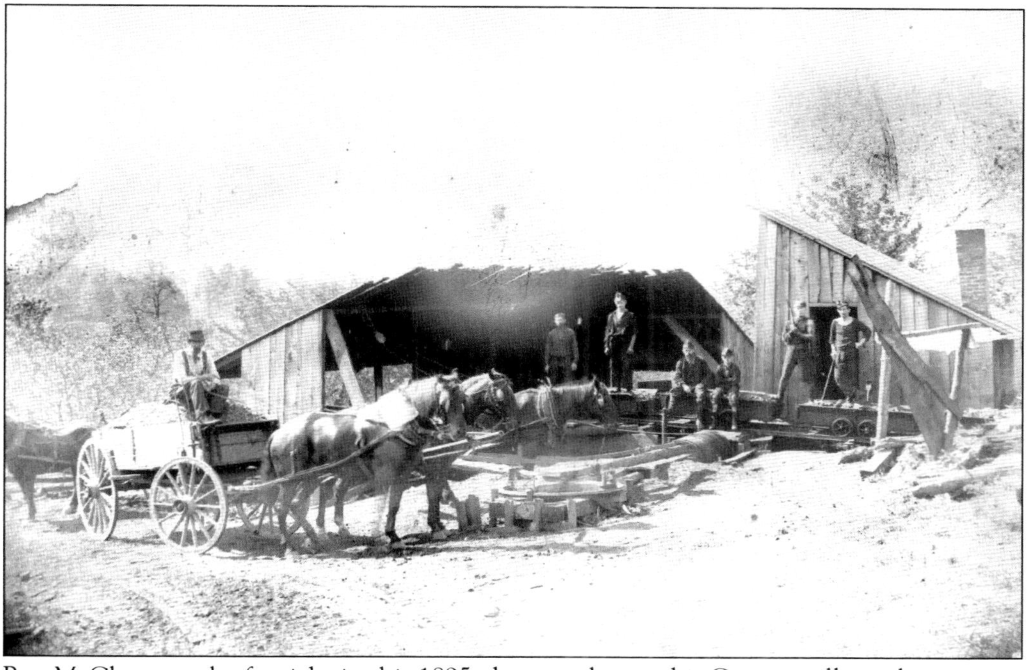

Roy McClure, on the far right in this 1895 photograph, ran this Curwensville coal operation. According to information found with the photograph, he eventually sold his land to the Alley Brothers and Company tannery. The Alley Brothers tannery was destroyed by fire in 1899. (Courtesy Clearfield County Historical Society.)

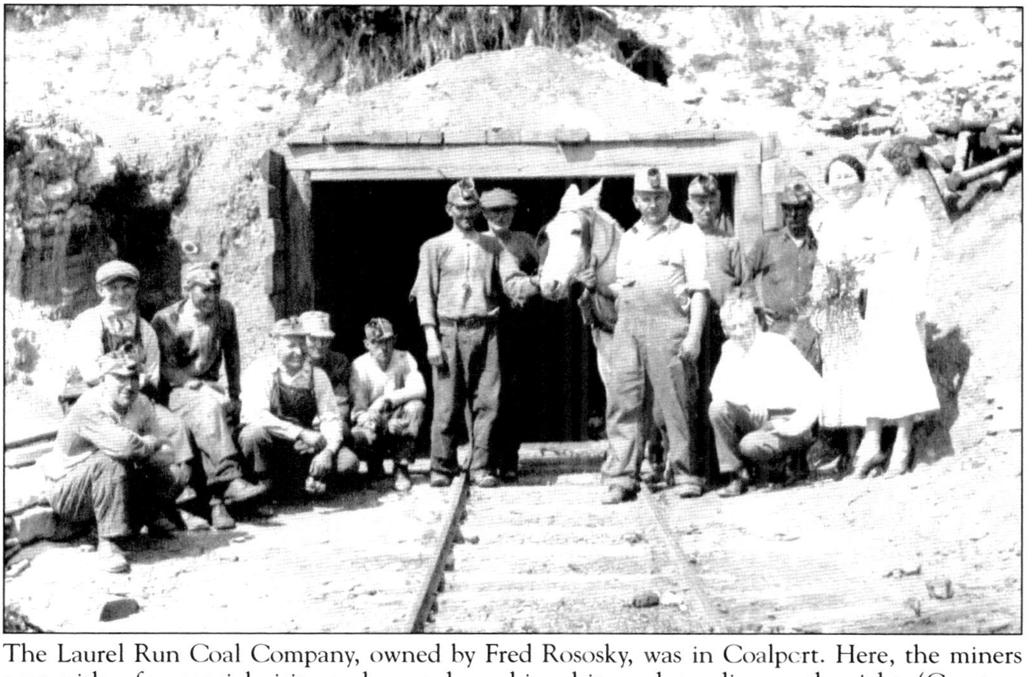

The Laurel Run Coal Company, owned by Fred Rososky, was in Coalport. Here, the miners pose with a few special visitors who are dressed in white and standing on the right. (Courtesy Coalport Area Coal Museum.)

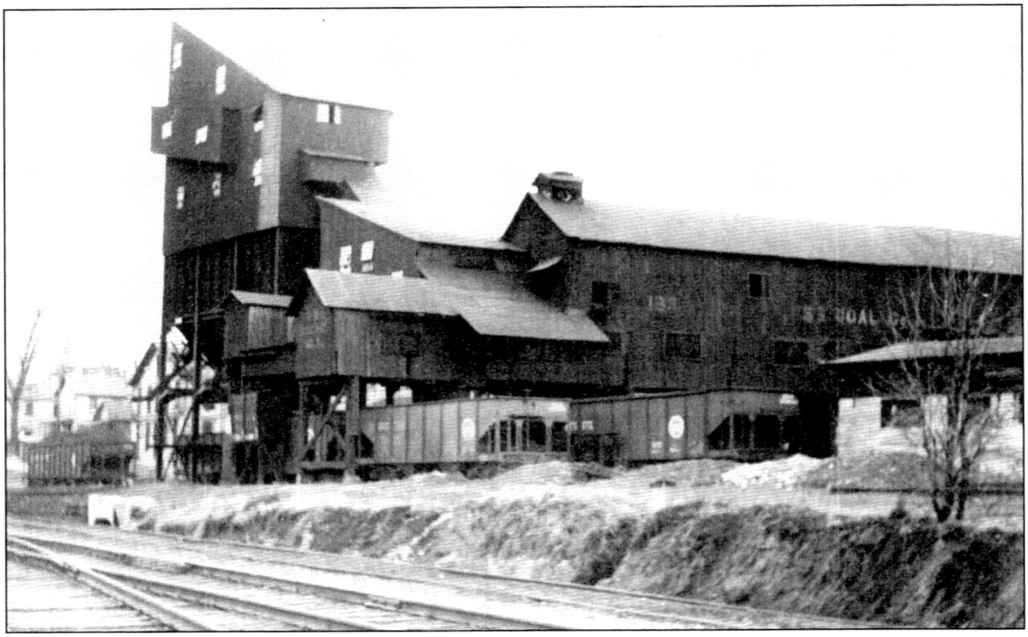

The Cambria Smokeless Mine in Coalport was also known as the Sunshine Mine. This mine, like many others, had a company store, located on Main Street, where the workers shopped. The store carried everything a family would need, and the cost of the items was then deducted from their paychecks. (Courtesy Coalport Area Coal Museum.)

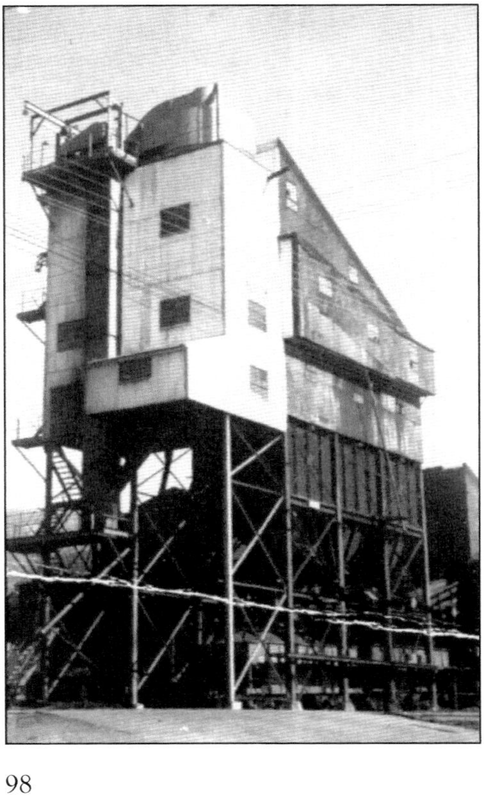

This photograph shows a closer view of the coal-cleaning plant at the Sunshine Mine at Coalport. It was owned by the Cambria Smokeless Coal Company from Johnstown. At one point, the mine employed between 500 and 600 miners. When it closed, many of the workers were transferred to a mine in Clymer. (Courtesy Coalport Area Coal Museum.)

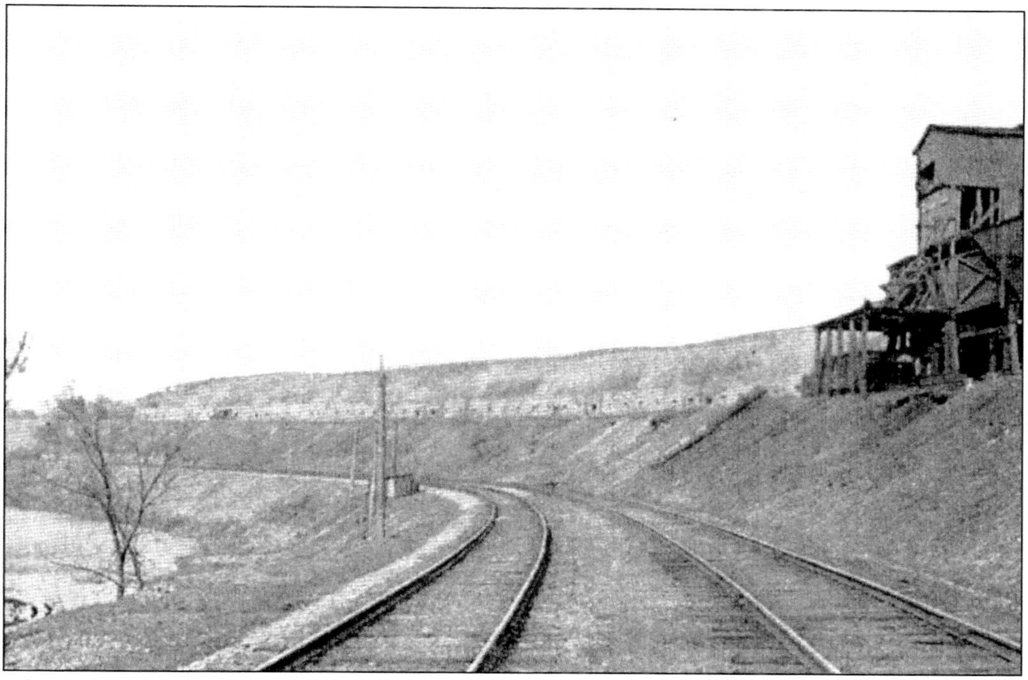

Along these tracks is the Irvona Coal and Coke Company mine No. 5 and the coke ovens that were located in Coalport. Coalport was named for the large amount of coal in that area. The first person to mine in this area was John Gill in 1810; he used the coal for his blacksmith business. Samuel Hegarty's company mined the first coal for shipping. (Courtesy Coalport Area Coal Museum.)

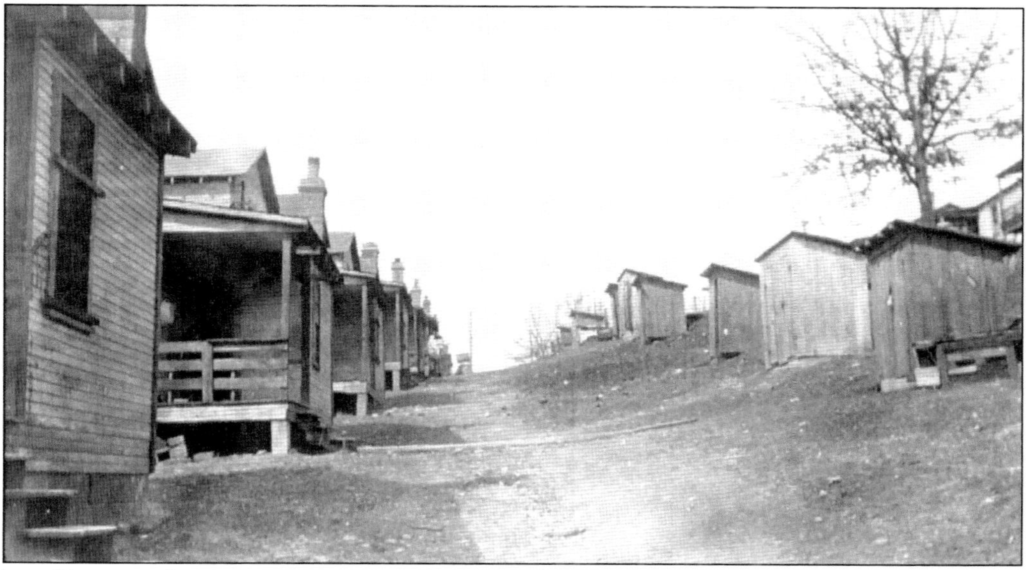

In addition to having company stores, many coal companies built homes for the miners and their families to live in. Behind these lines of houses were outhouses, as seen in this photograph of Coalport. Men known as honey dippers cleaned them out just twice a year. (Courtesy Coalport Area Coal Museum.)

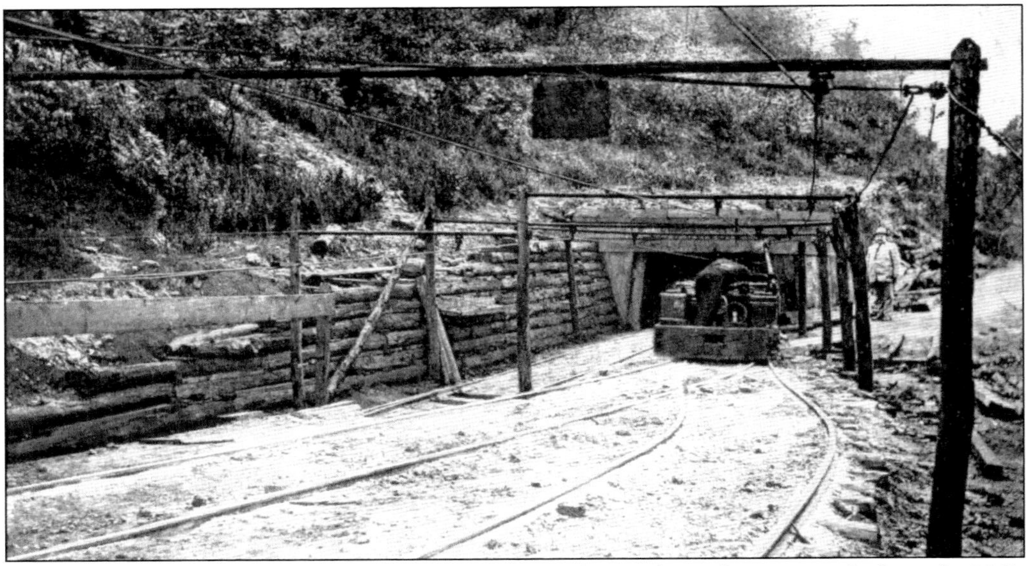

The Moshannon No. 1 mine in Osceola Mills is featured on this postcard. Osceola Mills started as a lumber town but made the transition, as many towns did, to a coal town. In 1862, an Osceola mine transported 7,239 tons of coal. In 1885, 3,663,466 tons were shipped from Osceola Mills. (Courtesy Osceola Mills Public Library.)

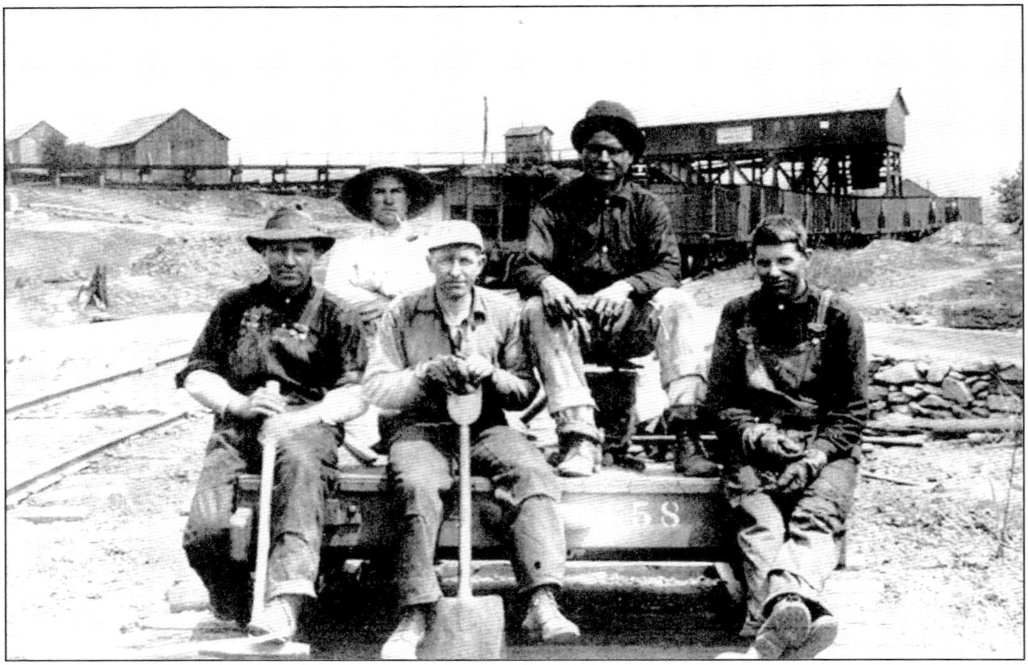

Henry Swoope bought the Morrisdale Coal Company's Madera mine in 1908 and called it the Sylvania Mine Company. At that time, among the assets of the company were 18 red houses, 20 additional mules, and 12 shanties. A few of the miners for the Sylvania mines pose in this undated photograph. (Courtesy Coalport Area Coal Museum.)

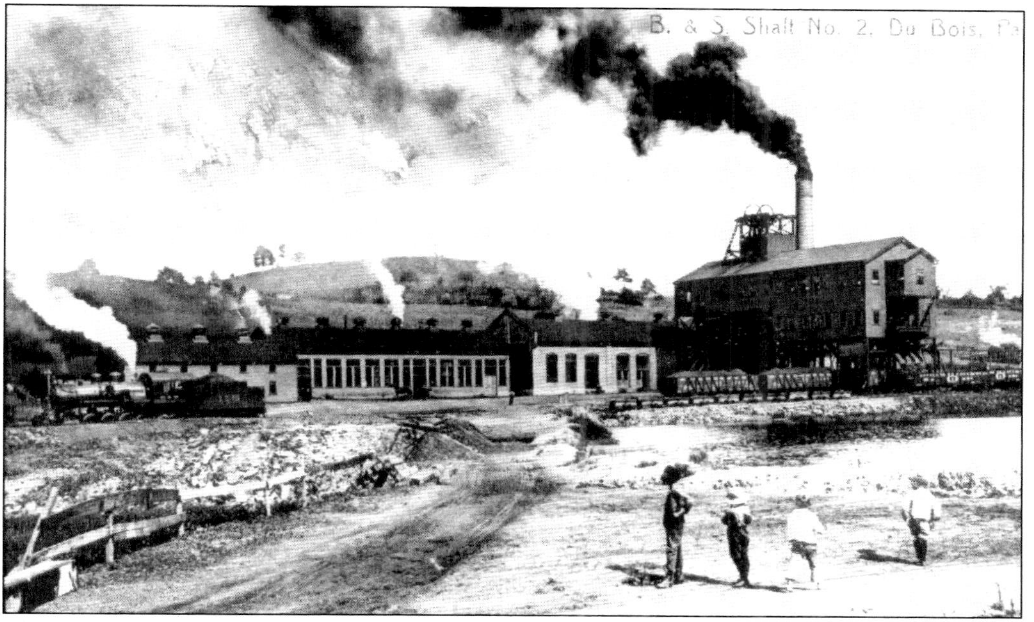

This postcard shows the Buffalo and Susquehanna Coal and Coke Company (B&S) shaft No. 2, located near the Oklahoma-Highland Street area at DuBois. The company employed 500 men between this shaft and the No. 1 shaft, which was located at the current site of the DuBois Mall. Both closed in 1929 following a labor dispute. (Courtesy Clearfield County Historical Society.)

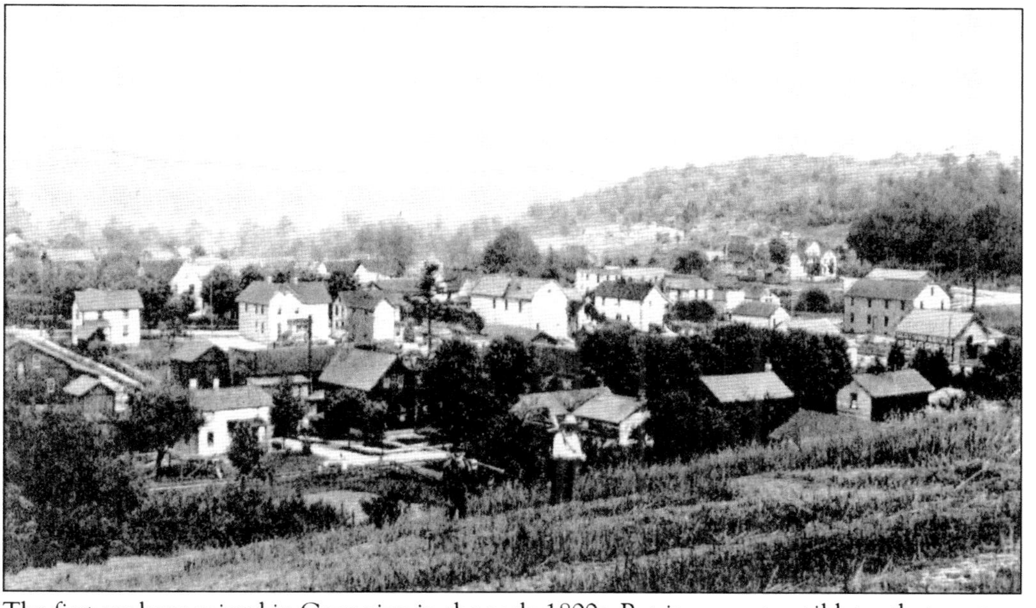

The first coal was mined in Grampian in the early 1800s. But it was not until later that century that coal mining became the most important industry in the community. Grampian Hills was the name given to the town by the county's first doctor, Dr. Samuel Coleman, who said the town reminded him of his home in Scotland. Eventually, the name became just Grampian. This view of the town dates from c. 1900. (Courtesy J. Duane Test.)

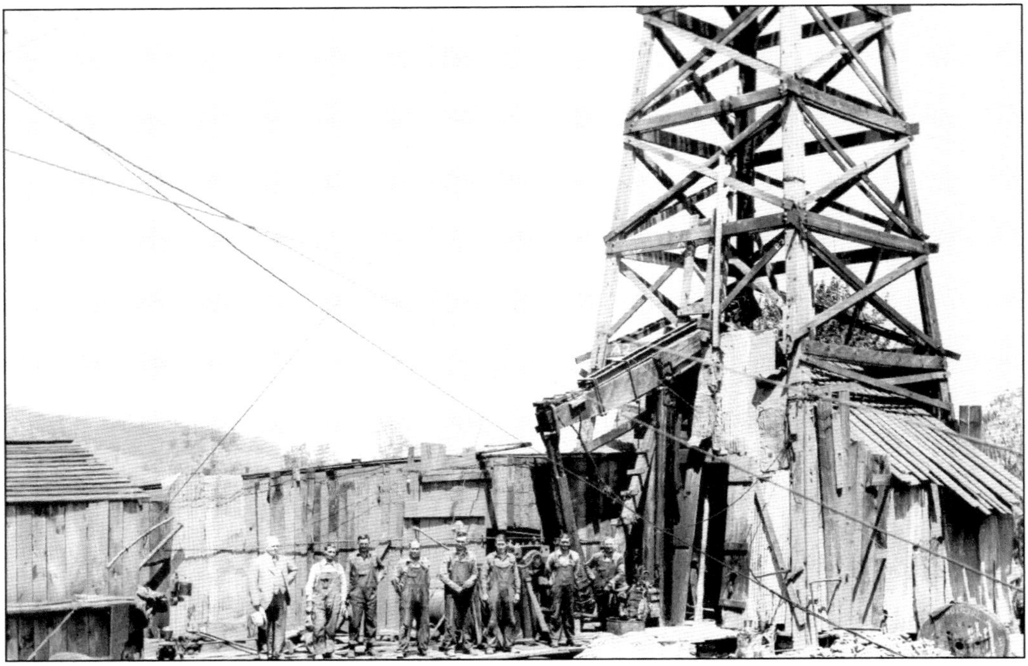

This photograph shows a deep well in Peale, which was located in Cooper Township. A good example of a coal town, Peale thrived in the 1880s, but as early 1912, the company began tearing down houses and shipping them to other coal towns. Peale was named for S.R. Peale, a director of the Clearfield Bituminous Coal Company. Mark Twain visited the town to see his nephew, Mark Clemens, who worked for the coal company. (Courtesy Clearfield County Historical Society.)

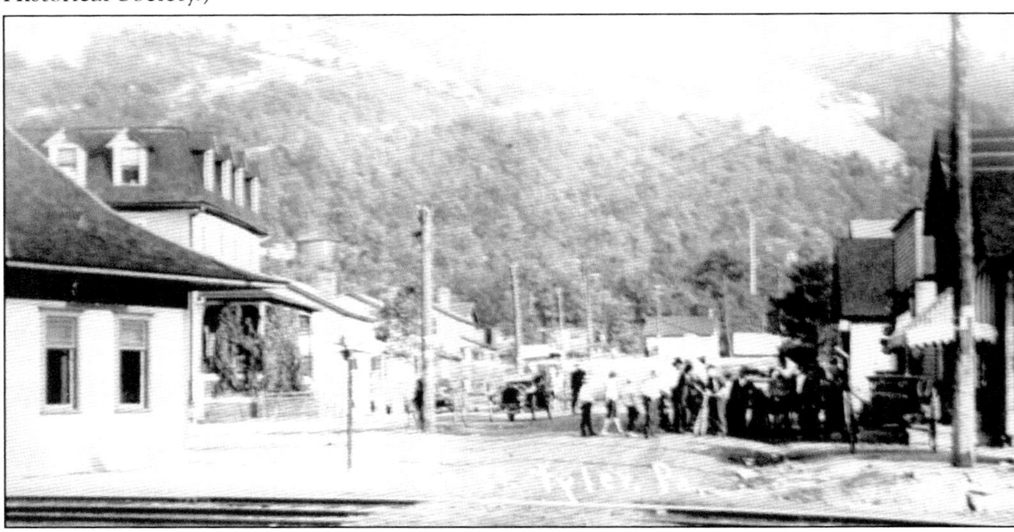

The small village of Tyler was once a bustling coal town. David Tyler started the town when he settled there in 1848. He began a lumber business, but it was not until the 1880s that the Clearfield Coal Company began operations. At that time, 500 tons of coal were mined per day. In 1929, the mine was shut down by a strike, and the equipment was sold to another coal company. This postcard shows the town's main street *c.* 1915. (Courtesy Autumn Watson.)

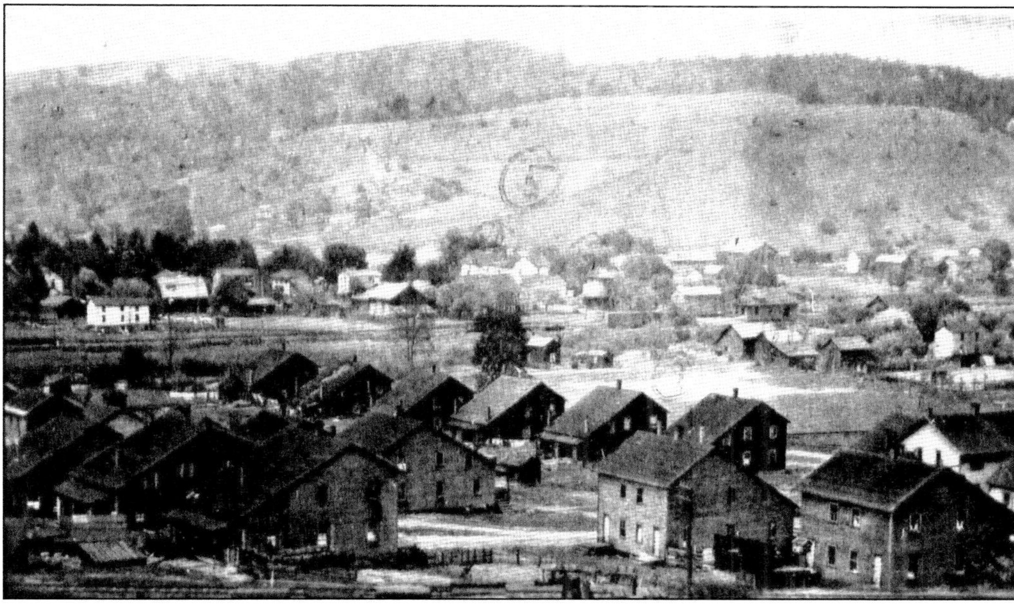

Penfield also started as a lumber town and became a coal town in the last part of the 1800s. This postcard shows the cemetery on the side of the hill. The Cascade Coal and Coke company store is in the bottom right-hand corner. A water tank for the B&S can be seen in the center, with the railroad station next to it. A baseball diamond is in the center. (Courtesy Autumn Watson.)

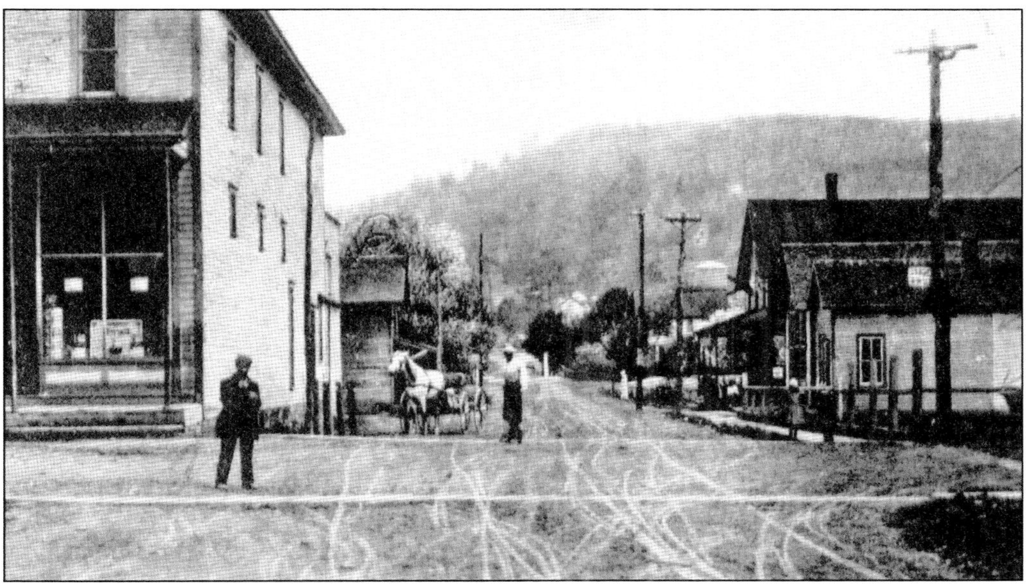

"Tucker" Dan Burkett is standing by the boardwalk in front of the Johnson and Overturf store in this postcard of Penfield's Clearfield Street. On the right is the Central Telephone Company office, Verge Wilson and Sam Boyle's butcher shop, George Town's hardware store, Mary Garry's antique shop, and McCulley's. (Courtesy Autumn Watson.)

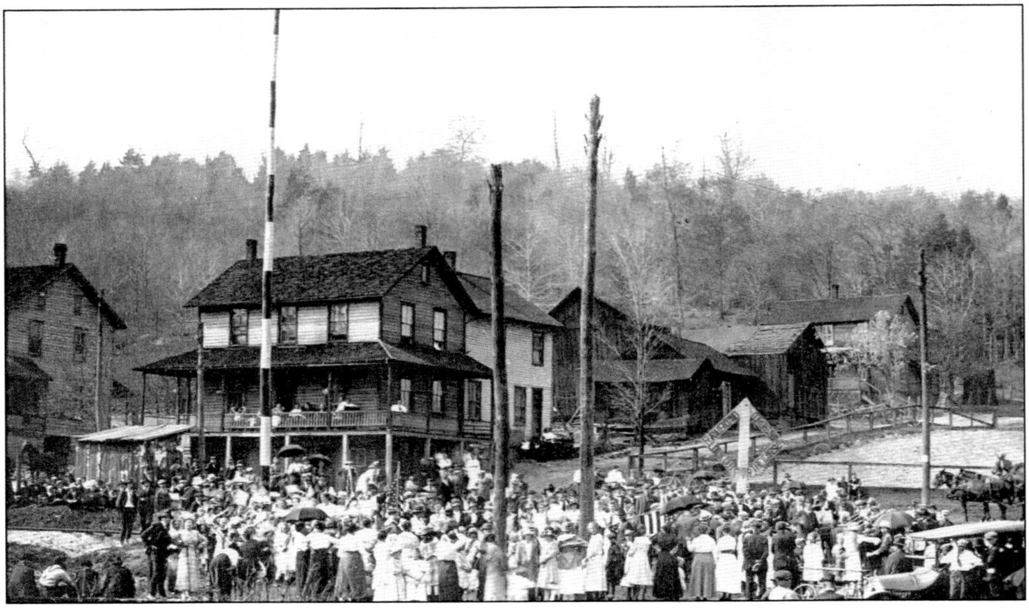

Residents gather for a flag-raising ceremony in this 1920s photograph of O'Shanter. O'Shanter's patriotism led to the residents' erecting a monument, or honor roll, in respect of those who served in World War II. The town was known as Mitchell before the O'Shanter Coal Company was formed here. As with many of the other towns, the railroad also once ran here, allowing students to ride to Clearfield High School. Below is a bird's-eye view of the village. (Courtesy Glee Norman.)

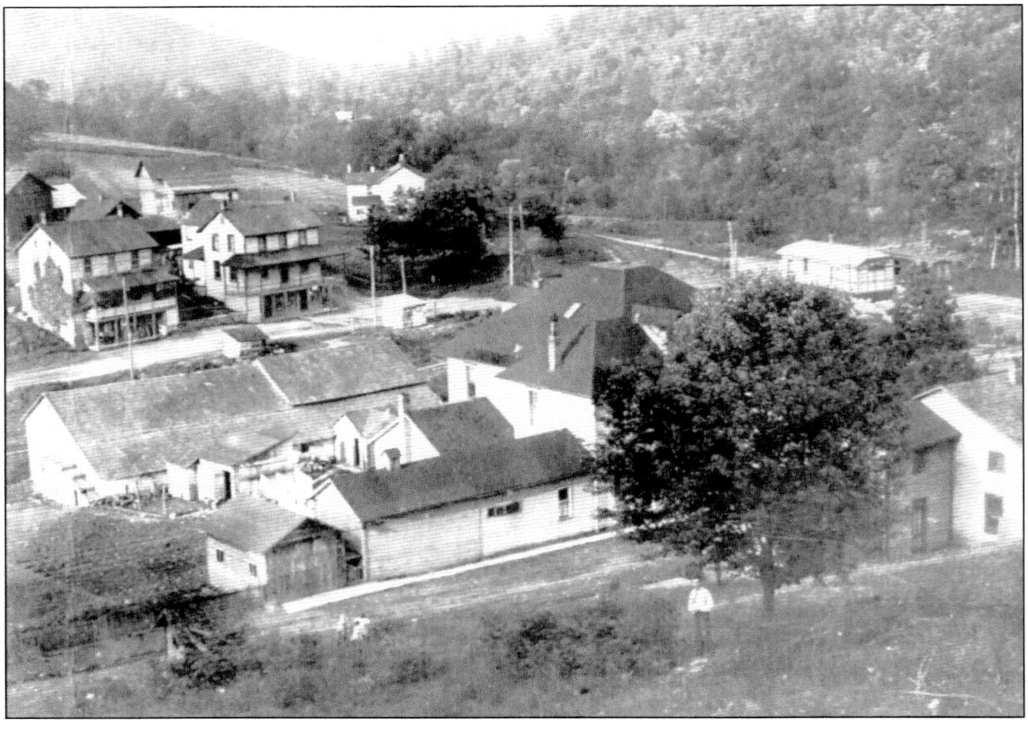

Eight

Businesses in the 20th Century

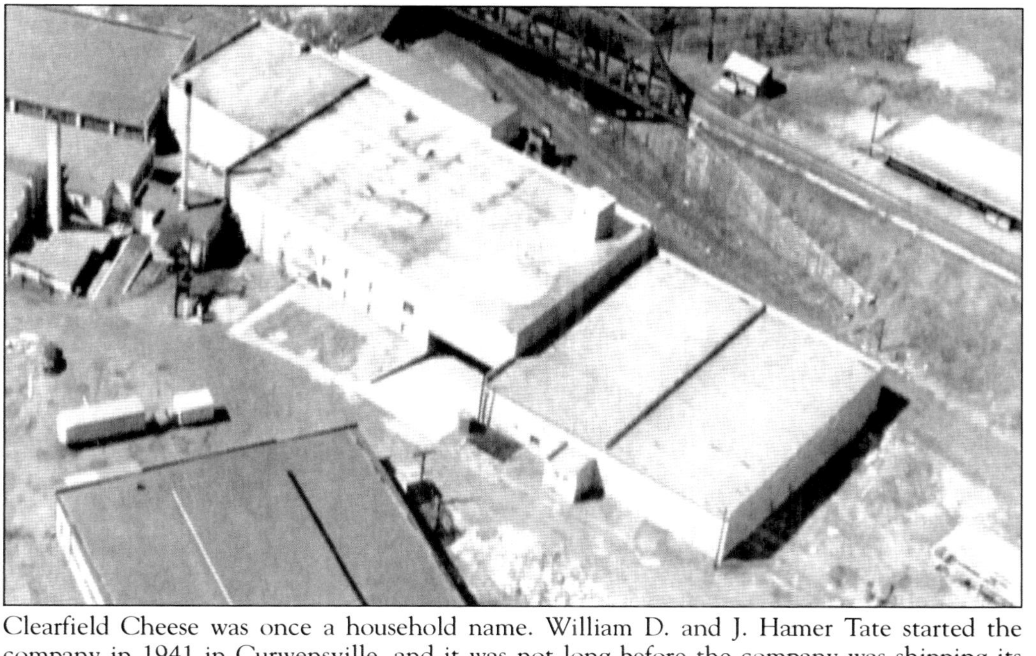

Clearfield Cheese was once a household name. William D. and J. Hamer Tate started the company in 1941 in Curwensville, and it was not long before the company was shipping its products all over the country. At one point, it was also sold in many foreign countries. In the 1950s, Clearfield Cheese revolutionized the industry when it started producing individually wrapped cheese slices. This photograph shows the plant in 1949. (Courtesy Curwensville-Pike Township Historical Society.)

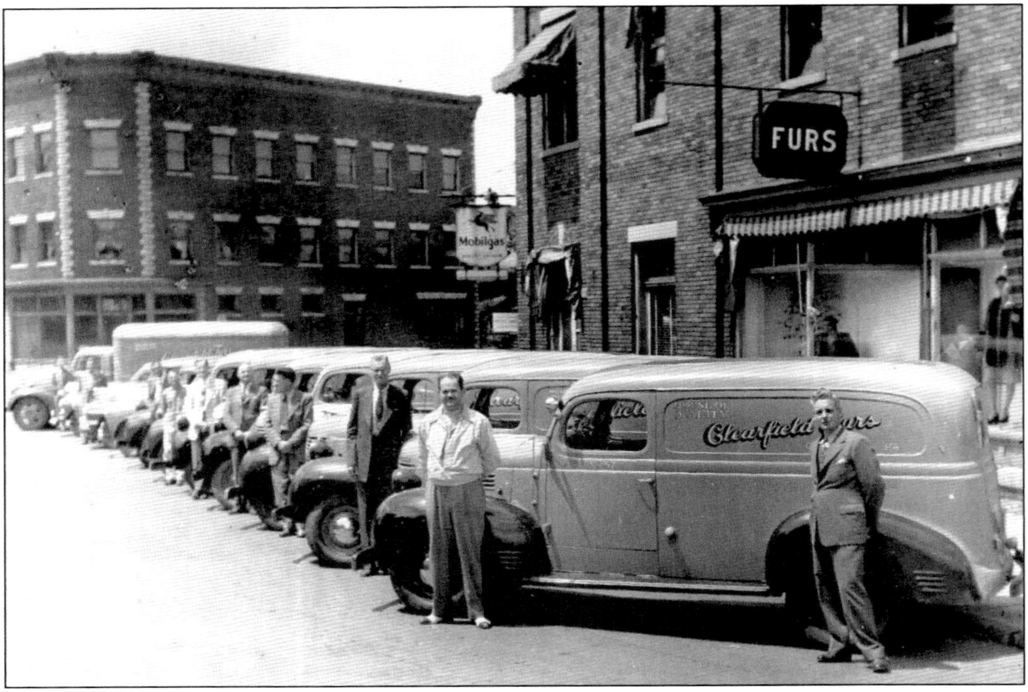

A fleet of Clearfield Furs vehicles waits outside the Nichols Street factory showroom. Clearfield Furs was started by Sylvan K. Williams as Clearfield Taxidermy in 1915. In the 1920s, it branched out into Clearfield Furs, which moved to the corner of Nichols and Front Streets. Seen here are, from right to left, Sylvan K. Williams, Theron Smeal, Art Lyle, Gene Davidson, Frank Smith, and Al Pyle. The other drivers are unidentified. (Courtesy Clearfield County Historical Society.)

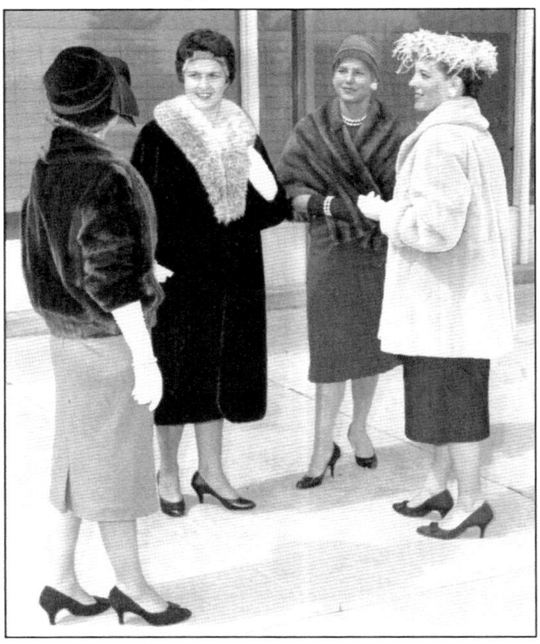

Models for Clearfield Furs visit during a break in a photograph shoot. The company did fashion shows for women's organizations and conventions all over the state. These models are, from left to right, Ruth Saricks, Pat Wallace, Thelma Williams, and Shirley Williams Bloom. In the 1940s, Clearfield Furs also had the stores Clearfield Furs in Bradford, Genevieve's in DuBois, and Woodworth's in Altoona. In 1949, these stores were closed and stores were opened in Pittsburgh and State College. (Courtesy Clearfield County Historical Society.)

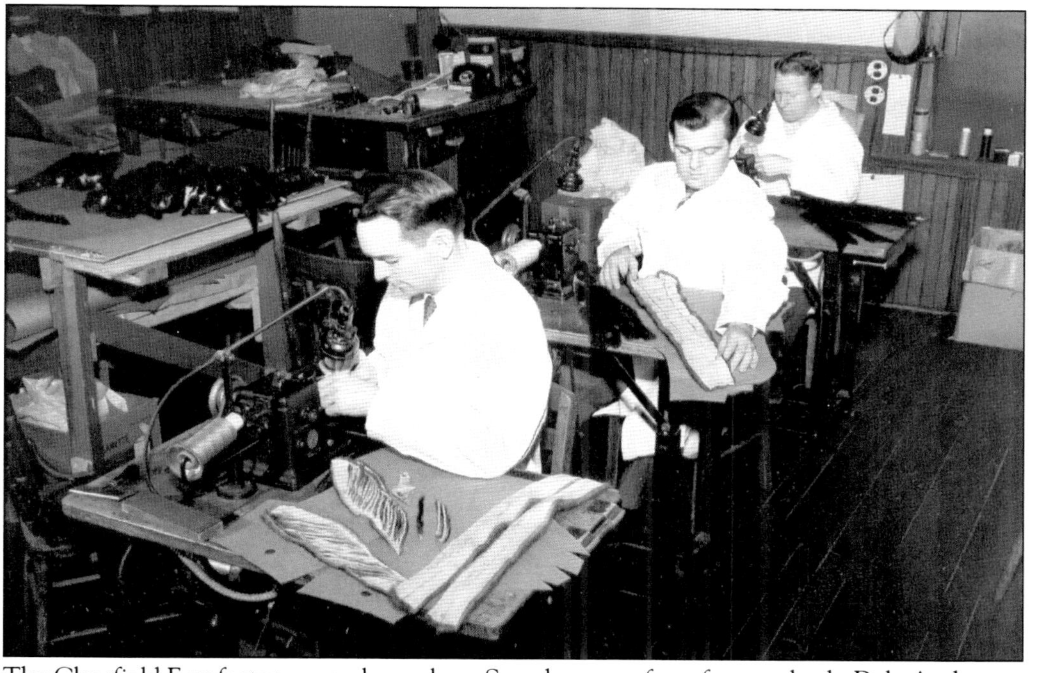

The Clearfield Furs factory was a busy place. Seen here are, from front to back, Dale Anderson, Jack Hepburn, and Bill Meagher. It became a family business when Sylvan Williams's brother Tom joined him, and their children, Eugene, Murray, Shirley, and Bob, also worked for the company. (Courtesy Clearfield County Historical Society.)

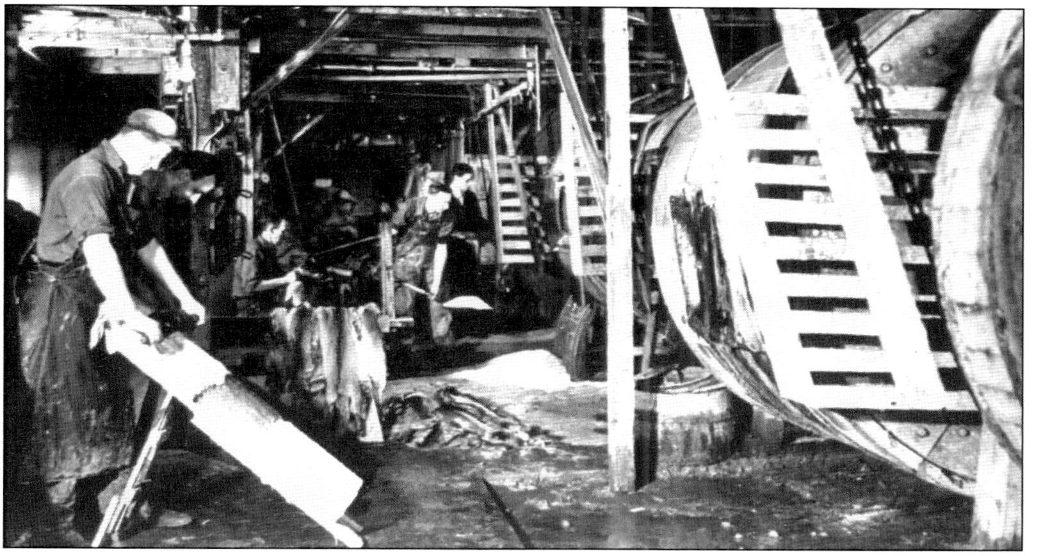

This scene is from Clearfield Taxidermy in the 1930s. From left to right are Art Caldwell, Chet McKee, Carl Cochrane, and Thompson B. Williams. Clearfield Furs created the first Penn State Nittany Lion mascot suit, which was made of real mountain lion skin, and they also developed the Pitt Panthers mascot suit. For almost 80 years, Clearfield Furs was an important part of the Clearfield business community. It closed in 1992. (Courtesy Clearfield County Historical Society.)

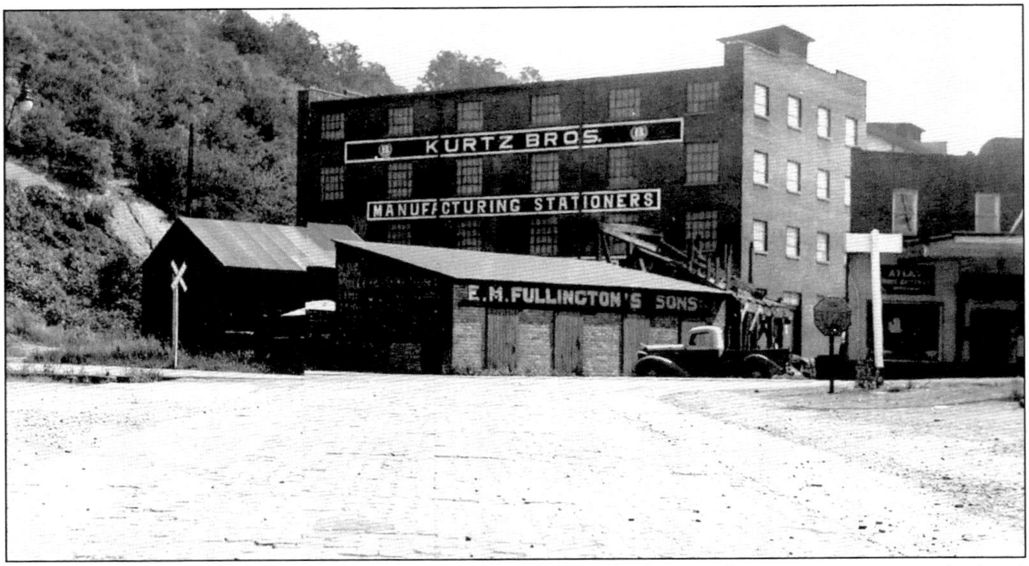

Another landmark Clearfield business is Kurtz Brothers, which specializes in stationery and school supplies. Three generations of the Kurtz family have worked this business, which started with Charles T. Kurtz (or Chas, as he often wrote it) in June 1894. It was then that he rented a small 200-square-foot place on Third Street for only $9 a month. (Courtesy Robert M. Kurtz Jr.)

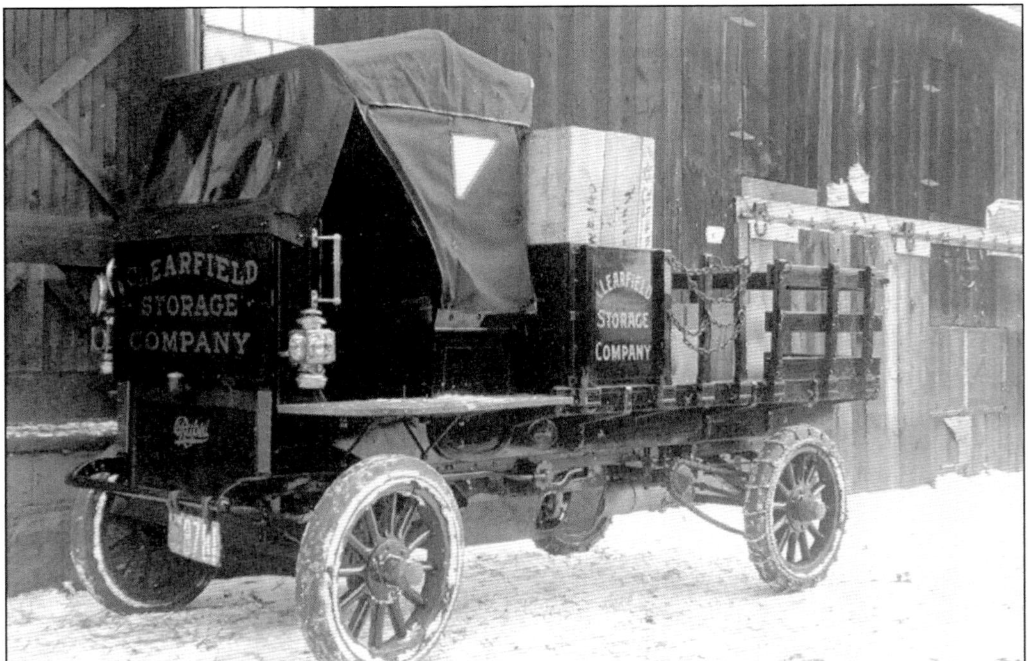

The Clearfield Storage Company, a division of Kurtz Brothers, was located at the Fourth and Reed Street building, which is the current site of Kurtz Brothers. In 1910, they purchased their first delivery truck. It was a solid-tire, two-cylinder, chain-driven vehicle made by the Rapid Motor Vehicle Company in Pontiac, Michigan. (Courtesy Robert M. Kurtz Jr.)

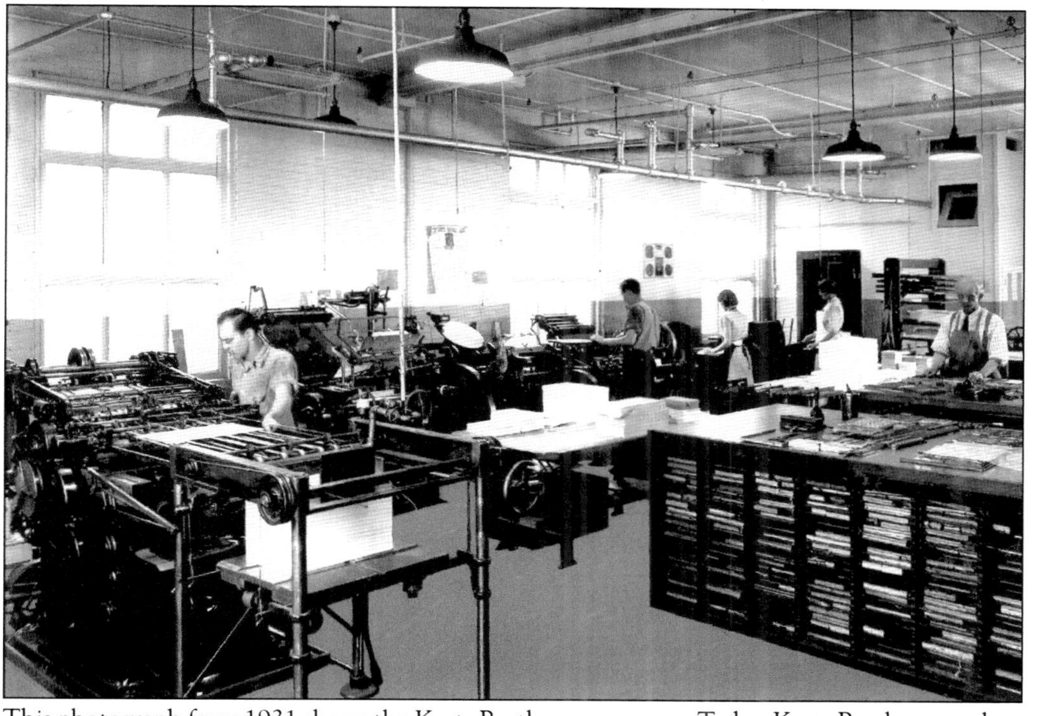

This photograph from 1931 shows the Kurtz Brothers pressroom. Today, Kurtz Brothers employs over 170 people and during the summer doubles that with seasonal workers. It is the biggest supplier of school products in the mid-Atlantic states, as well as Tennessee, Kentucky, Virginia, and of course, Pennsylvania. (Courtesy Robert M. Kurtz Jr.)

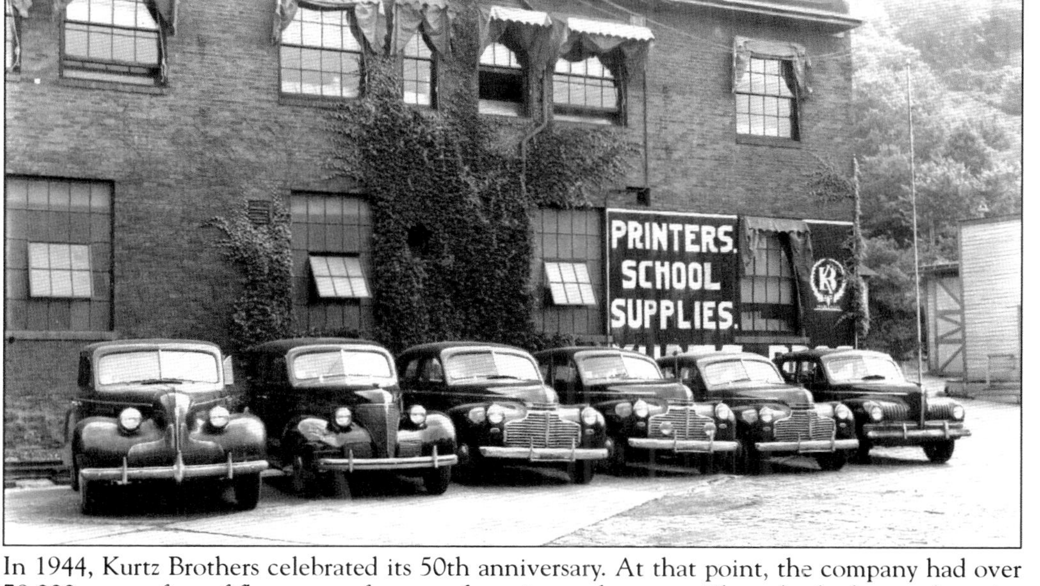

In 1944, Kurtz Brothers celebrated its 50th anniversary. At that point, the company had over 78,000 square feet of floor space for manufacturing and storage. They also had several service cars. From left to right are a 1939 Buick, a 1939 Chevrolet, three 1941 Chevrolets, and a 1941 Nash. (Courtesy Robert M. Kurtz Jr.)

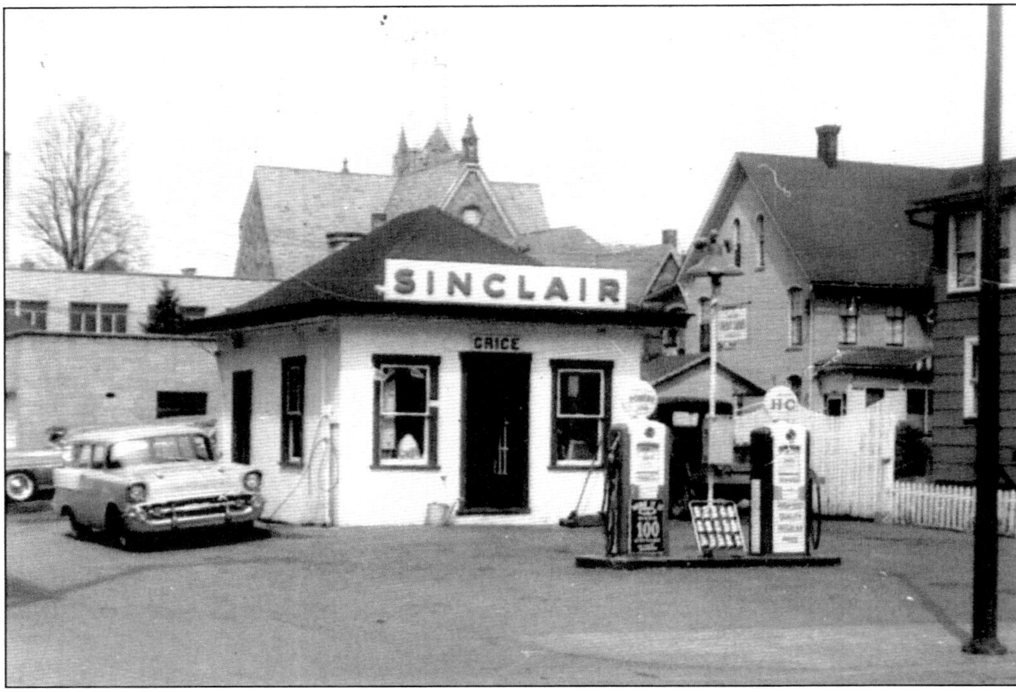

In 1955, Lynn "Scoot" Grice returned to Clearfield after serving in the army and reopened his uncle Tom Grice's gas station (above) on Third Street. As a hobby, he started loading ammunition and converting military rifles for civilian use. This proved successful, so eventually he and his wife, Janet, gave up selling gas, and the Grice Gun Shop grew. It moved to its current Reed Street location in the 1980s. Today, it is one of the biggest gun sellers east of the Mississippi. Below is the gas station during the 1936 flood, when it was under Shull ownership. Shull also had a photograph studio across the street. (Courtesy Lynn "Scoot" Grice.)

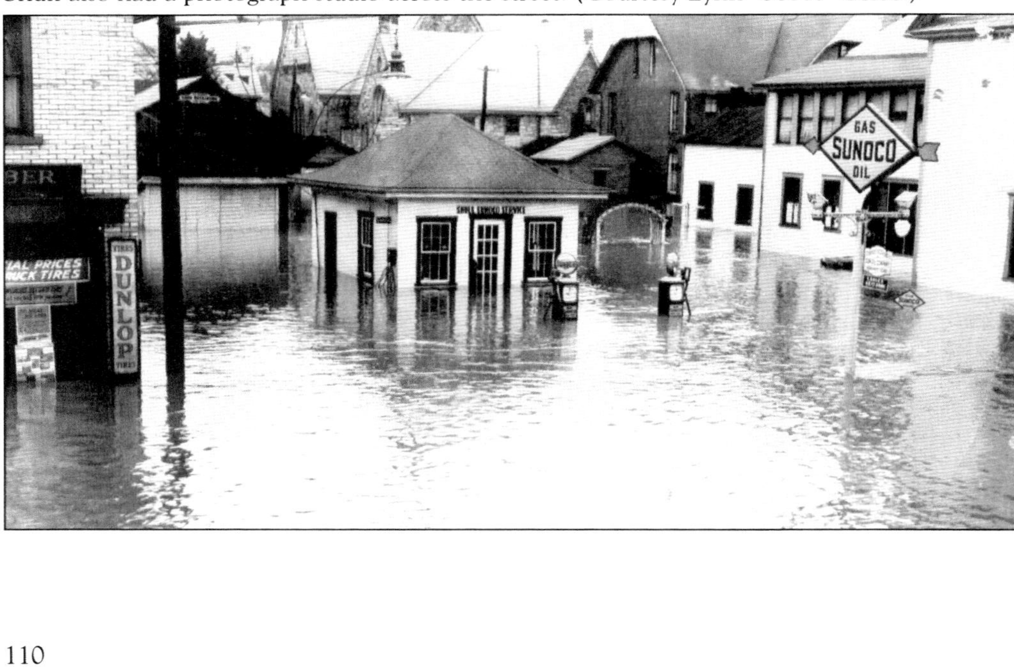

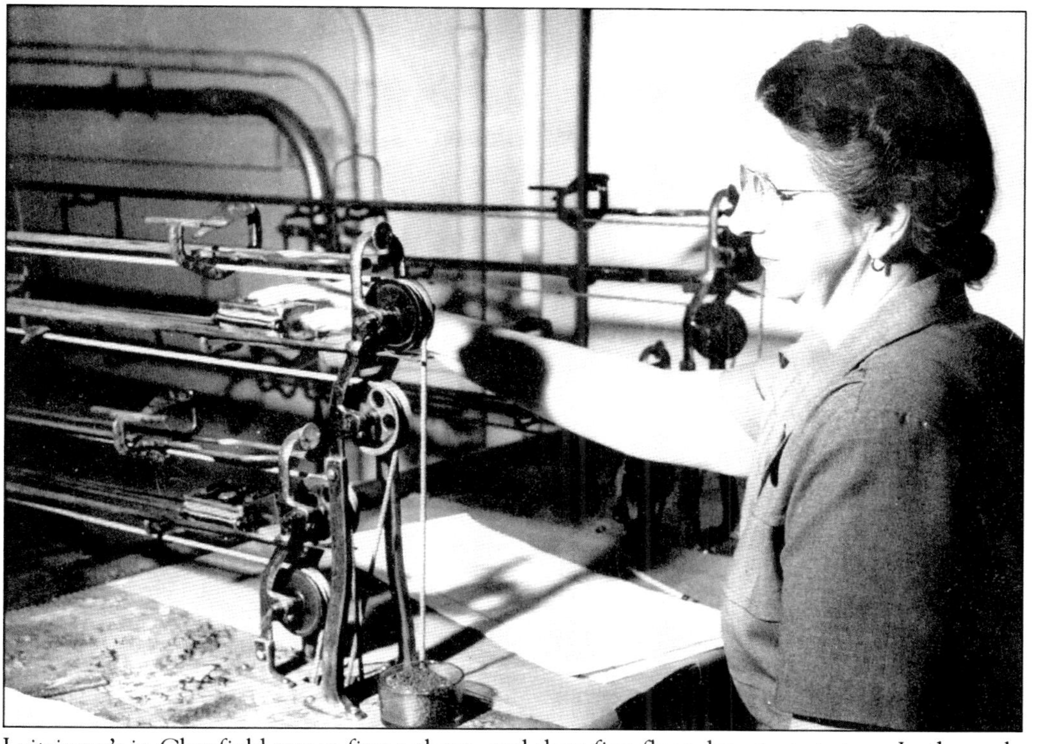

Leitzinger's in Clearfield was at first a three- and then five-floor department store. In the early days, they used an electric car system to process sales. The cars took payment to the cash department. As employee Emily Swales demonstrates, change was made and the car was sent back to the appropriate department. (Courtesy Jim Leitzinger.)

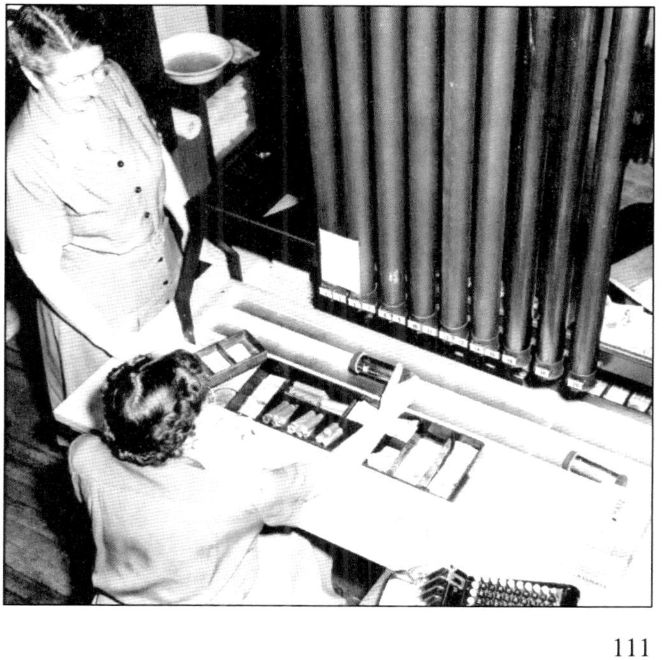

Leitzinger's replaced the electric car system in 1951. The new pneumatic tube system used a vacuum to move metal carriers from floor to floor. The elaborate tube system ran throughout the five floors and was used even in the 1990s. In this photograph, Emily Swales is watching another employee process a sale. (Courtesy Jim Leitzinger.)

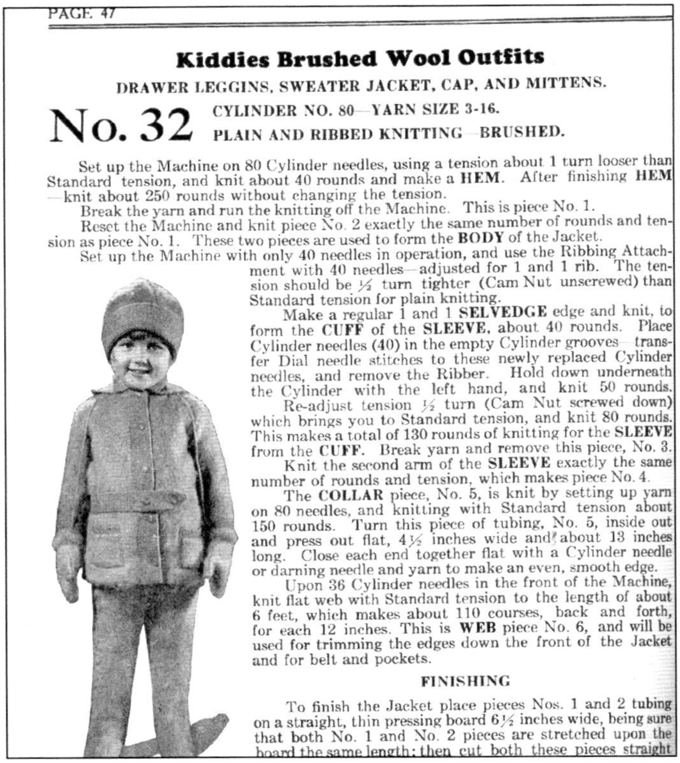

PAGE 47

Kiddies Brushed Wool Outfits

DRAWER LEGGINS, SWEATER JACKET, CAP, AND MITTENS.

No. 32 CYLINDER NO. 80—YARN SIZE 3-16.
PLAIN AND RIBBED KNITTING—BRUSHED.

Set up the Machine on 80 Cylinder needles, using a tension about 1 turn looser than Standard tension, and knit about 40 rounds and make a **HEM**. After finishing **HEM**—knit about 250 rounds without changing the tension.

Break the yarn and run the knitting off the Machine. This is piece No. 1.

Reset the Machine and knit piece No. 2 exactly the same number of rounds and tension as piece No. 1. These two pieces are used to form the **BODY** of the Jacket.

Set up the Machine with only 40 needles in operation, and use the Ribbing Attachment with 40 needles—adjusted for 1 and 1 rib. The tension should be ½ turn tighter (Cam Nut unscrewed) than Standard tension for plain knitting.

Make a regular 1 and 1 **SELVEDGE** edge and knit, to form the **CUFF** of the **SLEEVE**, about 40 rounds. Place Cylinder needles (40) in the empty Cylinder grooves—transfer Dial needle stitches to these newly replaced Cylinder needles, and remove the Ribber. Hold down underneath the Cylinder with the left hand, and knit 50 rounds.

Re-adjust tension ½ turn (Cam Nut screwed down) which brings you to Standard tension, and knit 80 rounds. This makes a total of 130 rounds of knitting for the **SLEEVE** from the **CUFF**. Break yarn and remove this piece, No. 3.

Knit the second arm of the **SLEEVE** exactly the same number of rounds and tension, which makes piece No. 4.

The **COLLAR** piece, No. 5, is knit by setting up yarn on 80 needles, and knitting with Standard tension about 150 rounds. Turn this piece of tubing, No. 5, inside out and press out flat, 4½ inches wide and about 13 inches long. Close each end together flat with a Cylinder needle or darning needle and yarn to make an even, smooth edge.

Upon 36 Cylinder needles in the front of the Machine, knit flat web with Standard tension to the length of about 6 feet, which makes about 110 courses, back and forth, for each 12 inches. This is **WEB** piece No. 6, and will be used for trimming the edges down the front of the Jacket and for belt and pockets.

FINISHING

To finish the Jacket place pieces Nos. 1 and 2 tubing on a straight, thin pressing board 6½ inches wide, being sure that both No. 1 and No. 2 pieces are stretched upon the board the same length; then cut both these pieces straight

The Gearhart Knitting Machine was invented by Joseph Emery Gearhart, who received a patent for it in 1889. That same year, he opened a small shop at West Decatur, where he manufactured the machines. The machines were so popular that in 1890 he moved to a plant on Nichols Street in Clearfield. He also opened a factory in Canada. Going under the name of the Gearhart Family Knitter, the invention and attachments were patented in 13 countries and sold around the world. Due to pressure from the competition to buy back items made by the machine, the company went bankrupt in 1926. Above is a sample of the items the machine made, and to the right is an illustration of the machine itself. (Courtesy Clearfield County Historical Society.)

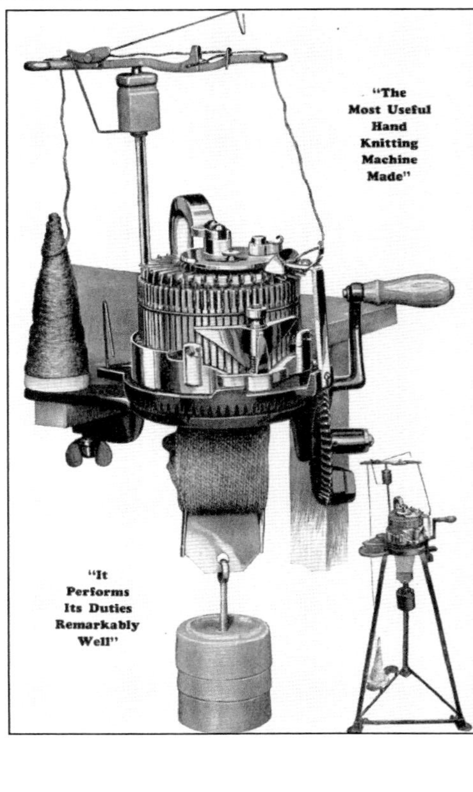

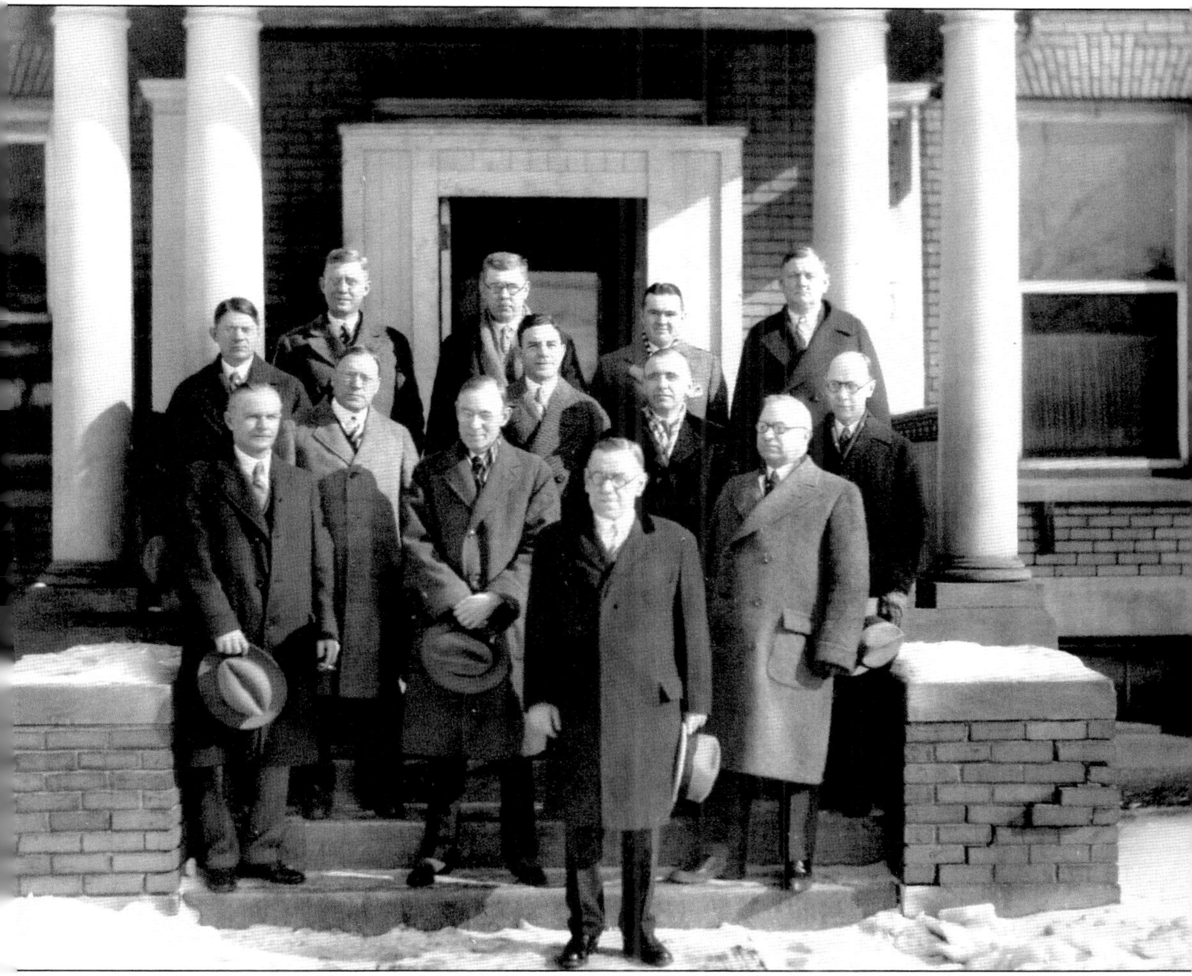

Clearfield Hospital's medical staff poses in this photograph from 1928. In front is S.J. Waterworth; on the first step are W. Scott Piper (left), John W. Gordon (center), and Ward O. Wilson; on the second step are Dr. G. Blaine Yeaney (left), J. Paul Frantz (center), and William Falconer; on the third step are W.E. Reiley (left) and J. Hayes Woolridge; and in the back are Dr. Fussell (left), Dr. Blair (second from the left), Harold S. Keeney (third from the left), and H.H. Lewis. The hospital started in 1900 with a 14-bed facility at Second Street and Ogden Avenue. In 1904, a donation of land from the Mossop sisters in honor of their brother, Fred, who was director of the early hospital, was used to construct a new hospital at the Turnpike Avenue site in 1906. The current hospital was built in 1949. (Courtesy Clearfield County Historical Society.)

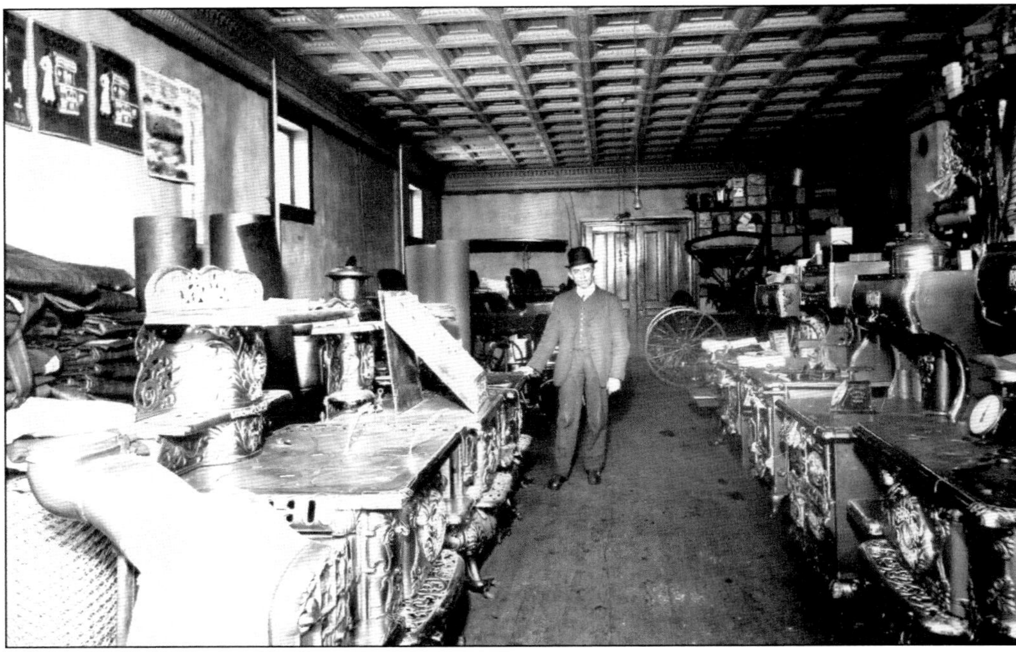

Hardware and appliance stores looked a bit different *c.* 1900, as seen in this photograph of the Routch and Swartzle Company. The store was located at 23 North Second Street in Clearfield. From 1906 through 1944, it sold hardware, stoves, ranges, washers, and radios. Minding the store in this photograph is George Routch. (Courtesy Clearfield County Historical Society.)

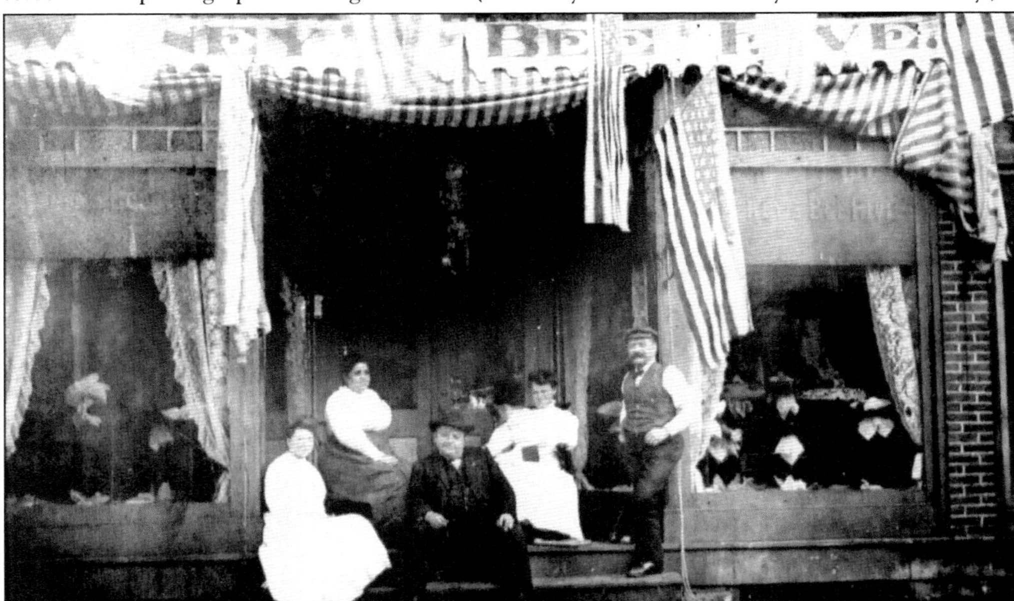

The Sweeney Millinery Shop was also known as the Bee Hive in Curwensville. This *c.* 1910 photograph shows Rose Sweeney; her husband, Will; her brother, Steve Graff; Mrs. Knight Staver (sitting in the rocking chair); and Staver's sister, Mrs. Robertson (sitting on the step). (Courtesy Clearfield County Historical Society.)

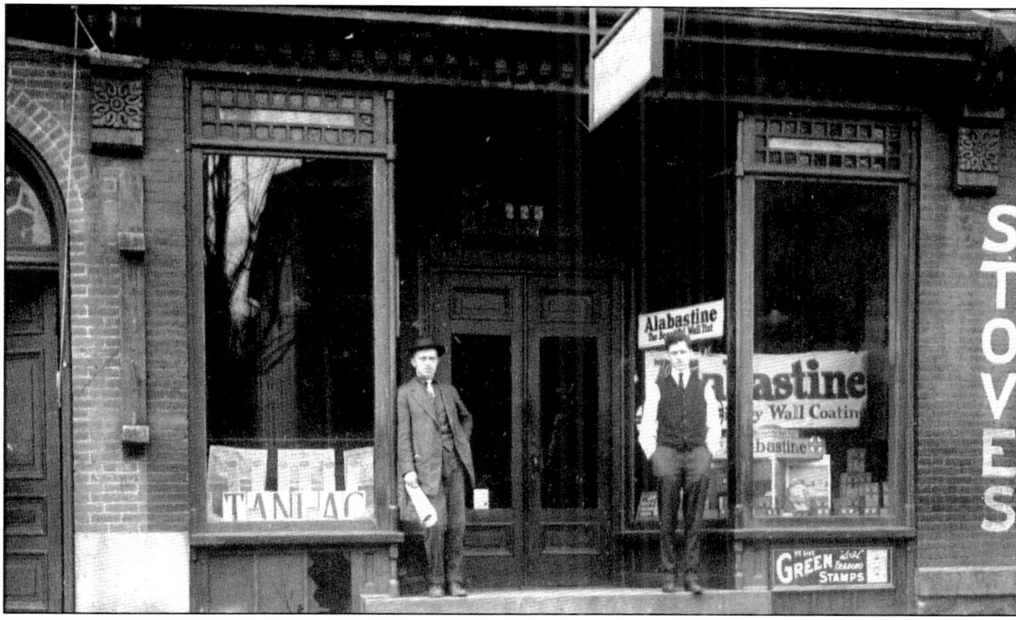

Relaxing in front of Wrigley's Drug Store in Curwensville are Harry Gates of Gates Hardware (left) and J.W. Murphy (right). Murphy was an apprentice of William Wrigley, and he later bought the store. For many years, it was Murphy's Drug Store and a popular hangout for teenagers. The store was famous for its sundaes, which had homemade toppings. Murphy's wife, Marie Addleman, made the syrups herself. The peanut butter fudge was supposed to be the best in the area. Cosmo "Gus" Guglielmi eventually bought the store and was the owner from 1954 to 1985. After that, it became Curwensville Pharmacy. Below is an inside shot with J.W. Murphy on the right, and William K. Wrigley is thought to be the man on the left. (Courtesy Pat Murphy.)

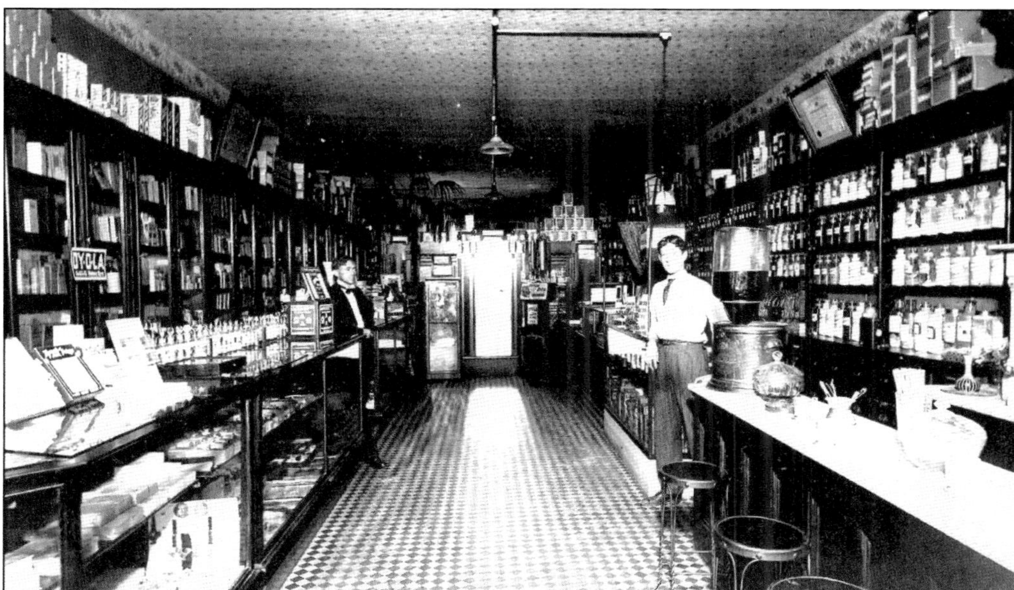

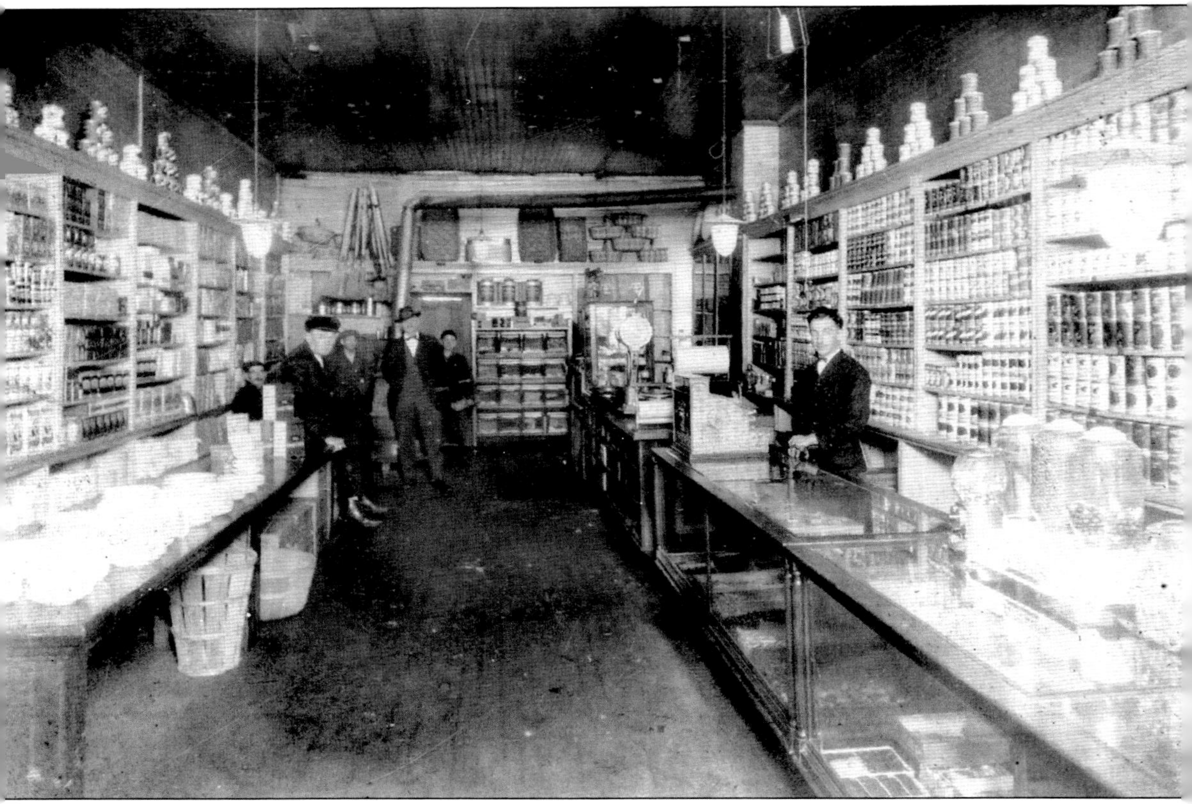

This little grocery store, run by Ralph Barnett (on the right), helped supply the residents of Kellytown for many years. As with many country stores, it was a gathering place where people shared local news and gossip. Ralph Barnett was quite a historian and told stories of his father, Dan Barnett, a well-known Civil War veteran. Kellytown, named for the Kelly Coal Company, was once a bustling coal town. (Courtesy Clearfield County Historical Society.)

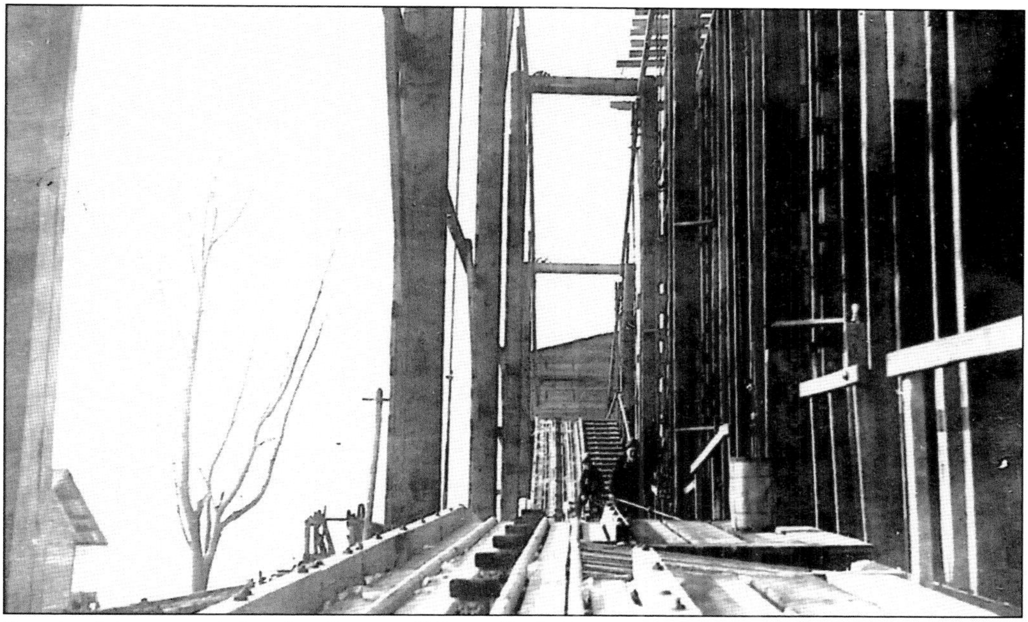

Berwinsdale, named for the Berwin White Coal Company, had a thriving business in the 1920s. The Berwinsdale Ice Company, an ice-cutting and storage plant, was owned by the Pennsylvania Railroad, which used the ice for its passenger and refrigerator cars. The ice would be taken from a pond and transported to the ice company by a team of horses. Workers scraped snow from the ice and used bars to split it into large blocks, which were then sawed into squares. Next, it was put on a conveyor (above), which separated the ice into a single row. The ice was kept in a large storage building. The equipment (below) was part of the process and might have carried the ice up to the conveyor. The business closed down sometime in the 1930s. (Courtesy Clearfield County Historical Society.)

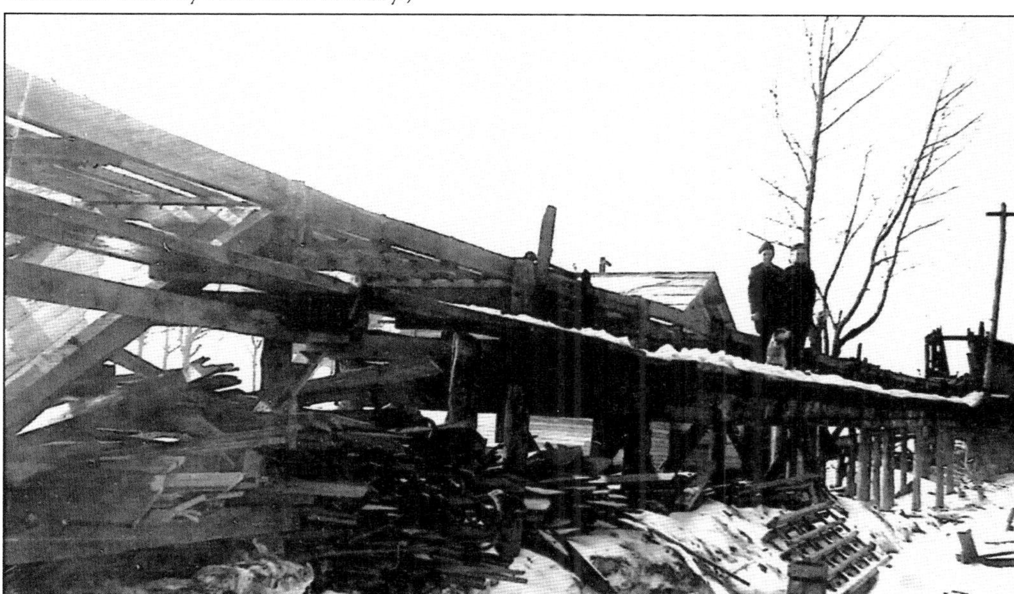

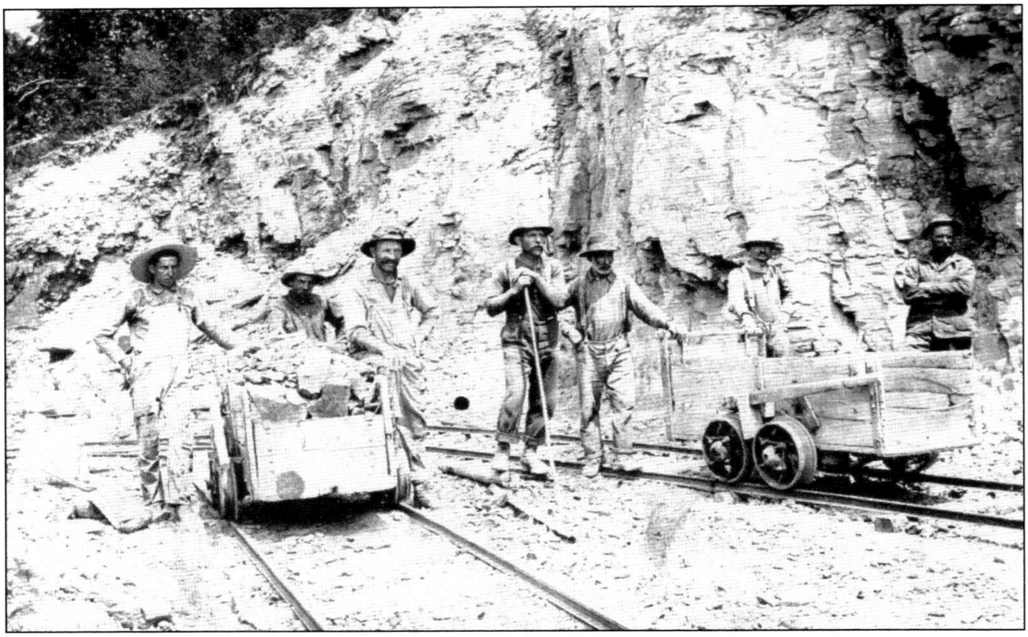

Men take a break from stripping clay shale at Krebs in this 1908 photograph. The men are, from left to right, Foster Wilson (next to his father), Alfred Wilson, George Jordan, John Haney, Calvin Parks, David Lets, and Scott Hess. The clay was used to make bricks. It took about four tons of clay to make 1,000 bricks. (Courtesy Clearfield County Historical Society.)

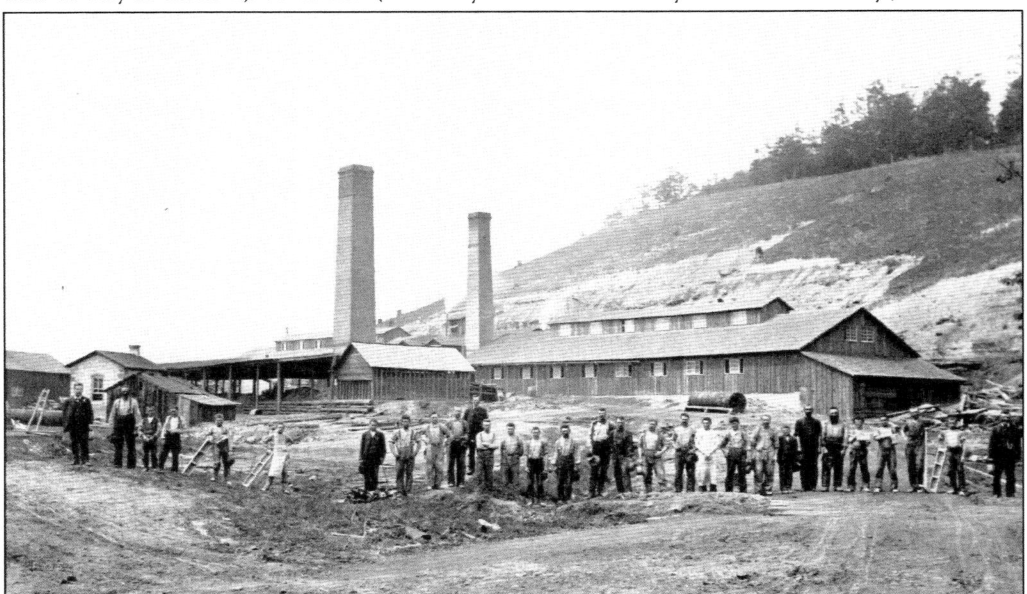

In the early 20th century, Clearfield Fire Brick Works was located at Fourth and Reed Streets, the current site of Kurtz Brothers. The first brick in the area was manufactured at the Hope plant in Woodland in 1867. In the early 1920s, Harbison-Walker Refractories had seven plants in Clearfield County, which produced 300,000 bricks a day. (Courtesy Clearfield County Historical Society.)

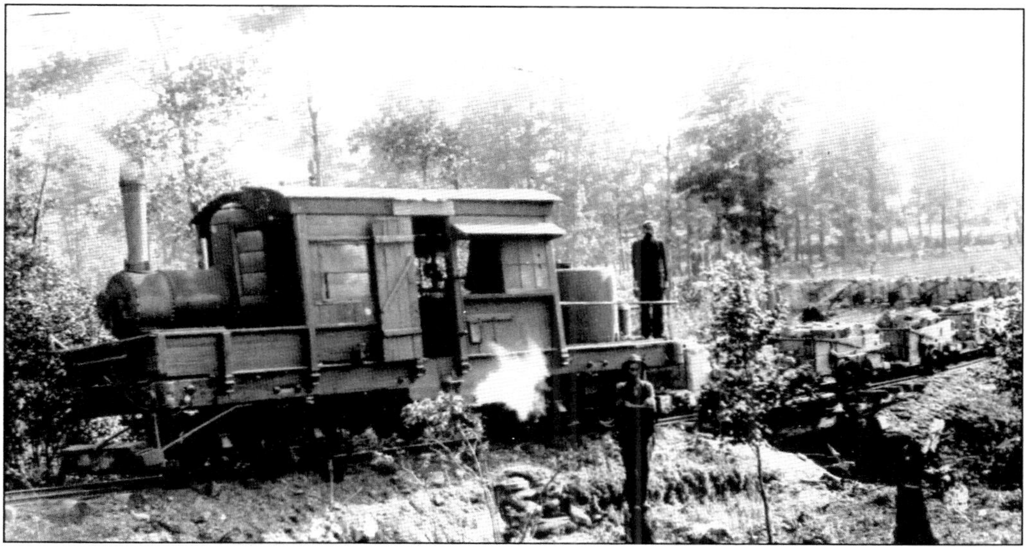

This photograph shows a Climax locomotive pulling a long string of clay cars at the General Refractories Company in West Decatur c. 1912. The clay pits were five or six miles west of the refractories, and the railroad was used between the two points. (Courtesy Clearfield County Historical Society.)

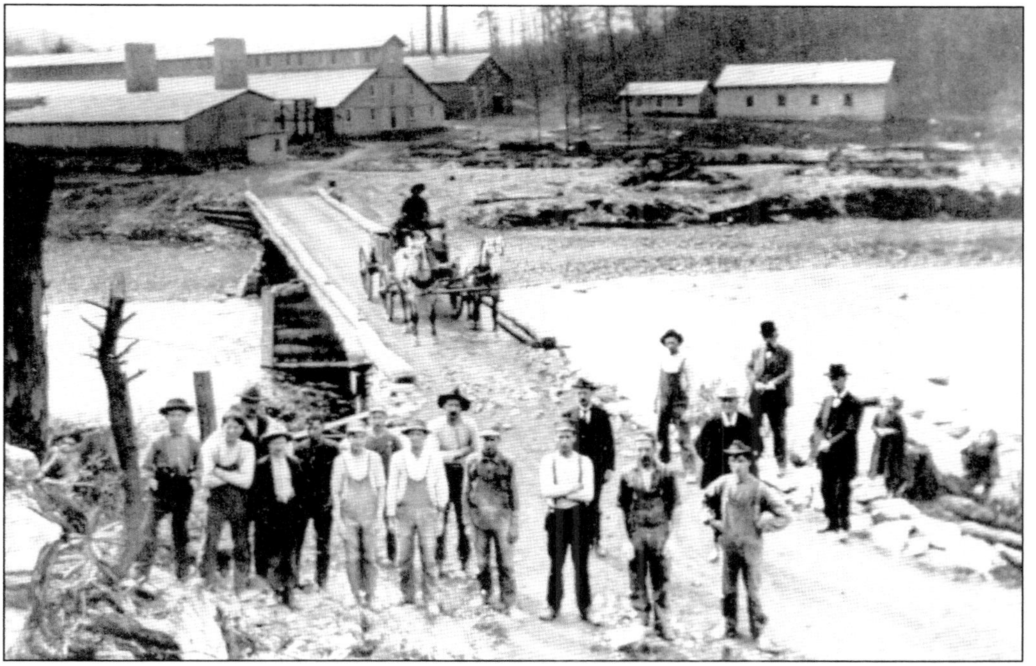

Workers pose near the Karthaus Fire Brick Plant in this undated photograph. They are, from left to right, Harry Rubly, Bill McKinzie, Charley McGovern, Charley Meeker, Pat Fitzgerald, Fred Chatam, Charley Shultz, Giles Shifter, Bill Shultz, Harry Reiter, Roy Reiter, Solomon Novey, John Gross, Ira Reiter, George Maurer, an unidentified official, ? McCulloughs, an unidentified official, Warren Kyler, and unidentified girls. Joe Bamat is on the wagon. The Mosquito Creek is in the foreground. (Courtesy Clearfield County Historical Society.)

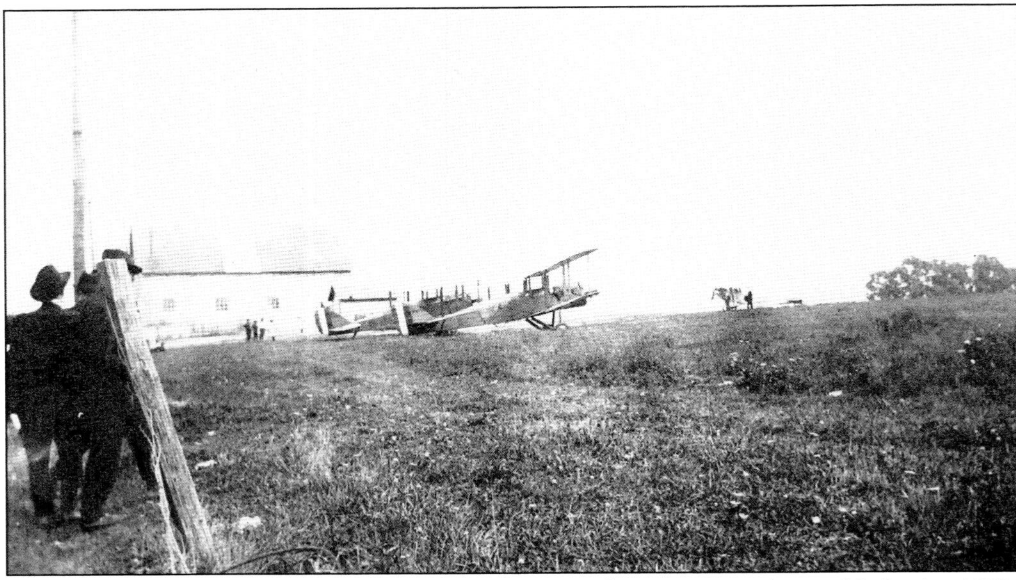

Kylertown Airport was once one of the largest air traffic centers in the world. In the 1930s, when there were 14 scheduled flights daily, you could fly to New York for only $15.50. In the 1940s, most air traffic was rerouted to larger fields. Ames Field was named for Charles Hayden Ames, an airmail pilot who was killed when his plane crashed into the Nittany Mountain in 1929. (Courtesy Clearfield County Historical Society.)

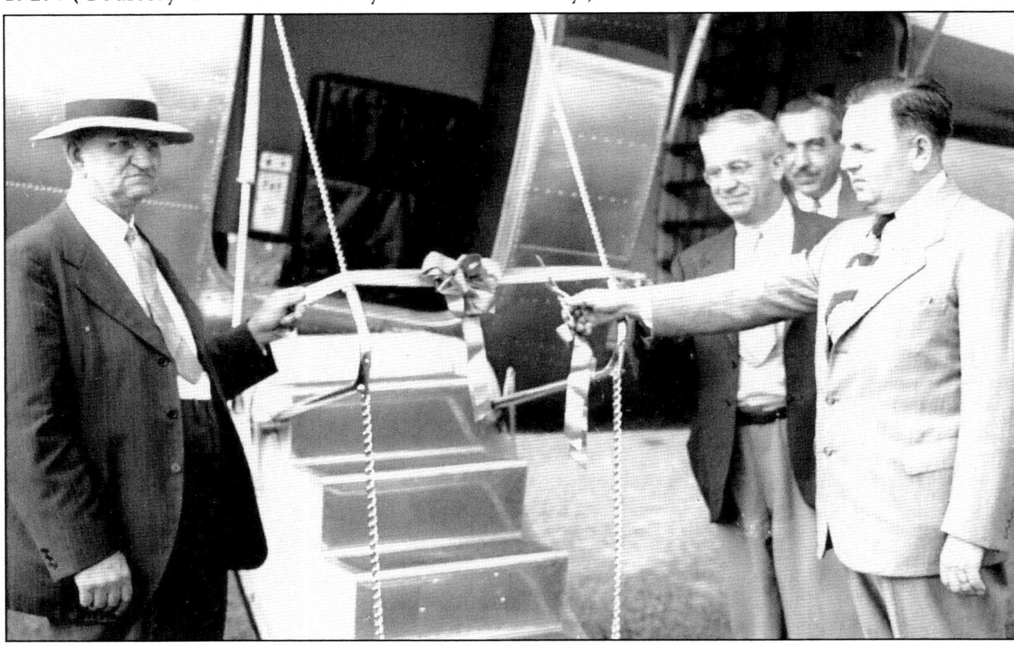

On June 20, 1949, Albert Airport near Morrisdale was officially designated as a stop on the All-American Airways route between Pittsburgh and Newark, New Jersey. Seen attending the ribbon-cutting ceremony are, from left to right, Carl Anderson of Clearfield, Mahlon Wells of Philipsburg, Paul Ruch of Clearfield, and Kenneth Barraclaugh of DuBois. The airport shut down in the 1950s. (Courtesy Clearfield County Historical Society.)

Nine

FAMOUS NATIVES

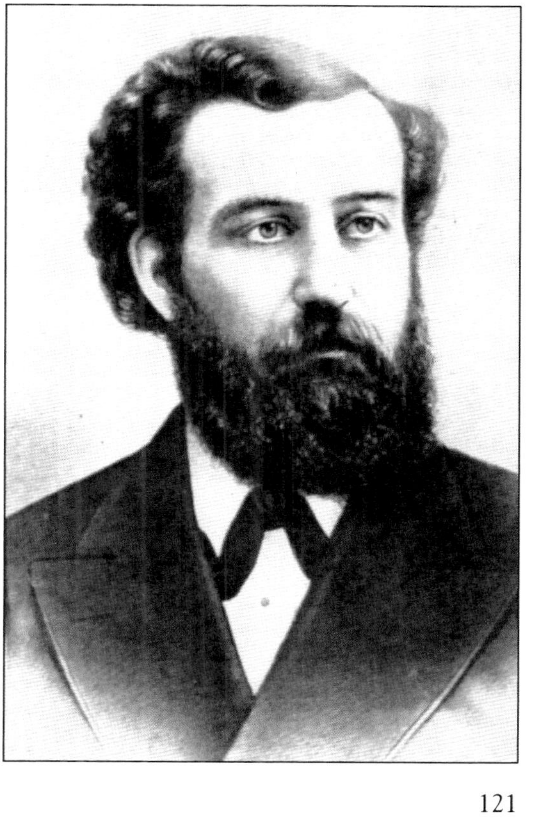

Philip Bliss was born in 1838 near Penfield, Huston Township. During his career, he was an editor of hymnals, director of music for Chicago's First Congregational Church, and a highly sought after evangelist and gospel singer. He is credited with writing 56 hymns. In his short career, Bliss earned about $30,000 in royalties, but legend says he gave much of this away to charity. (Courtesy Clearfield County Historical Society.)

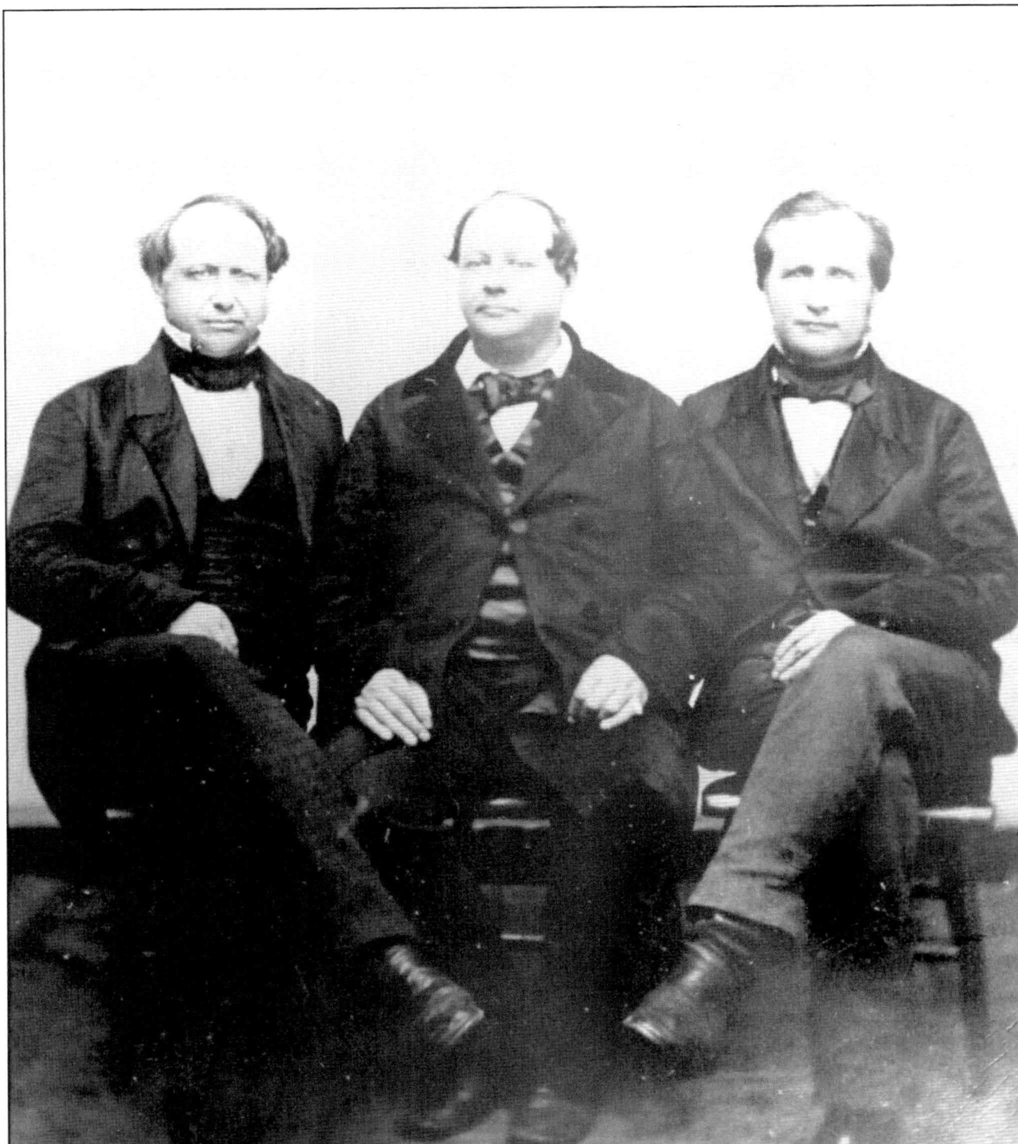

The Bush brothers, George W. and Jeb, are not the only brothers to serve as governors in different states. William Bigler (left) of Clearfield was the governor of Pennsylvania, and his brother John (center) was the governor of California. Composer Stephen Foster wrote a variation of his "Camptown Races" as the campaign song "Bigler Boys" when William and John were running for governor in 1851. William came to Clearfield in 1833 and started publishing a newspaper called the *Clearfield Democrat*. In 1836, he married Maria J. Reed, daughter of A.B. Reed, a prominent businessman who helped lay out Clearfield. After he went into business with his father-in-law, he became one of largest producers of lumber, or square timber, on the Susquehanna. Later, William turned to politics and served as both a state and U.S. senator. The town and township of Bigler are named for him. William and John's other brother, Washington, is on the right. (Courtesy Clearfield County Historical Society.)

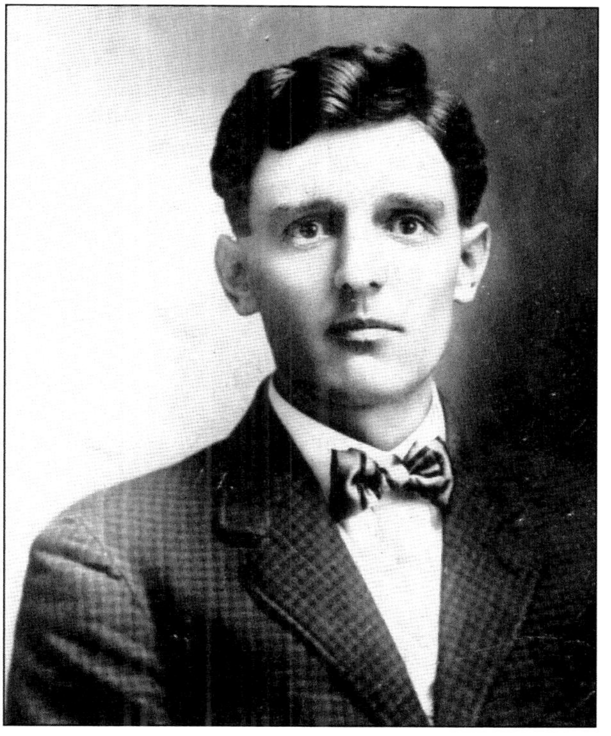

George Rosenkrans of Penfield was a world-renowned composer of band music and hymns. In fact, the National Music Educators Association listed him as one of the world's 10 most important composers in a 1970s report. While sitting at the presidential reviewing stand at the inaugural parade of Woodrow Wilson, he was pleased to hear many of the bands playing his marches. Also, his funeral marches were played at the funerals of several presidents. Unfortunately, when the demand for band music dwindled, Rosenkrans struggled financially. He died in 1955 as a pauper. (Courtesy Clearfield County Historical Society.)

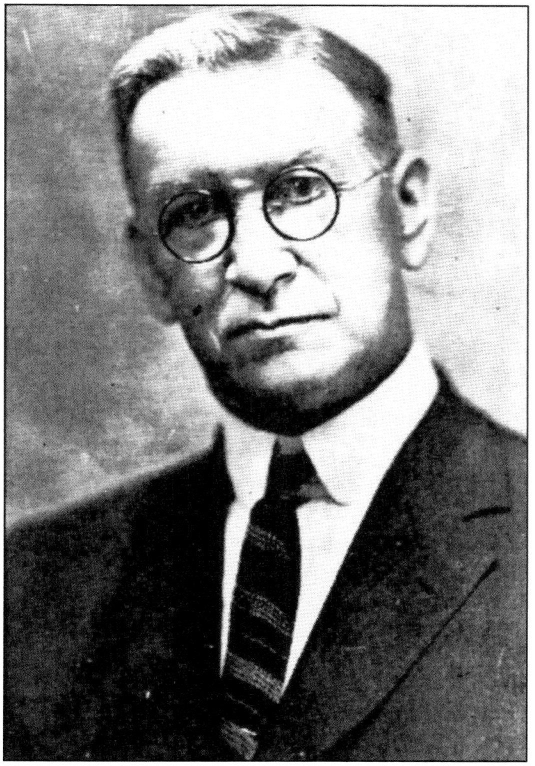

Artist Richard H. Burfoot came to the area in 1895. After marrying Edith Trezise of DuBois, he bought a home in Luthersburg. He was well known as a landscape and portrait painter. Among his works are portraits of President McKinley and many other governors, senators, congressmen, judges, and other prominent people. He had exhibitions in all the large cities of the east. (Courtesy DuBois Area Historical Society.)

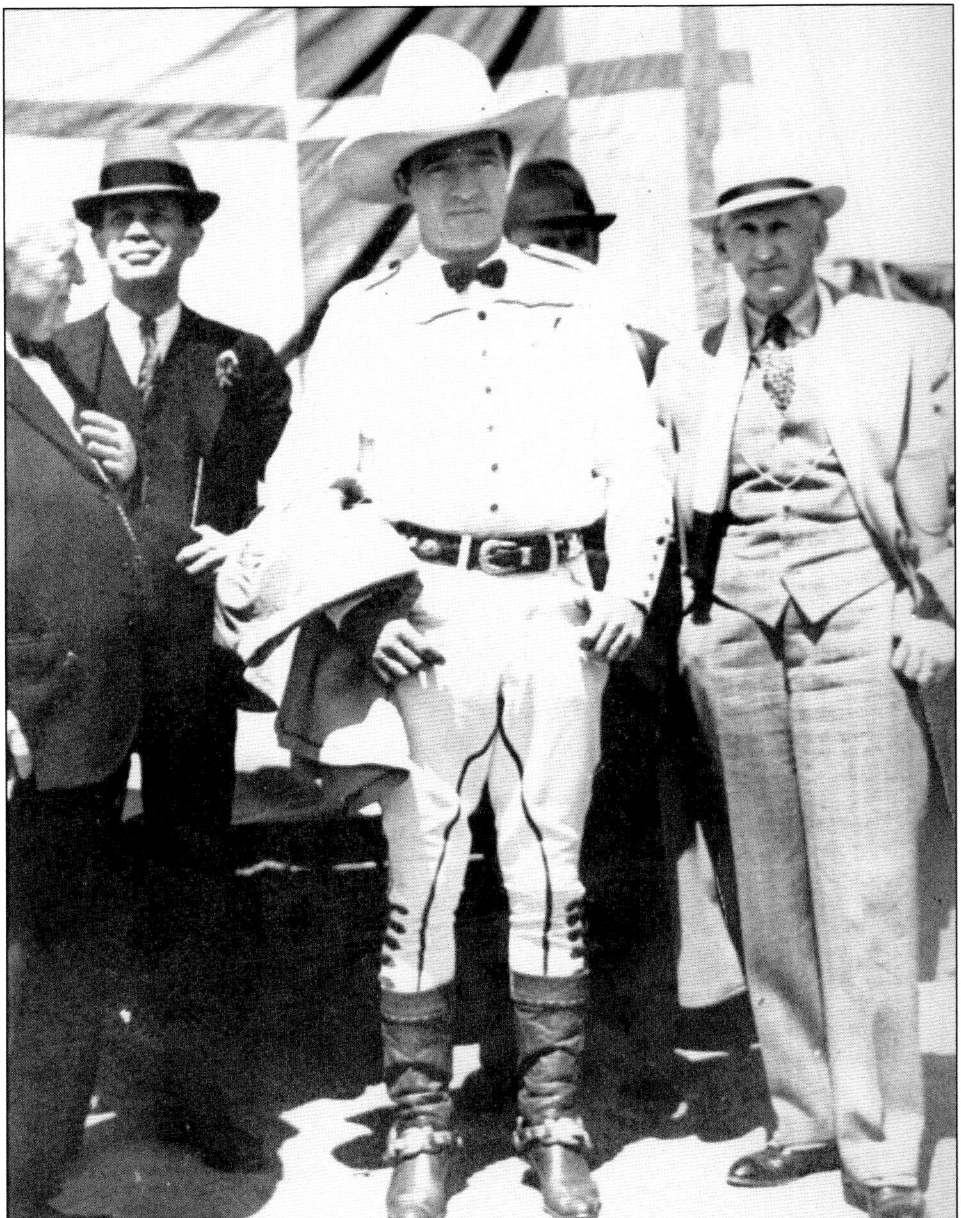

Although most biographies of cowboy actor Tom Mix list his birthplace as Texas, he was actually born at Mix Run in the DuBois area. His family moved to DuBois when he was eight. Because his father worked for John E. DuBois as a supervisor in his stable, Tom was able to work with horses and became an expert handler and rider. After spending time in the army, he moved to Oklahoma, where he worked on a ranch. Later, he appeared in a Wild West show, which led to his movie career. He made about 300 silent movies, but his career ended because of his high-pitched voice when talkies became popular. In 1930, Tom Mix, above in a white outfit and hat, returned to DuBois with his Tom Mix Circus. An annual Tom Mix Festival is held each September in DuBois in his honor. (Courtesy DuBois Area Historical Society.)

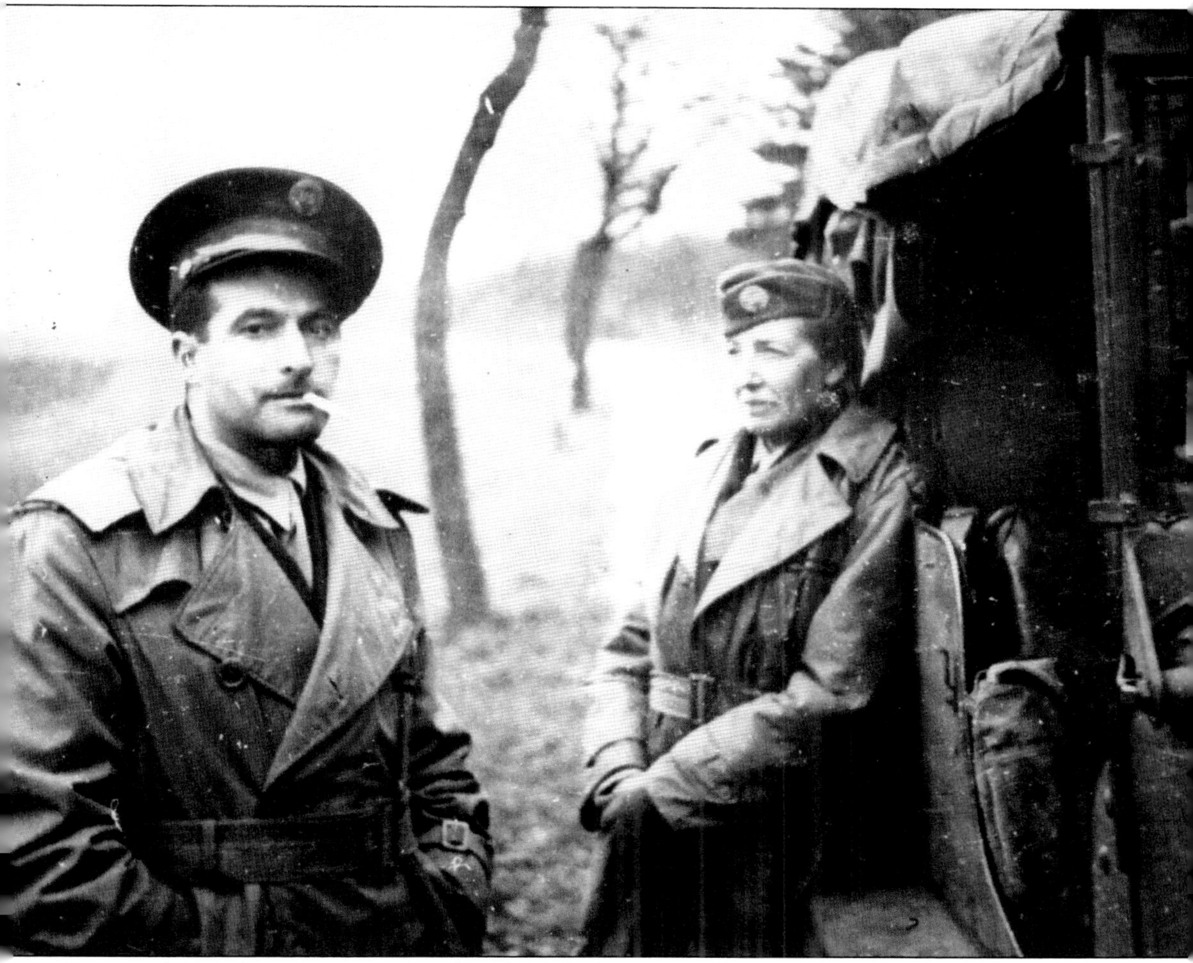

Nora Waln was born in Grampian, but she left the area to find worldwide fame as an author, magazine writer, and foreign correspondent. Among the magazines she wrote for are the *Saturday Evening Post*, the *Atlantic Monthly*, *National Geographic*, and the *New Yorker*. Her books were *The House of Exile*, about China, and *Reaching for the Stars*, about life in Germany in the 1930s. She was a war correspondent during both World War II and the Korean War. She began her writing career at *The Progress* in Clearfield, and in the early 1960s, she wrote a special series of articles for that newspaper. The above photograph was taken in Austria during the fall of 1945. The man on the left is said to be Dr. Otto Zausmer. She was married to George Edward Osland-Hill, an English diplomat. Born Nora Wall, she changed her name to the original family name of Waln. Her father was Thomas Lincoln Wall, known for his history book *Clearfield County, Pennsylvania: Past and Present*, published in 1925. (Courtesy Clearfield County Historical Society.)

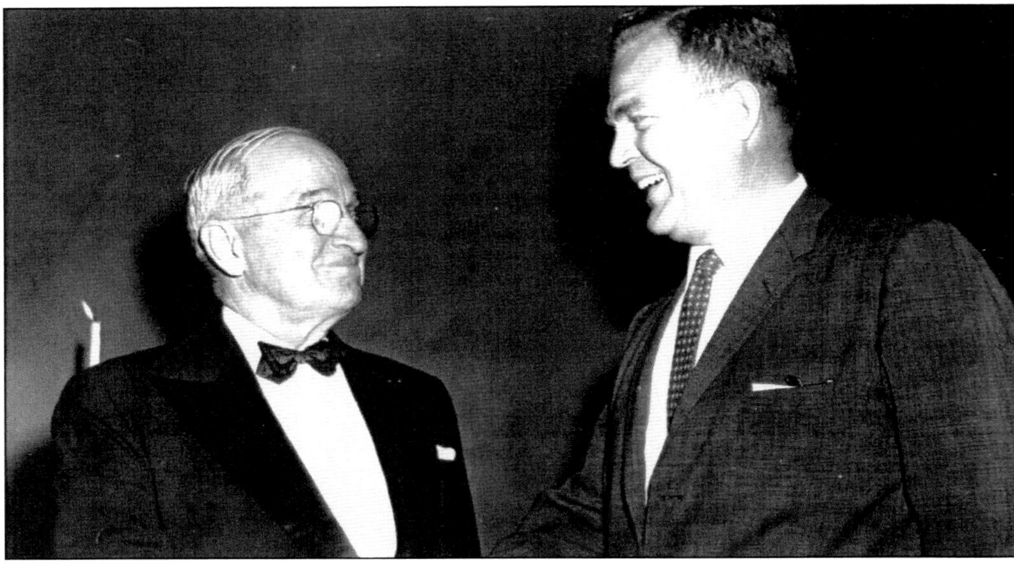

DuBois native Floyd "Toad" Boring, pictured above with Pres. Harry Truman and below (walking on the left) with Pres. Dwight Eisenhower in New Orleans, was in the Secret Service for many years. His law-enforcement career began when he joined the Pennsylvania State Police. He served in the Secret Service from 1943 to 1967. He was first assigned to the White House in 1944. When the driver was not available, Floyd was asked to drive the presidential limousine. He described President Truman as very friendly and said he knew all the agents by name. Floyd was on duty in November 1950, when two men attacked the Blair House, where President Truman was staying. He shot one of the assassins and helped stop the assault. In addition to Presidents Truman and Eisenhower, he guarded Franklin D. Roosevelt, John F. Kennedy, and Lyndon Johnson. After Kennedy was elected president, Boring was the first Secret Service agent assigned to him. However, he was off duty at home when President Kennedy was shot in Dallas in 1963. (Courtesy DuBois Area Historical Society.)

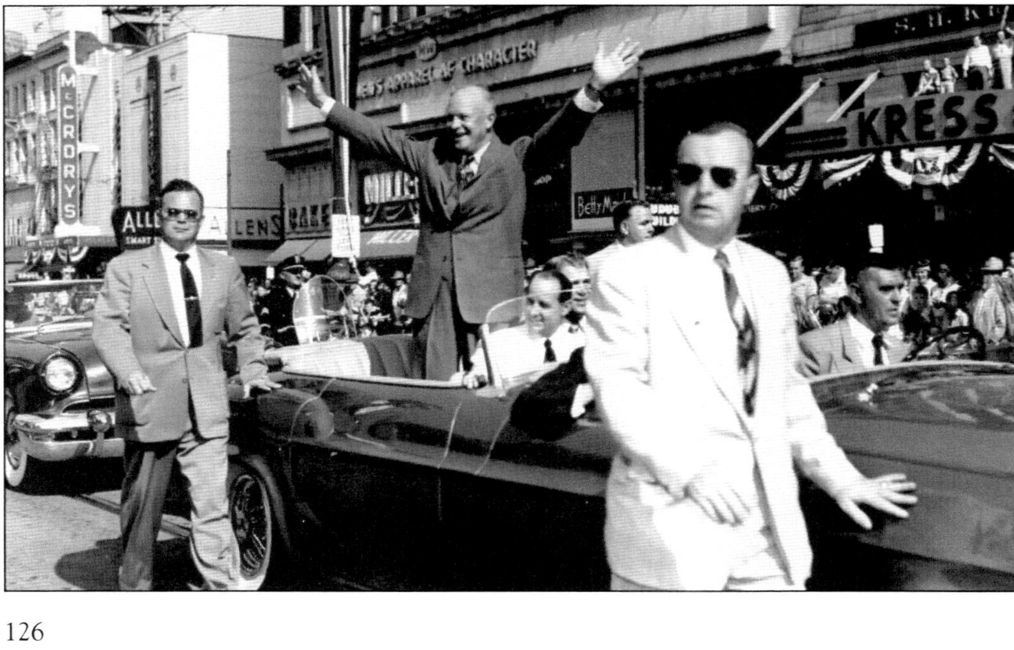

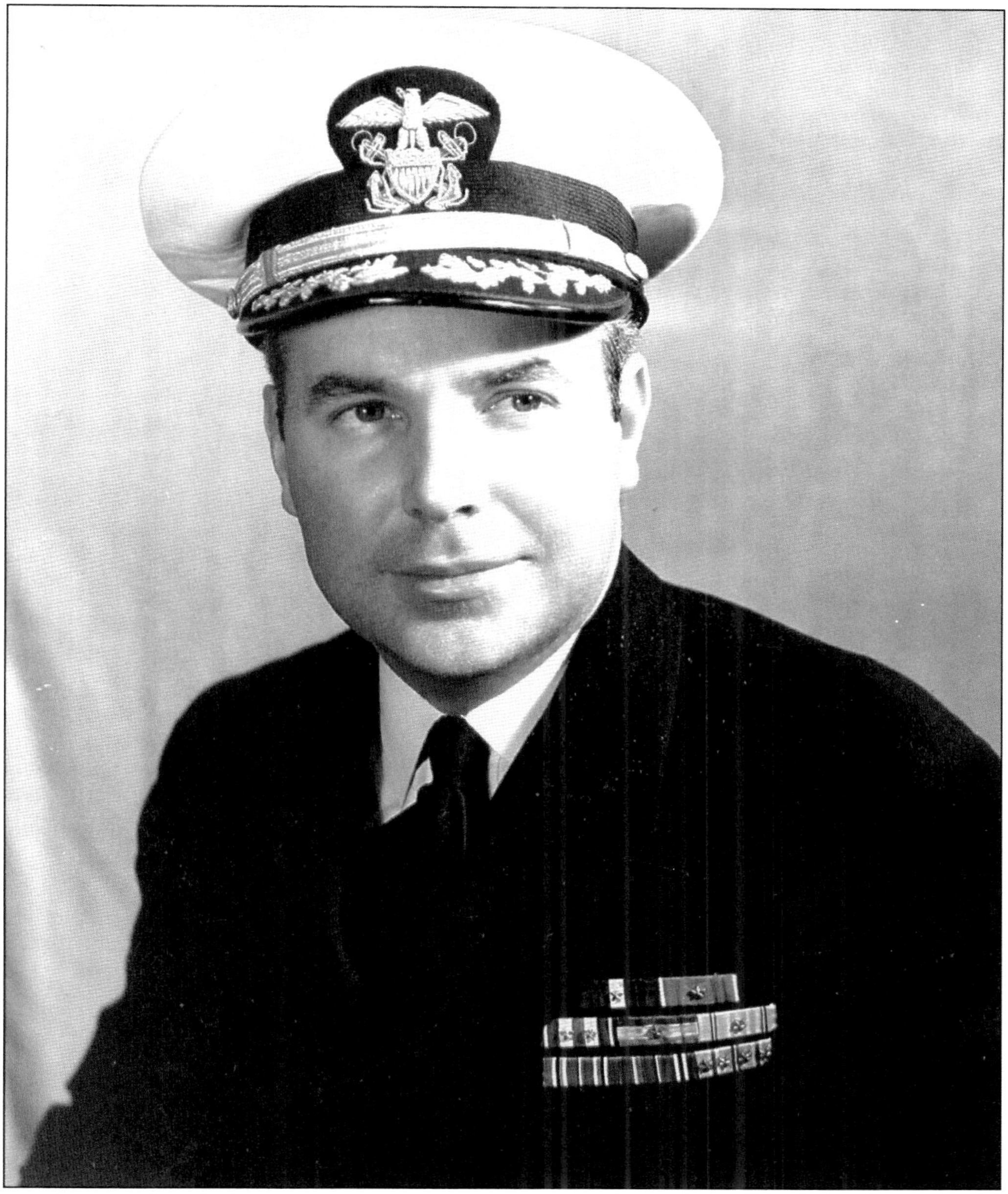

Rear Adm. Donald MacDonald (above) was born and raised in DuBois. After graduating from the U.S. Naval Academy in 1931, he was assigned to destroyers and then various battleships. In 1938, he was sent to Washington, D.C., where he first served as an assistant communications officer at the navy department and then as a White House aide to Pres. Franklin Roosevelt. During World War II, he was the commanding officer of the *O'Bannon*, which was involved in every major engagement from 1942 to 1944. It was the only ship that survived that amount of combat. As a result, he became a highly decorated naval officer. In 1948, he was named the captain of the presidential yacht *Williamsburg*, where he spent a lot of time with Pres. Harry Truman. His brother, Col. Charles H. MacDonald, was an ace pilot in World War II. With 27 aerial victories, he was the highest scoring P-38 pilot to survive the war. (Courtesy Evo G. Facchine.)

Further Information

For more information on author Julie Rae Rickard, go to http://thedestinyofmiro.tripod.com, e-mail her at thedestinyofmiro@yahoo.com, or write to her at P.O. Box 565, Clearfield, Pa. 16830.

Part of the proceeds from this book go to support the Clearfield County Historical Society, 104 East Pine Street, Clearfield, Pa. 16830. For more information on the Clearfield County Historical Society, go to http://www.rootsweb.com/~pacchsm or call (814) 765-6125.

Below is information on contacting other local groups that contributed to this project.

DuBois Area Historical Society, P.O. Box 401, DuBois, Pa. 15801, (814) 371-9006, http://home.wrkcs.net/history, e-mail: history@wrkcs.net.

Curwensville-Pike Township Historical Society, 836 State Street, Curwensville, Pa. 16833.

Curwensville Public Library, 601 Beech Street, Curwensville, Pa. 16833, (814) 236-0355.

Coalport Area Coal Museum, P.O. Box 248, Coalport, Pa. 16627, (814) 672-4378, http://wbweb.ciu10.com/cacm.

Osceola Mills Public Library, P.O. Box 55, Osceola Mills, Pa. 16666, (814) 339-7229, http://members.tripod.com/~aruathite, e-mail: omlibrary@adelphia.net.